D0449957

"*Jens Soering is not only helping us to see the injustice of America's prison system. He is helping American Christians see the Scriptures with new eyes through his faithful, counter-intuitive biblical study. These intimate interviews fairly demand of us that we reflect on what it means to be members of the 'Church of the Second Chance,' in need of spiritual parole.*"

—**Jason Byassee**, Assistant Editor, *Christian Century*,
Affiliate Professor of Theology,
Garrett-Evangelical Theological Seminary

"*Each of Jens Soering's books is a gem, and* The Church of the Second Chance *is his most interesting and unique work yet. His tour through the Scriptures, showing Jesus' passion for helping prisoners, is profound in its insights. No Christian can read it and not be compelled to care for and assist our brothers and sisters in prison.*"

—**Pat Nolan**, Prison Fellowship Ministries

Other books by Jens Soering, available from Lantern

One Day in the Life of 179212
Notes from an American Prison

The Way of the Prisoner
*Breaking the Chains of Self through Centering Prayer
and Centering Practice*

An Expensive Way to Make Bad People Worse
An Essay on Prison Reform from an Insider's Perspective

THE CHURCH OF THE SECOND CHANCE

A FAITH-BASED APPROACH TO PRISON REFORM

✝

Jens Soering

LANTERN BOOKS • NEW YORK

A DIVISION OF BOOKLIGHT, INC.

2008
LANTERN BOOKS
128 Second Place
Brooklyn, NY 11231
www.lanternbooks.com

Copyright © 2008 Jens Soering

All rights reserved. No part of this book may be reproduced, stored in a retrieval system, or transmitted in any form or by any means, electronic, mechanical, photocopying, recording, or otherwise, without the written permission of Lantern Books.

Printed in the United States of America

LIBRARY OF CONGRESS CATALOGING-IN-PUBLICATION DATA

Soering, Jens.
    The church of the second chance : a faith-based approach to prison reform / by Jens Soering.
        p. cm.
    Includes bibliographical references.
    ISBN 978-1-59056-112-6 (alk. paper)
    1. Criminals—Rehabilitation. 2. Prisoners—Religious life.
I. Title.
    HV9275.S57 2007
    261.8'336—dc22

                                                        2007042177

All biblical citations refer to the *New American Bible*, published by the United States Conference of Catholic Bishops, 3211 Fourth Street NE, Washington, DC, 20017.

To Tom,
with special thanks to
Decker, Jean, David, and Jim

ACKNOWLEDGMENTS

This book would not have been possible without my wonderful research elves: Richard Busch, Aaron Condon, Mary Edwards, Jean Franklin, Sarah Gallogly, James McFadden, and Candy Miller. Richard and Jean also provided invaluable advice in the latter stages of writing. Essential technical support was rendered by "Grasshopper" and Peg Cunningham. Thank you all so very much—and forgive me, please, for being such a pest.

Because prisoners in Virginia have only very limited access to typewriters and virtually none to computers, the manuscript of this book had to be produced by a professional typing service at a cost of more than $1,400. Special thanks to those of my friends who helped cover this bill: John and Meta Braymer, Richard Busch, Peter Cosby, Raymond Dufresne, Claude Ford, Jean Franklin, Ken Grabner, David Hilfiker, Bernd Kaut, James McFadden, Candy Miller, Rosemary Murphy, Joe Slattery, Walter Westbrook, and James Wiseman.

Contents

INTRODUCTION

Let's start with a pop quiz: what do Adam and Eve, Joseph, Moses, Samson, David, Daniel, and his three friends, Jesus, Paul, and Onesimus all have in common? Yes, of course, in one way or another each of them is an indispensable link in the long chain of people who brought us salvation through grace and faith in the incarnate Word. But what else do they share?

Do you "see but not perceive, … listen but not understand" (Mark 4:12, quoting Isaiah 6:9)? The answer is so obvious! All of these holy men and women, these heroes of our precious faith, our spiritual forefathers and foremothers, were … *criminals, or prison inmates, or both.*

- Adam and Eve were guilty of receiving stolen goods and petty theft, respectively. That infamous apple was taken and eaten contrary to the express wishes of the fruit's legal owner.

- Joseph was convicted of raping Potiphar's wife, though the Bible declares him to be innocent. After serving many years in prison, Pharaoh freed him without, however, officially exonerating him.

- Moses was guilty of capital murder. The slave driver he killed was a legitimate law enforcement officer, equivalent to a prison guard in our age.

- Samson committed robbery-murder, arson and acts of terrorism. He killed thirty men and stole their clothes to pay off a gambling debt; he burned down Philistine fields and vineyards with those foxes whose tails he set on fire; and he slaughtered three thousand civilians in a murder-suicide when he destroyed the great hall.

- David solicited murder by proxy. He commanded his general Joab to abandon Uriah the Hittite on the battlefield so he would be killed.

- Daniel and his friends were sentenced to death in the lion's den and the fiery furnace, respectively, for breaking their government's religious decrees.
- Jesus died a prisoner's death: he was tried in court just like an ordinary felon and then executed alongside two other criminals.
- Paul was an accessory to murder. He joined the lynch mob that stoned Stephen, watching over the killers' coats as they pelted a helpless man with rocks until he was dead.
- Onesimus, one of Paul's especially valued assistants, committed theft. As a slave, he was the legal property of his owner and thus broke the law by running away (Philemon, v. 12, 16, 19).

When the author of the Letter to the Hebrews writes so movingly of "the great cloud of witnesses" to our faith (Hebrews 12:1), he means the crooks and convicts above, among others. Their felony records did not bar them from places of honor in what we might call the Church of the Second Chance.

Of course, none of this should surprise readers of my third book, *The Convict Christ: What the Gospel Says about Criminal Justice.* That volume's premise is that God's Son gave his life for our sins in a very specific way: by becoming a "dead man walking," a death row prisoner, the lowest of the low. Working backward from that often-overlooked fact, *The Convict Christ* examines an astonishing *fourteen* episodes in the life of our Savior in which he either spoke about or interacted with outlaws or inmates. Jesus reached out in love to felons and prisoners because he "did not come to call the righteous but sinners" (Mark 2:17), including some outright villains:

- the Woman Caught in Adultery, whose offense was not considered a personal failure in those days, but a crime deserving the death penalty (John 8:1–11);
- Zacchaeus the tax collector, who admitted to several counts of embezzlement (Luke 19:1–10); and
- the Gerasene Demoniac, who attacked travelers on the road near the tombs where he lived (Matthew 8:15).

While Jesus gave these three miscreants an opportunity to turn their own lives around, however, God did something even more remarkable with the criminals and jailbirds we will examine in this book: he used them to advance his plan of salvation for all of humanity. Thus they not only got a second chance themselves, but became our Father's means of giving all of us a second chance, too.

Consider the tasks he assigned to the felonious subjects of our study:

- Adam and Eve peopled the earth.
- Joseph saved his whole family and thus preserved the entire Jewish nation.
- Moses led the slaves out of Egypt and gave them the Ten Commandments.
- Samson kept the flame of independence alive in the Israelites when the Philistines began to encroach on their land.
- David secured the kingdom and assured its future by producing an heir.
- Daniel and his three friends demonstrated how the Jews could preserve their religious identity even during their exile.
- Jesus reconciled us to our Father on the cross.
- Paul spread the Gospel throughout the Near East and into Europe.
- Onesimus, Paul's helper, stayed with him even after he was imprisoned (Philemon, v. 10, 13).

The deeds these men and women performed were often heroic and always historic—not at all what one would expect from mere outlaws and inmates. How did this riffraff find the courage to do what princes and priests did not? What helped them take their second chance and turn it into triumph?

Forgiveness. Mercy. Free pardon.

Pardon for *all* of humanity's sins is what Christ earned for us on Golgotha, of course. Just to make sure that we got the message, he chose a thief as the very first person he took with him to paradise (Luke 23:43). Each one of us is a sinner no less than that thief; we all need mercy as much as he did. If a "scumbag" criminal cannot be forgiven, then none of us gets a second chance, either.

Unfortunately, we tend to ignore this lesson. In our own eyes, we do not need to be pardoned quite as much as the thief because we think of ourselves as reasonably decent people, trying our best, etc. What distinguishes the other eight criminals and convicts featured in this book is that their life experiences saved them from making this spiritual error.

When they broke the law or went to prison, our protagonists all hit the proverbial rock bottom. They had to face their own weakness and sinfulness and *admit* that nothing they could do would lift them out of the depths to which they had sunk. Only God's mercy could save them—and when he granted it, their gratitude was so intense that they could not help but throw themselves completely into whatever mission our Father assigned to them.

If "he who has been forgiven little, loves little," as Jesus said, then he or she who has been forgiven very much also loves very much (Luke 7:47, NIV).

Paul nicely sums up this spiritual dynamic in his First Letter to Timothy, written many years after he stood as a lookout for Stephen's murderers: "I was once a blasphemer and a persecutor and an arrogant man, but I have been mercifully treated because I acted out of ignorance.... I am grateful to him who has strengthened me, Christ Jesus our Lord" (1:13, 12).

But gratitude for his own forgiveness does not suffice. Paul goes on to explain that the reception of divine pardon has now placed an obligation on him: "...*for that reason* I was mercifully treated, so that in me, as the foremost [of sinners], Christ Jesus might display all his patience, as an example for those who would come to believe in him" (1:16, emphasis added). That second step—the acceptance of a duty to pass on to others the grace and forgiveness one has received—this is what distinguishes Paul and the other criminals and inmates we will examine.

We shall not stop with a pleasant little Scripture study on the "Bad Boys and Girls of the Bible," however; if our faith is to have any meaning, we must apply God's word to our own lives and times. That is how Christ read the Torah, as a handbook for action: feed the hungry, heal the sick, chase the moneylenders from the Temple! Those of us who follow Jesus today would do well to read our Bible in the same spirit.

When it comes to the success that our scriptural scoundrels made of their second chance, for instance, we might ask ourselves why ex-convicts in America fare so much worse. Joseph was put in charge of all of Egypt after serving time for rape, but 60% of inmates discharged from U.S. correctional centers remain unemployed one year after their release.[1] What did Pharaoh know about reintegrating former prisoners that America has forgotten?

Even as you read these lines, criminal justice experts and legislators are debating that very question—minus the reference to Pharaoh, of course. They are struggling to come to terms with a correctional crisis that has been building for over thirty years, but is only now reaching a climax:

- Since the early 1970s, the number of inmates in U.S. jails and penitentiaries has grown *sevenfold*, from 300,000 to 2.3 million.[2]
- The land of the free now incarcerates a higher percentage of its own citizens than any other country on earth, bar none.[3]
- Although only 4.6% of the global population lives in America, 22% of the world's prison population is housed in U.S. correctional centers.[4]

And the number of convicts keeps on rising, by an average of 3.3% a year since 1995.[5] Another 13% will be added to the nation's penitentiary population between 2007 and 2011.[6] To hold them all, America now operates 1,208 adult prisons and 3,365 jails, with more opening up every year.[7]

Locking up such enormous throngs of people has not made this country any safer, however: the crime rate in 2003 was precisely the same as in 1973.[8] Of course, opinions will differ on whether that is good news or bad, depending on how fondly one recalls the early seventies. Either way, the fact remains that a 700% increase in the number of inmates produced a 0% change in levels of offending.

Instead of lowering crime, mass incarceration has only produced a new public safety problem: huge hosts of ex-convicts. Each year, prison departments throughout America discharge 672,000 inmates who have finished their sentences.[9] And 67.5% of those 672,000 will re-offend within three years of their release.[10]

So all those extra jails and penitentiaries built since the 1970s can truthfully be described as factories that produce 453,000 brand-new recidivists every twelve months. Not exactly a resounding victory in the "war on crime."

This Rube Goldberg device for increasing the amount of human misery in the world costs U.S. taxpayers $63 billion (with a "b") per year.[11] According to the Pew Charitable Trusts, the projected 13% expansion of the correctional system will cost an additional $27.5 billion (with a "b") annually.[12] These figures are high enough for politicians, social scientists and even some commentators to search for alternatives:

- Since the turn of the century, twenty-five states have carried out reforms like abolishing "mandatory minimum" sentences or restoring time off for good behavior.[13]
- Conservative criminologist John J. DiIulio Jr. has argued for the immediate release of all inmates locked up for narcotics offenses only.[14]
- Republican pundit Cal Thomas has called for all those who committed nonviolent property crimes and "public order" offenses to be punished by fines instead of prison.[15]

However, those twenty-five states' reform efforts have only slowed, but not reversed the growth of America's correctional population.[16] And even if DiIulio's and Thomas's proposals were actually implemented, they would still leave over one million men, women, and juveniles behind bars.

That would mean more than 300,000 prisoners would still be returning to society each year, and roughly 200,000 of them would still re-offend.

So must these hundreds of thousands of ruined lives simply be considered collateral damage, an inevitable level of wastage in a modern industrialized state? Is there really nothing that can help these ex-convicts, *and* the citizens whom they victimize after leaving prison, *and* the taxpayers who have to finance this exercise in futility?

Yes, there is help. All three groups—offenders, victims, and society at large—can break the cycle of despair through the careful, considered and Christian application of the same key that freed Joseph and Moses and Paul to do great things *after* they broke the law. Forgiveness. Mercy. Free pardon.

Of course, pardon does not make all punishment unnecessary. And although mercy is offered to all, it comes with a condition: "If your brother sins, rebuke him; and *if he repents,* forgive him," Christ taught the disciples (Luke 17:3). No grant of pardon is possible without the acceptance of responsibility by the offender, without the full and frank admission of his or her need to change.

But while forgiveness makes heavy demands of the sinner, it requires no less of a sacrifice from the sinned-against: letting go of anger and pain, relinquishing the status of victim, and giving wrongdoers a real second chance.

When Daniel's three friends emerged from the fiery furnace after breaking King Nebuchadnezzar's decree, "the king *promoted* Shadrach, Mesach and Abednego in the province of Babylon" (Daniel 3:97, emphasis added). And Christ did not replace stoning with a lesser punishment for the Woman Caught in Adultery, but simply told her, "Go now and leave your life of sin behind" (John 8:11).

This abundance of mercy is likely to provoke howls of outrage, as God himself pointed out:

> …though I say to the wicked man that he shall surely die, if he
> turns from his sin and does what is right, giving back pledges,

restoring stolen goods, living by the statutes that bring life, and doing no wrong, he shall surely live, *he shall not die.* None of the sins he committed shall be held against him; he has done what is right and just, he shall surely live. Yet your countrymen say, *"The way of the Lord is not fair!"* (Ezekiel 33:14–17, emphasis added)

What makes this passage so interesting is that forgiveness is applied specifically to criminal offenses ("stolen goods"), including those carrying the death penalty ("he shall not die"). For those of us who make an effort to live "by the statutes" and follow the rules, so much mercy for outlaws does indeed seem unfair.

The purpose of this book is to help us apply the standards of this seemingly unfair divine justice to America's prison system. In each of the nine chapters, we begin with a Bible study that examines how God and his Son handled a particular outlaw's case. Then we study one of a variety of problems besetting our jails and penitentiaries—everything from prison rape to mentally ill inmates. Finally, each chapter introduces us to a genuine hero laboring in the vineyards of prison reform and prison ministry today, or to one of five long-term inmates spending their time behind bars doing great things for their fellow convicts. Here is a preview:

- Adam and Eve's theft of an apple gives us the opportunity to review how Christian concepts of justice have changed through history. In our first interview, we meet someone who challenges our understanding of justice, punishment, mercy and redemption: George C., sentenced to sixty years for rape and burglary in 1984 and now the coordinator of two prayer groups at the correctional center where he and I serve time together.

- As noted earlier, the notorious ex-convict Joseph the Israelite was put in charge of Egypt and successfully steered that nation through an agricultural crisis. Today the Reverend Bill Twine's Onesimus House helps recently released inmates find work of a more humble nature so that these men, too, can rejoin society. In his interview,

Reverend Twine explains why his ministry has become both more difficult and more rewarding over the last twenty years.

- Forty years after he killed the slave-driver, Moses led the Israelites out of Egypt but never abolished the institution of slavery itself. A similar sort of blindness arguably prevents us from seeing the reality of prison today. When we meet Carlton L.—sentenced to thirty years for aggravated involuntary manslaughter in 1997 and now working as an inmate chaplain's clerk—our eyes may begin to be opened.

- The ending of Samson's life as a prisoner in the Philistines' great hall lets us consider the role and concerns of the victims' rights movement. Thanks to our interview with Linda L. White, a crime victim herself, we can now imagine a different conclusion to Samson's sad story.

- King David was arguably the worst of our biblical criminals, yet his very public repenting sufficed to rehabilitate him in the eyes of ancient Israelite society. At our correctional facility, Kent I.—sentenced to life and two years for murder in 1990—conducts a painting class for offenders who are trying to rehabilitate themselves today.

- Students of the Book of Daniel usually focus on the heroism of the three young men who preferred going to the fiery oven instead of betraying their faith. Just as interesting, however, is the reason they were put on trial: very prosaic motives of power and, ultimately, money. In our interview, Warden Charlie Campbell, who once oversaw the only coed correctional facility in the federal Bureau of Prisons, explains some of the financial motives behind the creation of the world's largest prison system in the U.S.

- Before he was executed, the notorious felon Jesus of Nazareth was stripped naked, dressed up as a king to humiliate him, beaten, and scourged. Sadly, the mistreatment to which inmates are routinely exposed today differs only in kind, not in intent or barbarity. Our interview subject is Ras Talawa Tafari, sentenced to forty-seven years for armed robbery and abduction in 1990—and confined in solitary isolation continuously since 1999, simply because he refuses to cut off his Rastafarian dreadlocks, symbols of his faith.

- During his sojourn in the jail at Philippi, Paul operated a classic faith-based initiative for his fellow inmates, a textbook example of early prison ministry. Dennis and Loretta Beeman tell us how they came to follow in Paul's footsteps by holding monthly Communion services at the facility where I am incarcerated.

- Onesimus's decision to run away from his legal owner not only constituted an act of theft but also challenged the foundation of a culture and society based on slavery—a very serious crime indeed. In the U.S. today, a dangerous felon like Onesimus can expect to be subjected to merciless policies like "three strikes" laws, parole abolition, mandatory minimums, or life without possibility of parole. But Bud T.—sentenced to one hundred and twenty-seven years for first-degree murder, malicious wounding, and numerous counts of aggravated sexual assault and sodomy in 1983—demonstrates that no offender is beyond hope and redemption.

By introducing you to the nine activists and prisoners above—all of them friends or acquaintances of mine—I hope to encourage you to form friendships with their counterparts in your area. Meeting personally with men and women like these is, I believe, the first and absolutely necessary first step toward addressing America's correctional crisis. Even in this, the most individualistic country on earth, we are still all members of one community: criminals, victims, and bystanders. Christians, perhaps more than any others, can breathe new life and purpose into the bond we share, because we who follow Jesus know that we are all one in him, our Lord and Savior. Truly, all of us are members of the Church of the Second Chance.

QUESTIONS FOR REFLECTION AND DISCUSSION

SCRIPTURE—The nine criminals and convicts selected for this book are only a few of the many miscreants found in the pages of the Bible. Think of Cain in Genesis 4, Jeremiah in Jeremiah 38, John the Baptist in Mark 6, Peter in Acts 4 and 12, and the apostle John writing the Book of Revelation on the prison island of Patmos. Can you find others? Why do you think so few have noticed this scriptural theme?

CRIMINOLOGY—Roughly 1,124 men and women are added to America's correctional population each week.[17] That amounts to more than 58,000 human beings lost to prison every twelve months—the same number lost in the entire Vietnam War. Why do you think no one has noticed that America is essentially fighting and losing a war against itself year after year?

SELF-EXAM—What do you think of the idea that it was the experience of divine forgiveness that inspired killers such as Moses, David, and Paul to bring others to God? Is it really necessary to undergo some sort of personal tragedy or trial in order to be as strongly motivated as they were?

INTERNET—One of the many reasons why this country's correctional system has spun out of control is that Americans are unaware how vastly different U.S. prisons are from those of other nations. Visit the Web sites of the International Centre for Prison Studies and Penal Reform International to get a broader view. See www.prisonstudies.org and www.penalreform.org.

IMMERSION—Find out the location of the jail and/or penitentiary nearest you and drive there. For now, there is no need to enter the facility; the point is to experience the reality of the place, its physical distance from your neighborhood, and its "invisibility." Pray for all those inside, inmates and staff, and pray for God's guidance as you begin to explore corrections.

Chapter 1

ADAM AND EVE AND DIVINE JUSTICE

Wᴴᴬᵀ ᴘʀᴇᴄɪꜱᴇʟʏ ɪꜱ original sin, the sin that Adam and Eve committed and transmitted to all humankind? Wise men and women have pondered that question for centuries and arrived at a great variety of answers:

- St. Paul, the great apostle to the gentiles, simply dodged the issue. While he discusses the effect of the Fall at length in Romans 5:12–21 and 1 Corinthians 15:21–24, he never names the transgression through which death entered the world.

- Theologians tell us that Adam and Eve committed the sin of disobedience: God issued a command—"you shall not eat [from] the tree of the knowledge of good and evil"—but the first man and woman did so anyway (Genesis 2:17). By defying their Maker's will so blatantly, our ancestors created a rift between God and humanity that was not healed until the coming of Jesus Christ.

- Cultural anthropologists point out that the serpent was one of the ancient deities of Canaan. Since the story of the Fall probably first took shape during the period when Israel was struggling to conquer the original inhabitants of the Promised Land, it makes sense to read this tale as one of numerous biblical warnings against worshipping foreign gods. Original sin, then, is deserting Yahweh and committing idolatry.

- Although Christians have now largely abandoned the age-old tradition of associating the Fall with sex, Freudian psychologists insist that the serpent is in fact a powerful phallic symbol. Original sin can thus be seen as the loss of sexual innocence, which leaves us feeling "naked" and forces us to hide our sexuality behind "fig leaves" (Genesis 3:7).

- To some feminist scholars, the story of the Fall is little more than gender-based blame shifting, designed to lend spurious legitimacy to patriarchal social systems. Original sin is not so much what Adam and Eve did or did not do in the Garden, but the way in which the authors of Scripture later distorted the tale to justify the repression of women.

While all the explanations above are interesting and quite possibly even true, they all overlook one plain and obvious fact: *Adam and Eve committed a crime.* Filching a piece of fruit that belonged to Someone Else was, to put it bluntly, a case of petty theft. Or, given the fact that the purloined apple conveyed knowledge of good and evil and therefore was a highly sophisticated data-storage device, perhaps a closer analogy would be stealing the ultimate Apple iPod. Nothing petty about *that* theft!

Amazingly enough, few Bible scholars comment even in passing on the felonious nature of original sin. One of the purposes of this book is to correct this oversight by unearthing the criminal justice theme in familiar Bible passages.

To understand God's response to our ancestors' thievery, we must first disabuse ourselves of the notion that the death that entered the world through Adam and Eve was a judicial punishment for their offense. This misunderstanding has arisen repeatedly throughout the history of biblical exegesis, but it is not supported by a close reading of Scripture. Instead, we find that death was the natural consequence of original sin, a product of the gulf that now separated God and humanity.

When Yahweh issued his injunction against eating the forbidden fruit, he did not speak of a legal penalty but used the passive voice to warn Adam what effect noncompliance would inevitably have: "the moment you eat from it you are surely doomed to die" (Genesis 2:17). Paul explained the link between sin and death in terms of causation, not retribution: "through one person sin entered the world, and through sin, death, and thus death came to all" (Romans 5:12). No doubt that is why he described death as the "wages of sin" (Romans 6:23), a metaphor that suggests (admittedly negative) compensation rather than punitive action.

At the primordial sentencing hearing that God conducted after the fruit thieves' confessions and guilty pleas, he announced specific punishments for each of the criminal conspirators, but did not impose the death penalty. The serpent was sentenced to crawl in the dirt and live in enmity with the woman; Eve, to painful childbirths and subjection to her husband; and Adam, to hard labor as a farmer (Genesis 3:14–18). If death had been among the penalties for their offense, His Honor the Judge would surely have said so.

Not even the thieves' banishment from Eden was part of the official sentencing order recorded in Genesis 3:14–19. Yahweh expels the first man and woman from Paradise, not to punish them further but to keep them from taking fruit from the tree of life (Genesis 3:22). We might consider this an early form of crime prevention, with the archangel Michael serving as Neighborhood Watch (Genesis 3:24).

If a close reading of the story of the Fall reveals God to be an unexpectedly mild judge, then those final five verses of the third chapter of Genesis hold another surprise in store for us: Yahweh, that stern, Old Testament deity, initiated the first rehabilitation program for criminals as well as the earliest ex-offender reentry initiative.

At the end of his sentencing speech, God makes a play on Adam's name: the Hebrew word for "ground" is *adama*, so God reminds man that "you [shall] return to the ground from which you were taken; for you are dirt, and to dirt you shall return" (Genesis 3:19). In the next verse, "the man called his wife Eve because she became the mother of all the living" (Genesis 3:20). In Hebrew, the name *Hawwa*, or "Eve," is related to the word *hay*, or "living."

This naming is significant because it demonstrates that Yahweh did not withdraw all his favor from Adam. Before the Fall, our Creator gave man the right to give names to every living creature (Genesis 2:19, 20)—an enormous privilege, since a name conveys essential identity in Hebrew thought. I propose that allowing Adam to exercise this authority directly after his punishment was God's way of showing that even a recently convicted thief is still a full human being.

So what did Yahweh do after affirming the basic human rights of convicted thieves? Scripture tells us, "For the man and his wife the Lord God made leather garments, with which he clothed them" (Genesis 3:21). Adam and Eve's nudity, we must remember, was the biblical author's metaphor for the moral consequences of eating the forbidden fruit: "Then the eyes of both of them were opened, and they realized that they were naked" (Genesis 3:7). As a criminal myself, I can assure you that nearly every offender experiences this painful realization immediately after doing wrong: we cannot help but see our own sinfulness, our innocence passing away before us. Our first reaction is to hide our pain and shame, much as the first man and woman did when they "sewed fig leaves together and made loincloths for themselves" (Genesis 3:7). Like their improvised leafy clothes, however, our flimsy self-justifications cannot disguise our guilt.

A merciful God can remove that guilt, of course: "though your sins be like scarlet, they may become white as snow" (Isaiah 1:18). But even a fully healed wound leaves a scar, a memory that we once fell and had to be restored. When we stand before our Father, we do so as forgiven sinners, not as men and women who have never sinned at all.

God may not be able to undo the past and give us back our original innocence, but he can and does make "leather garments" for us— new, divinely manufactured second skins that replace our lost innocence with our Father's own moral protection. In Adam and Eve's case, moreover, those clothes were not just a symbol of spiritual restoration but also a very practical shield against the day's heat and the night's cold. Now these two ex-offenders could start their new lives as parolees beyond Eden with the assurance of their Creator's love *and* an essential survival tool.

Of course, it is one thing to recognize this biblical incident as an inspiring example of divine forgiveness, but quite another thing for us to be as forgiving ourselves. In theory at least, we know that we must forgive "not seven times but seventy-seven times" and that "if you do not forgive others, neither will your Father forgive your transgressions" (Matthew 18:22, 6:15).[1] But how do we actually apply this divinely merciful kind of justice in the real world, to real crimes?

RETRIBUTION AND RESTORATION

Most of us favor the "eye for an eye" school of thought in these matters, much like the author of this letter to the editor of *USA Today*:

> My religion preaches, "Justice, justice thou shalt pursue." In looking at the [Scott] Peterson case, one wonders where that justice is..... The [death row] inmate is never subjected to any horror or misery comparable to what he mercilessly meted out to his victims.... [I]t is regrettable that we'll have to wait perhaps two decades for the [death] sentence to be carried out.[2]

When a convicted criminal lays claim to God's forgiveness through faith in Christ, our human sense of justice is offended, even outraged. Jeffrey Dahmer's jailhouse conversion, for instance, earned this reaction from journalist Bob Lonsberry:

> Did you hear he got religion? He made his peace with his maker. Lucky for him we have different makers. I think mine requires a little more than a prison conversion and a dunk in the pool to make up for butchering a dozen and a half innocent people.... [W]hy is it these dogs never get religion before they slaughter people? Why does it always come too late to do anybody any good? Whose side would God be on? Who does he welcome on judgment day? Are we supposed to believe that God embraces the murderer and sends the victim to hell?—Not in any heaven I want to be part of.[3]

As scholar and author Walter Wink has pointed out, the Old Testament provides plenty of support for this point of view:

> [There are] six hundred passages of explicit violence in the Hebrew Bible, one thousand verses where God's own violent actions of punishment are described, a hundred passages where Yahweh expressly commands others to kill.... [Retributive violence] is easily the most mentioned activity and central theme of the Hebrew Bible.[4]

Nor does this theme disappear entirely in the New Testament: the Book of Revelation as well as some of the Epistles speak of God's violent judgment of a deliberately sinful humanity.

But if divine justice were to consist of nothing more than pitiless retribution, what would we make of the hundreds of instances of and references to God's mercy and forgiveness in the Old and New Testaments?[5] How can Christ explicitly reject the Old Testament's "eye for an eye" and command us instead to "offer no resistance to the one who is evil" and turn the other cheek (Exodus 21:24; Matthew 5:39)? Is God the Son being untrue to God the Father when "mercy triumphs over judgment" (James 2:13)?

Of course not. The key to resolving the apparent contradiction between mercy and judgment is that godly punishment always has a *restorative purpose*, as both King Solomon and the author of the Letter to the Hebrews emphasized:

> My son, do not disdain the discipline of the Lord
> or lose heart when reproved by him;
> for whom the Lord loves, he disciplines;
> he scourges every son he acknowledges.
> (Proverbs 3:11–12; Hebrews 12:5–6)[6]

Thus punishment is not a *retributive* balancing of the scales, a repayment of one evil for another, but a kind of gift from God "for our benefit" (Hebrews 12:11)—the benefit of the offender! "At the time, all discipline seems a cause not for joy but for pain," our scriptural author acknowledges (Hebrews 12:11). But to end our examination of divine justice with that "pain" is to miss the whole point: "later it brings the peaceful fruit of righteousness to those who are trained by it" (Hebrews 12:11). St. Thomas Aquinas declares that "punishments are meant to be medicinal.... [T]he primary aim of punishment must be to achieve some good, either the sinner's correction, or at least his restraint so that others may enjoy peace and justice be defended and God honored."[7]

Of course, the restorative purpose and function of punishment is not some quirky New Testament innovation of our Father's but the central, if often overlooked motif of Old Testament justice as well. "Though Yahweh punishes sinners, there is no text in the Old Testament where his justice is equated with vengeance on the sinner," notes Professor J. R. Donahue of the Graduate Theological Union. "Yahweh's justice is saving justice, where punishment of the sinner is an integral part of restoration."[8] According to Professor Jürgen Moltmann of the University of Tübingen, "God's creative justice" heals and restores the victims *and* transforms the perpetrator, bringing about "a great Day of Reconciliation."[9]

On the individual level, too, ancient Israelite legislation on non-capital crimes usually aimed at "restoration," not mere retaliation: "since he has incurred guilt by his sin, [he shall] restore the thing that was stolen or unjustly retained" or even "restore his ill-gotten goods in full, and in addition give one-fifth of their value to the one he has wronged" (Leviticus 5:22; Numbers 5:5, 6). Professor Christopher Marshall of Victoria University, Wellington, sees laws like this in the context of Old Testament "social justice" concerns,

> such as care for widows, orphans, aliens, and the poor, the remission of debts, the manumission of slaves, and the protection of land rights. In this connection, covenant justice could be understood as positive succor for, and intervention on behalf of, the poor and the oppressed.[10]

Unfortunately, then as now, that concept of Godly justice was hard to uphold in daily life, as the prophet Zechariah noted with dismay:

are committing a form of idol-worship inside those courthouses. As serious and dedicated a Christian as Charles Colson, founder of Prison Fellowship Ministries, justifies the death penalty as necessary to "balance the scales of moral justice which have been disturbed" by premeditated murder. [15] Those scales are nowhere to be found in Scripture, however.

In the New Testament, scales or balances are mentioned only once: in Revelation 6:5, where death (not God) carries them to measure out starvation rations during the end times. The Old Testament uses *mozen*, or balances, fifteen times, almost always in reference to merchants cheating their customers; one exception is a beautiful poetic image in Isaiah 40:12 that describes our Creator's sovereignty. In only one passage, Job 31:6, do we find the man of sorrows complaining, "Let God weigh me in the scales of justice; thus will he know my innocence!"

But that is precisely what God refuses to do; in fact, the whole Book of Job is one long refutation of man's attempt to impose his sense of right and wrong on our Creator's actions! "Who is this that obscures divine plans with words of ignorance?" asks God. "Where were you when I founded the earth" (Job 38:2, 4)? Impartial scales were never our God's symbol of justice—not in Job's time, nor in Paul's.

Three Theories of Atonement

Because most of us do not like having to depend on a mysterious Creator's inexplicable mercy any more than Job did, we keep sneaking back to the altar of Themis to borrow her "fair" and simple scales. St. Anselm of Canterbury even used the concept of justice-as-a-metaphysical-balancing-act to explain how the cross freed us from sin, in what is called the "satisfaction" theory of atonement. According to Professor Harold J. Berman of Emory University and Harvard University, Anselm's *Cur Deus Homo* describes God as "bound by his own justice. If it is divinely just for a man to pay the price for his sins, it would be unjust, and therefore impossible, for God to remit the price." [16] Under this view of the cross, Christ actually *satisfied* God's demand for payment, instead of "*obliterating* the bond against us, with its legal claims" (Colossians 2:14, emphasis added). His death balanced out our sins, as it were.

In the hands of the Protestant Reformation, Anselm's "satisfaction" theory became the "penal substitution" theory. "Our guilt and its punishment were imposed on Christ, and his righteousness was imputed to us," Marshall summarizes this thesis. Significantly, "in popular Christian thought, some version of penal substitution remains the dominant form of explaining—and proclaiming—the work of the cross."[17]

And the theory of "penal substitution"—along with its image of God as a "hangin' judge" who insists on stiff retributive punishment—had a profound impact on the way Western criminal justice systems developed. "As [this theory] entered the cultural bloodstream,... [harsher] punishment was demanded because God himself had demanded the death of his son," according to Professor Timothy Gorringe of Exeter University.[18] This had direct and detrimental effects on courts and prisons: "Wherever Calvinism spread, punitive sentencing followed."[19]

There are, of course, some very obvious logical problems with both the "satisfaction" and the "penal substitution" models. Under both of these theories, atonement is seen as a forensic transaction in which God the Father acts both *in* God the Son (2 Corinthians 5:19) and *against* him at the same time. Moreover, God the Son essentially saves us, not from the devil, say, but from God the Father, who is eager to send us to hell. And if God really is "bound by his own justice"—*compelled* to punish *somebody* for humanity's sins—can he still be said to be an omnipotent deity?

Only in recent decades have some theologians begun to resolve such contradictions by studying the distorting effect that the Latin Fathers' Greco-Roman model of justice had on our Christian atonement theories. In order to properly understand "Paul's theology of justifying righteousness," for instance, it "is crucial to recognize that [it] is constructed on Jewish rather than Greco-Roman presuppositions,"

Professor J. D. G. Dunn of the University of Durham tells us.[20] Thus when Paul speaks of Jesus dying "for us" and "for our sins" (1 Corinthians 15:3; 1 Thessalonians 5:10), as he so often does, the operative model is the ancient Israelite scapegoat ceremony, not the scales of Themis.[21] Jesus died *on behalf of* us (our corporate representative), not *instead of* us (our penal substitute).

By grounding his understanding of the cross on Hebrew concepts of covenant and relationship rather than on the Greco-Roman idea of metaphysical justice, Marshall arrives at the "redemptive solidarity" theory of atonement:

> Christ suffers the penalty of sin not because God transfers our punishment onto him as a substitute victim, but because Christ fully and freely identifies himself with the plight and destiny of sinful humanity under the reign of death and pays the price for doing so. The thought is not one of legal imputation of guilt to Christ but of Christ's costly solidarity with humanity in its shameful and culpable condition. [22]

If the crucifixion is indeed not an act of punishment demanded by a stern Judge, but a loving Father's way of restoring a broken covenant, then our view of divine justice generally must change, too. The cross reveals that God does not seek to give each person precisely that punishment which he or she deserves; instead, he makes any sacrifice necessary to heal his damaged relationship with us. Translated to the human level, this means that true, divine justice is about "promoting the fellowship of the human race, and about furthering community," as St. Ambrose explains in *De Officiis*.

So what of America's enormous correctional system? Is "furthering community" and restoring *shalom* the aim of this country's prisons? Or do they embody the "eye for an eye" spirit of ancient Israelite cleansing rituals?

In fact, what of the concept of incarceration itself? Does God's justice allow the caging of his beloved sons and daughters at all? Teacher, author, and social activist Lee Griffith puts this issue in beguilingly simple terms:

Ultimately, there are not two kingdoms but one—the kingdom of God.... "Freedom to the captives" is not proclaimed [by Christ] in some other world but in our world [Luke 4:18]. The matter finally comes down to a peculiar question: Are there prisons in the kingdom of God? And if there are no prisoners there and then, how can we support the imprisonment of people here and now? For in fact the kingdom of God is among us here and now. [23]

George G., the subject of our first inmate interview, is also "among us here and now," and his testimony raises some troubling questions: does God's justice really demand that he remain behind bars? And even if we apply a purely human, utilitarian standard of justice, what purpose is being served by his continuing incarceration? Is George G.'s case perhaps a kind of canary in the coal mine, a sign that something has gone very, very wrong with America's criminal justice system?

INTERVIEW WITH "GEORGE G."

George G. was sentenced to sixty years for rape and burglary in 1984.

Q: Tell us a little about your life before you were arrested for your current offense.

A: I was born in 1958. My father was a carpenter, and my mother worked in the food industry. In 1974, at age sixteen, I was arrested for grand larceny; I stole some money from an apartment. The judge certified me as an adult and sentenced me to five years in prison.

Q: What was it like to walk into a penitentiary for the first time?

A: It was kind of scary, like anything you don't know or haven't done before. But a human being can adjust to anything, I guess.

Q: Describe your life there.

A: In the morning I went to GED class; in the afternoon I worked on a farm gang, planting corn or growing peanuts; and in the evening we had recreation on the yard or in the gym.

Q: There was no counseling, no programming to help a kid who was a first offender?

A: No, nothing like that. I don't think they even had a psychologist there. The only program was church, and I went to that once in a while.

Q: Was there any violence?

A: Oh, yeah, we had a lot of fights—a lot! One of them I can still remember clearly, more than thirty years later. There was this great big guy called Sugar Bear who knocked out another guy on the yard. Then he got on top of him and kept on beating and beating and beating him, even though he was totally unconscious. That got bloody, real bloody.

Q: Nobody tried to stop him?

A: Well, the guards came eventually. But you have to understand that there were hardly any officers who came on the yard; they'd rather stay in the buildings. So the yard was a kind of free-for-all.

Q: None of the other inmates tried to stop Sugar Bear?

A: No.

Q: The infamous convict code at its finest! Tell our readers a little about that code.

A: Well, it's really more of a survival code: do not involve yourself in anybody else's business, no matter what.

Q: Even when an unconscious man is being beaten close to death right in front of you?

A: Yeah. The thing is, even though you might see things in prison that you know aren't right, you are in an environment where *nothing* is right. So what are you going to do?

Q: Well? What did you do?

A: I built a wall around myself and didn't get close to people. I lived totally within myself. As long as you stay on this side of the window, this side of the wall, you can make your own world inside anything that you want it to be. You can't alter what you see, but you can fantasize.

Q: That sounds a little like the crimes you were arrested for in 1984.

A: Sure, it all ties in. But this is not to say that prison is to blame for what I did later.

Q: Would it be fair to say that prison did not make your pre-existing psychological issues any better?

A: It probably made them worse.

Q: So what happened after you got out of prison the first time?

A: I stayed out of trouble until 1984, when I was arrested for my current offense. I worked as a carpenter during those years, building houses. I didn't have any alcohol and drug problems, but I would drink a little alcohol and smoke a little pot at parties, just to be sociable. In 1982, I got married, but we separated after about a year.

Q: Tell us about your crime.

A: In 1984, I was arrested on a peeping tom charge and released on bond. Several days later, the police questioned me again about another offense that I didn't have anything to do with. But during that questioning, I decided to tell them everything.

Q: What do you mean by "everything"?

A: Between coming out of prison in 1978 and being arrested in 1984, I had been doing some things that I knew were wrong, and I wanted help rather than being out there and continuing to do these things. A guilty conscience played a part, because I knew I was living a double life. But mostly I wanted help, so I could stop.

Q: Stop doing what, precisely?

A: Raping women. You see, I had no self-esteem, no self-confidence. I could see no good in myself. Whatever I did, I could only see the flaws; it was always wrong. So I had to have a fantasy. I would watch people and be a peeping tom and build a fantasy relationship with that person, in order to love and be loved. In that position, as a peeping tom, there can be no rejection. You can be loved as much as you imagine.

Q: When did the peeping tom activity start?

A: Early in my childhood, when I was twelve. It began with a girl living up my street; I would go and watch her play drums. As a child, I did this every night. I never got caught, ever, until 1984. Nobody knew about this.

Q: Did you do this even after you came out of prison the first time, in 1978?

A: Yes, almost every night, except when I was dating my wife before we were married. But if she said or did something during the date that made me feel rejected—even an innocent comment, or being late—I would go out that night and watch people.

Then, after we were married in 1982, I stopped completely. But after we separated in 1983, I started back and continued until I was arrested in 1984.

Q: So how did the peeping tom activity escalate to rape?

A: The rapes only happened when the peeping tom fantasy was unsuccessful—if the person wasn't home, or if she went to bed early. None of the people I watched ever noticed me, so being discovered wasn't the reason. But if one of these other things happened to stop the fantasy and make me feel rejected and hopeless—that was important, the feeling of hopelessness, the feeling that no one would ever love me—then I would attack someone.

Q: Describe one of the rapes, in general terms.

A: On one occasion, I attacked a woman in a parking lot. Everyone I attacked was a complete stranger, because I thought anyone I knew already wouldn't love me. So I only attacked people I didn't know, because with them, I could fantasize that they loved me. I would have sex with the victim, but I would never beat her or hurt her sadistically. I always kissed my victims, because it was part of my fantasy to be loved.

Q: How many such attacks were there?

A: There were three, and also some attempted assaults. I told the police about them, but I wasn't charged with them.

Q: And the police did not know that you were connected with any of these earlier crimes—the three rapes and the attempted assaults?

A: No, they had no idea. They were really surprised when I told them all that stuff! But I wanted help, so I could stop doing these things.

Q: What happened after you confessed to all these attacks?

A: I went to court and pleaded guilty and went to prison.

Q: What sentence did the judge give you?

A: Sixty years. I became eligible for parole in 1992, and I have been turned down every time I've gone up again since then. They give me the same reason they give everyone else: "the serious nature and circumstances of the crime," every single time. My mandatory release date is 2014.

Q: Did you have an opportunity to apologize to the victims in court?

A: I don't know if they were in court when I pleaded guilty. I told the judge I was sorry, but it was all so rushed. I wrote all the victims letters, though.

Q: How did you manage to do that?

A: Back in 1984, when the police served a warrant for the charges on you, the names and addresses of the victims would be printed on that. Crazy, huh? I'm sure they don't do that anymore. Anyway, I had all the victims' names and addresses, so I wrote them letters to apologize. But at that point, I didn't really understand what I had done, or why I'd done it.

Q: Tell us about your life after you pleaded guilty, your life in prison.

A: From 1984 to 1989, I was in Mecklenburg Correctional Center, Virginia's supermax at that time. I arrived right after the big death row escape that they made the movies and TV shows about.

Q: Mecklenburg was extremely tough during those days, wasn't it?

A: It sure was. About three months after I got there, I got into a verbal argument with a particularly dangerous inmate, a well-known killer. I don't know why, but I faced right up to him on the middle of the ball field outside—and we didn't fight! Somehow, I guess I gained his respect. Looking back, I think it was God protecting me, standing by me. A year later, he was killed by another inmate in a dispute over a shower mat. But because I had stood up to him I never had any problems with all the other inmates.

Q: How did you spend your time?

A: Oh, the usual. I smoked some pot, and sold a little, too, so people would like me. But then, in 1988, I started taking college courses that the local community college was offering there. [Interviewer's Note: No supermax prison offers community college courses today. Also, inmates with long sentences no longer qualify for free community college courses, regardless of what type of prison they are housed in.] My second semester, I took psychology because I wanted to understand why I had done my crimes. Then one day the instructor showed up in the counselor's office.

Q: Why was that?

A: He said that he'd read my file and was interested in me because I had confessed to things I didn't need to confess to—things that the police hadn't even known about. That showed him that I wanted help. So for three years, we did one-on-one therapy. At first, we did it twice a week, but then the instructor was transferred to Brunswick Correctional Center. He arranged for me to be transferred to Brunswick, too, and once I got there in 1990, we continued with the therapy once a week.

Q: Did you finish your college education at Brunswick?

A: No. Brunswick offered an apprenticeship program in plumbing that I really wanted to take, so I went into that. You can't get fully certified until you get out and take a written test, but you can do the apprenticeship and the 8,000 hours on the job while you're inside. I've done way more than 8,000 hours by now, of course; I finished the apprenticeship in 1994 or '95.

Q: So what does your work at Brunswick consist of? You're kind of an institution around here, as you know.

A: Well, I'm on call twenty-four hours a day, working independently at night and on weekends when my supervisor isn't here. Last night, for example, I worked for four hours in the kitchen on the dishwashers. They trust me to work on my own, without anyone there to keep an eye on me.

Q: What do you do in your spare time?

A: I build model boats from scrap pieces of cardboard, Styrofoam and little things I find in the trash. I've been doing that since I was at Mecklenburg Correctional Center. It's helped me build self-esteem; I began to see that I could build something really beautiful, something that other people liked. I've sold one boat for as much as $150, but most of them I've given away to people who have helped me. Like the psychology instructor, or my counselor, or my boss at work. Apart from building boats, I like to work out in the weight room, and I go to Bible studies and prayer services.

Q: Tell us about how you found your way to God in here.

A: Well, first you have to understand that it's impossible to love God if you don't love yourself. Impossible! So before I could learn to love God, I had to learn to love myself. I had to learn not to base my self-esteem on what other people thought of me; that's what I'd been doing all my life until then.

Q: Is that what you learned in the therapy—how to love yourself?

A: Yeah, you could say that. It was after the therapy was over, in 1994 or so, that I turned my life over to Jesus. I was sitting in my cell, reflecting on all the changes in my life. I was no longer dependent on others for how I saw myself, I liked the boats I was making—but there was still something missing in my life.

Q: And that something was God?

A: Sure. Our heavenly Father. That's what brought it to a head, actually. I'd had a bad relationship with my father while I was growing up, and he hadn't visited me at Mecklenburg Correctional Center or Brunswick Correctional Center. But I had started talking to him on the phone from 1990 onward about the therapy I'd been doing with that instructor from the college course. Then, in 1993 or 1994, he began to visit me, and we rebuilt our relationship. We built a relationship that both of us had always wanted.

Q: How did that come about?

A: Through forgiveness. My father had to forgive me for the way I had turned out—his son, convicted of rape, in prison. And I had to learn to understand him and the things that had happened while I was growing up. His father had probably raised him the same way he raised me, so he didn't know any better. He had done the best he could.

Q: So reconciling with your earthly father helped you develop a relationship with your heavenly Father?

A: That's right. I had to heal the *natural* father–son relationship first, before I could have a *supernatural* father–son relationship. After all the stuff that my dad and I had gone through, I just got a feeling that God loved me the way my father loved me—only more so.

Q: And where did you go from there, from that feeling of being loved by God?

A: I got baptized in 1994 and started going to all the services they offered at Brunswick Correctional Center at that time. But I never found anything that represented father–son love. It was all just a bunch of rules—"religion."

Q: But you found one religious program that did satisfy you, right?

A: Yes, the Bible study led by Nahmen N., a German immigrant who came to the U.S. in the 1950s. He started in the ice business and ended up owning a restaurant, becoming really successful. Then he found the Lord, quit his business and bought a farm near Brunswick. He lets prisoners who've been released stay at houses on his property until they find their feet; he's been doing that for about ten years now. And, of course, he does the Bible study here.

Q: What attracted you to Nahmen's Bible study?

A: His honesty. He's very down-to-earth. He sees himself as no different from us prisoners; he's still dealing with problems in his own life and all that. With him, religion wasn't just a list of dos and don'ts, it was a family, a relationship. He became a kind of spiritual father figure to me.

Q: Shortly after that, your own father died, didn't he?

A: That's right, in 1995. I miss him very much, and I'm so glad that I was able to love him as a father and have him love me as a son before he died. He was able to forgive me and *forget* the past— leave it behind completely. That's what our heavenly Father does, too. It says so in Ezekiel: "None of the sins he has committed shall be *remembered* against him." We are washed completely clean by Christ's blood.

Q: And you were able to forgive your father, too, before he died.

A: That's right. I was able to love him. There had been so much anger in my life until then—mostly at myself. But that's gone, too. Once I understood why I did what I did, then I could forgive myself, because I know that those things can never happen again.

Q: If you could talk to your victims now, what would you tell them?

A: I would want them to know that it was never in my heart to hurt them. In my fantasy, it was a love relationship. That's what I was always searching for: love. I think, maybe, if they knew why I did what I did, maybe they could forgive me.

Q: After about ten years of attending Nahmen's Bible studies at Brunswick Correctional Center, you and two other guys started something new, something of your own, didn't you?

A: Yes. The Lord had us put together a "Soaking Prayer" program that meets every Friday, with Nahmen as our sponsor. I did some of the administrative side of that, because I've been at Brunswick for so long and the staff here know they can trust me. The two other guys are more experienced with the kind of prayer that we do.

Q: I attended one of your "Soaking Prayer" sessions, and I would describe it as a Pentecostal prayer service that involves speaking in tongues and the laying on of hands. It's a very emotional atmosphere, and really quite moving and powerful. But how would you describe it?

A: Well, we call it "Soaking Prayer" because we want to soak in the presence of God. Through his word, we know that the love of God has been shed into our hearts. We have been fully reconciled to God through the death of his son. Christ has blotted out our sins, so God holds nothing against us and loves us completely. Me and the two other guys, we bring this to the men who attend the "Soaking Prayer" sessions—we give them what God has given us. We want them to experience our heavenly Father's love and mercy and forgiveness.

Q: What would you do if you were to experience some very earthly forgiveness—if you were released from prison?

A: I would probably return to doing woodwork and carpentry to support myself. But my top priority would be continue with the Bible study and soaking in the presence of the Lord. That's what's most important. And I would try to get permission to come back to prison through the front door, as a minister.

Q: Do you think about those possibilities a lot?

A: Not really. I don't look far into the future. I concentrate on bringing as many people as possible from the darkness into the light now, right here. It's one day at a time, one person at a time.

Q: But you do want to be released, don't you?

A: Yes, but even if I never make parole, I'm fine with that, too. I feel I'm more free in here than a whole lot of people on the street. It's what's on the inside that counts, not the environment. I'm enjoying my life, and I have peace.

QUESTIONS FOR REFLECTION AND DISCUSSION

SCRIPTURE—Review the various interpretations of original sin at the beginning of this chapter. How do they relate to each other? How does each relate to the author's proposition, that original sin manifested itself as a theft? Could all of these theories be complementary?

CRIMINOLOGY—The author of the letter to the editor quoted in this chapter regrets that a death-row prisoner "is never subjected to any horror or misery comparable to what he mercilessly meted out to his victims." Imagine a court and legal system based on the principle that every crime must be balanced with an equivalent punishment. Work through a list of offenses and consider how, on a practical level, each sentence would be imposed. Is it actually possible to operate a real-world criminal justice system if punishments have to fit the crime?

SELF-EXAM—Review to what extent "justice" has become equated with "punishment" in your own mind. Test this by watching local TV news. Can you imagine replacing "justice = punishment" with "justice = restoration of covenant/relationship"?

INTERVIEW—George is a sex offender and thus the epitome of evil— at least according to his Department of Corrections file and current public perceptions. Can you imagine having him move in next door to you? How would you feel? What would you say or do?

INTERNET—Virtually all denominations have position papers or official statements on criminal justice. Download your own denomination's statement *and* that of the denomination that you judge to be the furthest removed from yours doctrinally.

IMMERSION—Go to a courthouse and spend an hour or two observing the proceedings in two or three courtrooms. Try to schedule your visit to coincide with bail hearings. Measure what you see against the yardstick of "justice = restoration of covenant/relationship." As you leave, take a look at Themis.

Chapter 2

JOSEPH AND COMMONLY HELD
BELIEFS ABOUT PRISON

LIKE GEORGE G., our previous interview subject, Joseph the Israelite also served time for rape (Genesis 39:20). Unlike George, however, Joseph did not commit the crime of which he was convicted—and that surely should make us pause. Could it really be just a coincidence that the very first prison inmate we encounter in the Bible is the victim of a miscarriage of justice?

Perhaps the authors of Scripture meant to warn us against our inclination to condemn and dismiss anyone who wears the convict's striped garb. How do we know—really *know*—that the monster we saw on *America's Most Wanted* last night is as guilty as TV producers and prosecutors made him appear? He could be another Joseph!

A convict like me might interpret Genesis 39:6–20 this way: woman attempts to seduce man; man refuses; woman screams rape; man goes to prison. As a story about a sexual offense that may or may not have occurred, this passage is surely trying to tell us something about...well, crime. Right?

Wrong, if you ask most Bible scholars. According to Professor Walter Brueggemann of Columbia Theological Seminary, for instance, Genesis 39 is actually a kind of cultural allegory: Joseph represents Israel, the "people of the dream," while Potiphar's wife stands for Egypt, the "rulers of the Empire." Brueggemann devotes much time to the ancient scriptural author's subtle use of the words "lie" and "hand," and he has much to say about the tension between divine power and imperial might.[1] But amid all the fascinating facts and insights, he passes over the simple fact that *Joseph got screwed by the system.*

Yet miscarriages of justice like Joseph's are clearly of concern to God, since the Bible contains many stories of wrongly imprisoned and/or executed men: Jeremiah, John the Baptist, Jesus, Peter, Stephen and Paul, for example. If the Good Book is to be believed, the pre-exilic Israelite courts (Jeremiah 37 and 38), the indigenous Palestinian courts under Roman occupation (Mark 6), the Roman military courts (John 18 and 19, and Acts 24 and 25), the Temple courts (Acts 4, 5, and 7), and the Roman provincial courts (Acts 16) were *all* as unjust as the ancient Egyptian courts (Genesis 39). What the sheer number of these cases suggests to me, if not to Brueggemann, is that God wants us to be extremely cautious about trusting judges and juries—and that includes American judges and juries, too.

According to a comprehensive study of miscarriages of justice by the University of Michigan's Professor Samuel R. Gross, "there are thousands of innocent people in prison today."[2] Another study, by Professor Stephen A. Drizzin of Northwestern University and Professor Richard A. Leo of the University of California, Irvine, even offers an estimate of the number of wrongful convictions: "if we reviewed prison sentences with the same level of care that we devote to death sentences, there would have been 28,500 non-death-row exonerations rather than the 255 that have in fact occurred."[3]

This figure of 28,500 only seems high if we forget that it represents a mere 1.2% of the 2.3 million men and women behind bars in this country. In any other profession, an error rate of 1.2% would be considered admirably low. What taxi driver gets lost only once in every one hundred trips? What doctor misdiagnoses only one out of every one hundred patients? What mutual fund manager picks only one bad stock in a hundred?

Indeed, if judges and lawyers are just as imperfectly human as the rest of us, then there are almost certainly *far more* than 28,500 unjustly imprisoned inmates languishing in U.S. penitentiaries. In 2005 the state of Virginia DNA-tested biological evidence from thirty-one *randomly chosen* case files dating from the mid-1980s. Two of the thirty-one convicts, or 7%, turned out to be innocent.[4]

For most Christians, the material above makes for uncomfortable reading because it challenges our commonly held beliefs about the legal system. We tend to think of American courts as "the best in the world"—but Joseph the Israelite and those 28,500 wrongly convicted inmates force us to question that belief. As Joseph's story continues, we find other commonly held beliefs challenged as well.

Genesis 39 and 40 suggest that the reality of penitentiary life differs markedly from what most of us imagine:

- Even though Joseph himself was an inmate, the chief jailer put him "in charge of all the prisoners in the jail, and everything that had to be done was under his management" (Genesis 39:22). In this case, even the guards recognized that some convicts, at least, are neither lazy nor untrustworthy, but honest, able, and intelligent.
- When two of Joseph's fellow inmates had troubling dreams, he "noticed that they looked disturbed" and volunteered to help them by using his gift of interpretation (Genesis 40:6). Apparently, not all prisoners are heartless sociopaths who exploit other convicts' weaknesses whenever possible.
- After Pharaoh freed Joseph and placed him "in charge of the whole land of Egypt" (Genesis 41:41), the Israelite ex-convict wisely steered his host country through a time of national emergency. Some inmates, it seems, do not spend their whole sentence planning their next crime after release.

Of course, the three points above are only scriptural hints and suggestions, not a fully elaborated biblical critique of corrections. But they do suggest that we should question our assumptions about prison, the most important of which may be that there is no alternative to current U.S. penal policies.

THE AMERICAN WAY IS THE ONLY WAY

Judging by the incarceration rates of those nations that use prison only as a last resort, America could easily do without the vast majority of its jails and penitentiaries. Japan, for instance, survives quite nicely while locking up only 58 out of 100,000 of its citizens, and the five Scandinavian countries remain perfectly pleasant while confining just 39 to 75 out of 100,000.[5] By comparison, the U.S. keeps 737 out of 100,000 residents behind bars.[6] To what purpose?

What the incarceration rates of Japan and Scandinavia suggest is that only *one in ten* of America's convicts probably *needs* to be in prison to protect the public. For that small minority, a few jails and penitentiaries should be kept open. But nine out of ten correctional centers could be closed.

To those who would argue that the above line of reasoning ignores different levels of offending in the U.S. and overseas, a close look at the International Crime Victim Survey, conducted in seventeen industrialized countries, might be instructive. This study found that crime rates in "first world" nations all fall within a range of 15 to 25%, with 21% being the average.[7] Since the latter happens to be precisely America's rate, too, the land of the free turns out to be no more and no less lawless than comparable countries.*

At least one U.S. jurisdiction manages to maintain law and order with an incarceration rate very close to European levels: Maine. While the Pine Tree State is not typical of America as a whole, it is one of the forty-eight contiguous states and is only a short drive away from Boston, a major urban area with all the usual crime-generating social problems. Yet Maine has found it only needs to lock up 144 out of 100,000 of its residents, *one-seventh* the national U.S. rate of imprisonment.[9]

When it comes to corrections, then, the American way clearly is not the only way: not only Europe but even Maine manage to maintain public safety at much lower levels of incarceration. So why does this country nevertheless lock up such a disproportionate number of

---

* Note that the International Crime Victim Survey employs the household survey method, which excludes murder. Because of the greater availability of guns in the U.S., homicides are significantly more common here than in other industrialized nations.[8] This study effectively filters out much of the distortion in crime rates caused by America's peculiar love of firearms, allowing a fairer comparison of underlying levels of offending.

offenders? What are the myths that sustain current penal policies? Let us examine a few of them.

Prison Reduces Crime

Between 1991 and 2001, the number of inmates in the U.S. rose 51.6%, and the crime rate dropped 29.5%.[10] But that does not mean the former *caused* the latter, any more than the cock's crow causes the sun to rise. According to criminologists, *only 15 to 27%* of the 29.5% decline in crime can be attributed to the rise in the incarceration rate: a buoyant economy, a smaller population of crime-prone teenagers, and changes in law enforcement practices account for most of the reduction.[11]

This point is so important that it bears repeating: *only about one-quarter of the drop in crime is due to higher rates of incarceration.* To put this in numbers:

- increasing the size of America's prison system by more than half (51.6%)...
- ...lowered crime by only 4.4 to 7.9% (that is, 15 x 29.5 and 27 x 29.5, respectively)

Why do prisons get so little credit for decreasing crime? Because those states that experienced enormous growth in their penitentiary populations lowered their crime rates no more—and in some cases less—than those states whose incarceration rates increased by more modest margins.[12]

State	Rise in Incarceration Rate	Decrease in Crime Rate
U.S. average	51.6%	29.5%
Texas	139.4%	34.1%
California	42.5%	42.4%
New York	10.9%	53.2%

Figures from New York City illustrate the disconnect between prison and crime even more dramatically. Between 1993 and 2006, the number of homicides in the Big Apple fell by 70% even as the inmate population dropped from 21,449 to 14,129. "What we've seen in New York is the fastest drop in crime in the nation, and we did it while locking up a lot fewer people," boasts Corrections Commissioner Martin F. Horn.[13]

According to Jonathan Turley, law professor at George Washington University and a columnist for USA Today, "It would be hard to make the case that the rising prison population has lowered the crime rate. I expect that there is some impact, but the population of criminal actors in society is so large that it would be difficult to show a pronounced effect." Former New York Corrections Commissioner Michael Jacobson also "does not believe there is a direct cause and effect [relationship] between incarceration and crime rates," and conservative criminologist James Q. Wilson concludes that "very large increases in prison population can only produce modest reductions in crime rates." [14]

According to the Vera Institute survey of current criminological research, Reconsidering Incarceration: New Directions for Reducing Crime, "The most sophisticated studies available generally agree that increased incarceration rates have some impact on reducing crime rates, but the scope of that impact is limited…. [C]riminal justice policymakers appear to have placed undue emphasis on incarceration."[15]

Prison Teaches Criminals a Lesson

As with any assumption, we should start by questioning what exactly we mean when we say, "Prison teaches criminals a lesson." For instance, precisely what lesson is prison supposed to teach?

If "crime doesn't pay" is the proposed message that correctional facilities are meant to send, then we can easily imagine other means of communication: fines, house arrest by GPS bracelet, community service, etc. All of these methods effectively convey the central point—"breaking the law is more trouble than it is worth"—but they do so at far lower cost and without many of the negative side effects of incarceration.

Prison is also commonly thought to teach felons, "Do not commit crime again." But by that standard incarceration is spectacularly unsuccessful: the national recidivism rate is 67.5%. In fact, a stay behind bars actually makes criminals *more* likely to re-offend. The American Bar Association's *Justice Kennedy Commission Report* found that "prison has a negative effect on offenders' later income, employment prospects and family involvement, all of which is predictive of future criminality."[16] Many states bar ex-convicts from professions as innocuous as landscaping and barbering, and drug offenders usually cannot get food stamps or public housing assistance. The Legal Action Center, the Urban Institute, and the Sentencing Project have done much to reveal these so-called collateral consequences of incarceration, which make successful reentry so difficult for the thirteen million Americans with felony records.[17]

Less commonly known are the psychological handicaps that inmates acquire as a result of their sojourn in prison. According to the *British Journal of Criminology*, convicts are subject to institutionalization, a process "characterized by apathy and reduced motivation, coupled with extreme dependency on routine and the support of the institution—which may render the man unfit to cope with the outside world upon release."[18] Dr. Craig Haney, of the University of California, Santa Cruz, reports that some ex-prisoners configure their living spaces at home to re-create the look and feel of their cells: "The rooms were always small and dark.... The beds were made in the same way. Shoes were always stacked by their bed, just like in prison."[19]

Since incarceration is meant to be a painful experience, we should not be surprised that it traumatizes many of those who are subjected to it. And we should also not be surprised if that trauma expresses itself in a new offense. Paradoxically, the very structure of prison is such that it works against itself: the harsher jails and penitentiaries are made, with the goal to "teach criminals a lesson," the more they impair the ability of inmates to learn whatever it is that prison is supposed to teach them.

Prison Deters Many People Who Would Otherwise Commit Crimes

Here again several fundamental questions present themselves before we even consider whether this commonly held belief about prison is actually true. For instance, if deterrence is our goal, then why not choose another deterrent—one that is less expensive, and the side effects of which are less harmful than prison? And why do we assume that it is necessary to scare people into compliance with the law? Positive (as opposed to negative) reinforcement has been proved to be effective: in very large-scale studies of AFDC (Aid to Families with Dependent Children) payments, researchers found that burglary and homicide rates fell as welfare disbursements increased.[20]

Deterrence, by contrast, has little empirical support. If the prospect of a term behind bars actually dissuaded potential offenders, then more prisons should lead to less crime. However, we know that this is not the case:

- In these pages we repeatedly note that the U.S. correctional population septupled over the last thirty years, while the crime rate today is almost exactly the same as in the early 1970s. Amazing, really—literally millions of people disappeared behind bars over those three decades, but criminals kept on breaking the law as if nothing had changed!

- As we saw in the chart above, Texas expanded its prison system thirteen times as much as New York in the 1990s (139.4% vs. 10.9%), but lowered its crime rate significantly less (34.1% vs. 53.2%). A genuine deterrent would have yielded a crime reduction proportional to the size of the threat; a bigger stick should have produced proportionally greater compliance.

- If prisons really served as an effective warning, then the neighborhoods surrounding each jail or penitentiary should be oases of perfect peace and tranquility, and correctional officers should be the most law-abiding people on earth. Neither is the case, of course—far from it.

Why does prison not deter potential offenders? Because the vast majority of criminals do not rationally calculate the consequences of their actions when they break the law. Of those felons who get caught and go to prison, 20% are mentally ill;[21] 37% were under the influence of alcohol at the time of their crime, while 33% were on drugs;[22] 19% are completely illiterate and another 40% functionally illiterate.[23] Add to all this the fact that the average convict's IQ score is eight to ten points lower than the general population's, and we can begin to understand why deterrence does not work![24] Society may think tough punishments send potential offenders a warning message, but the sad truth is that most of them are too crazy, too drunk, too high, too uneducated, and too dimwitted to hear that warning.

Not only is deterrence ineffective, but it also has several significant negative consequences. For instance, by raising the specter of merciless retribution, society may be dissuading criminals from seeking treatment for the psychological conditions that contributed to their offending behavior. The hope of getting therapy is what led George, our first interview subject, to confess to several sexual assaults of which the police were unaware. In the early 1980s, when rehabilitation was still the official goal of prison, his expectation of help was not unreasonable. Today, by contrast, no rapist would dare turn himself in voluntarily, given the currently popular demonization of sex offenders.

Perhaps an even more significant problem with prison as a deterrent is that it has become counterproductive through overuse. As we will see in the next chapter, incarceration is so common among black men in particular that many members of the African-American community simply accept it as inevitable. Prison is no longer a threat to be avoided but a regular feature of everyday life.

On Black Entertainment Television (BET), nearly every other video shows defendants singing on the witness stand or convicts rapping behind bars. Major artists like Lil' Kim, C-Murder, and Drama have served or are serving time, and their record labels trumpet their convictions as establishing their "street credibility." According to a fellow inmate, his sons think it is "cool" to visit their daddy in the penitentiary. They and their friends wear orange jumpsuits as a fashion statement, not as a sign of shame and disgrace.

Prison as a deterrent? Hell, no—prison is where all my home-boys are!

Prison Incapacitates Offenders; They Cannot Harm Anyone as Long as They Are Locked Up

That final qualifying clause—"as long as they are locked up"—is the problem, of course: over 95% of all inmates are released eventually, so incarceration merely delays the inevitable. With more than 672,000 prisoners returning to society each year, of whom 67.5% then recidivate, we can safely say that incapacitation simply is not happening.

Even worse, prison frequently puts the wrong kind of convict out of action, as we will see in Chapter 4. Murderers, sex offenders, and older inmates of all types may or may not *deserve* to remain behind bars, but their low recidivism rates mean that they do not need to be *incapacitated*. If the prevention of new crimes by known felons were the goal of prison, society would do better to keep those inmates locked up whose original offenses were less serious, but who are statistically more likely to re-offend. That would be manifestly unjust, of course, which is why incapacitation is not a practical argument for incarceration.

More significantly, it is simply untrue that prison stops convicts from harming others. For instance, there are currently two million boys and girls who are growing up with one or both parents behind bars.[25] One in thirty-three children has lost a father or mother to prison; for African-American kids, the figure is one in eight.[26] In most cases, the incarcerated parent is the father, and his absence condemns his offspring to a childhood of many hardships and few opportunities:

kids raised by their mother alone are six times more likely to be poor than similarly situated boys and girls raised by both parents.[27]

"When I come across kids not doing well in school, six out of ten will have someone in prison," says Richmond, Virginia, school social worker Bill O'Sullivan. Younger children sometimes regress to bed-wetting or throwing temper tantrums; older boys and girls may use drugs or skip school. "No two kids react the same," O'Sullivan says, but many—far too many—end up "mad at the world." [28]

Is it any wonder that many of those impoverished children of convicts later become criminals themselves? Sixty percent of rapists, 72.1% of adolescent murderers, and 70% of all long-term inmates grew up without a father in the home.[29] A child whose parent has been incarcerated is six times more likely than other kids to wind up behind bars himself, according to testimony before the U.S. Senate.[30] Thus, by failing to fulfill their parental duties, prisoners are indirectly causing new crimes to be committed in the future. And those crimes inevitably will "produce" yet more prisoners.

Moreover, prisons themselves are hardly free of crime: according to repeated large-scale anonymous surveys, 20% of male inmates, or roughly 400,000 men, are "pressured or forced" into sex by other prisoners each year, and one in ten is raped outright.[31] "Due to fear of reprisal from perpetrators, a code of silence among inmates, personal embarrassment and lack of trust in staff," however, the Bureau of Justice Statistics received only 8,210 officially documented reports of such incidents in 2004.[32]

Is prison rape a "real" crime? Some claim it is not: if you believe Professor Mark Fleisher of Case Western Reserve University, the typical prison inmate "doesn't interpret sexual pressure as coercion…. Rather, sexual pressure ushers, guides or shepherds the process of sexual awakening." That bit of "wisdom" cost the American taxpayer $939,233, according to the Department of Justice, which commissioned Fleisher's study.[33]

To those subjected to sexual assault behind bars, things look a little different. "Prison destroyed me," says one survivor. "They [i.e., the inmates who raped him and infected him with HIV] took my health. They took my manhood. I keep on fighting. But there are some things I'll never get back." Another victim reports, "On a purely emotional level, I have issues with self-confidence and trust since that day.... It's something that I'll never really recover from, no matter how hard I try." "The physical pain was devastating," says a man raped at knifepoint in an Arkansas prison. "But the emotional pain was even worse.... They'd stolen my manhood, my identity, and part of my soul."[34]

In addition to the suffering inflicted on victims, prison rape also harms society at large because it contributes to the spread of infectious diseases among inmates who will eventually be released. Other forms of transmission include consensual sex—44 to 65% of convicts voluntarily participate in some form of sex—as well as tattooing and intravenous drug use with stolen syringes.[35] Thanks to such fun and games, 8.1% of all New York prisoners, for example, are known to be infected with HIV.[36]*

The prevalence of HIV behind bars is directly responsible for the disproportionate rise of HIV infection rates in the African-American community, according to a study by Professors Rucker C. Johnson and Stephen Raphael of the University of California, Berkeley. While HIV was approximately as common among whites as it was among blacks in the mid-1980s, today African-American men are seven times as likely to be infected as Caucasian men, and black women are nineteen times as likely to have contracted the disease as white women. An analysis of 850,000 men and women who were infected with HIV between 1982 and 1996 reveals the cause of this divergence to be the much higher rates of African-American incarceration during those same years.[38] But since tens of thousands of Caucasian HIV carriers also leave prison each year, the white community's infection rate will eventually rise, too.

---

* The Bureau of Justice Statistics reports an HIV infection rate of only 2.2% for state prisoners nationwide. Why is their figure so much lower? Because "many jails and prisons have backed away from testing inmates for fear that they will be required to pay for treatment," according to the *New York Times*.[37] New York's correctional department, by contrast, tests all inmates systematically, so its data can be trusted.

HIV is only one problem, however: other contagious diseases being bred behind bars include hepatitis C, a fatal liver illness that has infected 39% of inmates in Virginia;[39] drug-resistant strains of syphilis and staph spreading in California's jails;[40] and good old-fashioned tuberculosis, which killed hundreds of convicts, guards and civilians in a well-documented outbreak in New York in 1989.[41] Every year 1.5 million people are released from jails and penitentiaries nationwide carrying potentially life-threatening illnesses.[42] Just as prison cannot truly incapacitate criminals, so too can walls and razor wire not confine viruses and bacteria.

In the end, incapacitation must fail because it is based on the illusion that prison can somehow make offenders vanish. But "out of sight, out of mind" never really works. Ever since Freud revolutionized the field of psychology, we know that personal problems cannot be effectively repressed but are better dealt with openly. The same principle holds true for societal problems like crime and criminals.

A Brief Interlude about AIDS and the Dangers of Doing Research in Prison

In 2006, the Centers for Disease Control and Prevention (CDC) published a study of AIDS in the Georgia Department of Corrections claiming that, over a seventeen-year period, only 88 inmates out of 45,000 became infected with HIV during their incarceration.[43] This piece of "research" should concern all of us because, if left unchallenged, it could set back AIDS prevention efforts behind bars, leading to higher infection rates both in and outside of prison. Moreover, in the process of debunking the CDC's "findings" below, we can learn a little about what penitentiary life is really like, as opposed to what is commonly believed.

Anyone with prison experience will realize that the CDC study contains three enormous "red flags"—indicators that something is terribly wrong with the "data" being collected.

- Half of the infected prisoners claimed that their sex partner was a staff member.

    What this "finding" suggests is that sexual activity between guards and inmates is rampant behind bars. In fact, nothing could be further from the truth: over the more than two decades I have spent behind bars, I have become aware of only about a dozen relationships between female staff members and male convicts, and just one between a male officer and a male prisoner. The overwhelming majority of guards have enough sense to avoid such potentially career-ending entanglements, while most inmates are only willing to take the risk if the romantic prize is a woman. For sex with another man, a fellow convict makes much more sense than an officer!

- Nearly three-quarters of prisoners in the CDC study describe their sexual activity as consensual.

    Sure they do! If they were to tell the truth, they would be labeled as snitches, so they keep their mouths shut—or lie. Remember, 400,000 inmates are forced into having sex *each year*.

    Social scientists researching prison rape know that the most important factor in designing their studies is to find some way to assure inmates that no one—not even the scientists themselves—can identify which prisoner turned in a particular questionnaire. To the convict mind, the idea that researchers would dust the answer sheets for fingerprints is not that farfetched! Lying is always the safest option.

- Almost one-third of prisoners in the CDC study said they used condoms or improvised protection, like rubber gloves or plastic wrap.

    When I discussed this with some acquaintances of mine, they burst out laughing. Condoms are contraband, so they are not available; the idea of using rubber gloves or plastic wrap was considered too ridiculous to be worthy of a coherent response. In the penitentiary, you live fast and die young, which means going "bareback."

The subject of this chapter is commonly held beliefs about prison, and just how wrong most of them are. In many ways, "the big house" is a *terra incognita* where even CDC epidemiologists can lose their way. So much of what passes for "data" in the field of corrections is simply junk: for instance, Arkansas, North Dakota, and South Dakota officially reported that there were *zero* assaults between inmates in those three states in 2000![44] Federal statistics on prison rape are nearly as absurd, as we saw above. In its report *Confronting Confinement*, the Commission on Safety and Abuse in America's Prisons devotes a twelve-page section and a separate two-page sidebar to a discussion of the "stunning gaps in the research and data" about corrections.[45]

The CDC researchers who conducted the study of HIV in Georgia's penitentiaries apparently were not aware of the general unreliability of correctional statistics. Nor did they take into account that "many jails and prisons have backed away from testing inmates for fear they will be required to pay for treatment."[46] If the CDC scientists had taken note of this, their findings would undoubtedly have been very different.

According to *Corrections Today*, the American Correctional Association's official journal, "There are three primary ways of examining the prevalence of HIV within correctional systems in the published literature: administrative data, seroprevalence data and the HIV/AIDS Reporting System (HARS)." The first and third methods measure only "administratively known" and "new 'officially' diagnosed" cases. When researchers use these figures, supplied by prison medical staff, they arrive at infection rates of 1.9 to 2.9%—pleasantly low.[47]

By contrast, studies employing the seroprevalence data method use "a sample of blood taken for various [other] purposes." Thus the tested population consists of a relatively random cross-section of all inmates in a given facility. In one such study of male prisoners in Maryland in the early 1990s, the seroprevalence method determined the HIV infection rate to be 7.9%—not 1.9% or 2.9%.[48]

That figure of 7.9% nearly matches the 8.1% reported by the New York correctional department which, as we saw earlier in this chapter, tests its *entire* inmate population. So we can reasonably conclude that the seroprevalence method is far more accurate than the administrative data or HARS methods. And that fact—surely known to highly educated epidemiologists and AIDS researchers—raises some very interesting and troubling questions.

Why is it that the seroprevalence method is only rarely used in studies of HIV infection rates in prison? Why is the public almost always given figures in the 1.9 to 2.9% range—not in the 7.9 to 8.1% range? And what are the likely effects of hundreds of thousands of prisoners being infected with HIV?

Prison Punishes

Even if incarceration does not make society safer, it could perhaps be justified on purely retributive grounds. Unquestionably, prison punishes—but are we honest about the form that punishment takes? Getting raped by other inmates, having painful medical conditions ignored by private correctional health care companies, being driven to the edge of insanity or beyond in a supermax-style isolation cell—these are not exceptional occurrences but part of everyday life behind penitentiary walls. If judges' sentencing orders were truly reflective of reality, they would include items like the above—perhaps with specific instructions on how many times this particular offender is to be sodomized by his cellmate, and whether he should be infected with HIV or syphilis or both. Or is that a little too much "truth in sentencing"?

In addition to the question of whether prison provides a just form of punishment, we must ask whether two wrongs could possibly make a right: Precisely how does one harm (prison) "make good" another harm (crime)? Also there is the problem of equivalence: even if "an eye for an eye" is fair, what relationship is there between "grand theft auto" and "five years in the slammer"? And for some categories of criminals, we must also ask, is punishment appropriate at all?

Earlier we noted that 20% of U.S. inmates, or roughly 400,000 men, women and youths, are afflicted with some variety of mental illness. Thanks to the badly mismanaged closure of large psychiatric facilities in the 1970s and '80s, "Lots of people are winding up in the criminal justice system because mental health services are not available," says Hazel Moran of the National Mental Health Association.[49] What is this country's largest psychiatric services provider? the Los Angeles County Jail.[50]

In 1955, America housed 559,000 mentally ill people in state hospitals. If the same patient-per-capita ratio applied today, there should be 930,000 residents receiving treatment in such facilities today. Instead there are only 60,000 patients in psychiatric hospitals; the rest are in prison or on probation.[51]

Even behind bars, however, they definitely remain patients. Twice a day, every day, dozens of them line up outside every prison's medical department to receive their psychotropic drugs at special "mental health pill calls." Those medications make them docile enough for the guards to manage—and also for other convicts to exploit.

Want a cheap high that standard correctional urinalysis cups cannot detect? Find yourself a mentally ill inmate and play cards with him; he will be so grateful to you for befriending him, and so dopey from his meds, that he will not notice how his gambling debt is mounting up. When he is in hock to you for some unimaginably enormous sum—say $20, a whole month's prison wages for sweeping floors—continue to play the role of friend and offer him a way out of debt!

Every time he goes to pill call, have your vic spit his psychotropic pills back into his hand and bring them to you. Take half the pills yourself and sell the other half to your stickman. Meanwhile, your mentally ill buddy will need extra tobacco to get him over the shakes from missing his meds. So you give him a few roll-ups and generously raise his debt level.

Of course, your friend will eventually start to act out because he is no longer getting his psychotropic drugs. Good Samaritan that you are, you help him fill out a sick-call slip and explain to him what to say to the staff psychiatrist to get his dosage increased. Then you let him keep a few of those extra pills to stabilize him, making a great show of what a kindhearted gesture this is. Your buddy will reward you with puppylike devotion, trust me!

At this point, you can easily persuade him to perform a few sexual services for you and your stickman, too. He will hardly object: many mentally ill people have a history of such exploitation by their caregivers from childhood onward. Since there is no overt threat of force, this sort of activity is considered consensual by those who try to measure the incidence of prison rape.

Hey, boys will be boys—and they are just inmates, anyway.

Why does America condemn 400,000 human beings to years and decades of this nightmare existence? One reason may be money: according to David Fahti of the ACLU National Prison Project, it costs $95 per day to house a mentally ill person in Wisconsin's supermax prison, for instance, but roughly $363 per day to house him in a secure psychiatric hospital. Corrections officials admit that "well over half" of the inmate population at some supermax facilities has diagnosable mental illnesses.[52]

Another reason why so many psychologically disabled people end up behind bars is the refusal of criminal courts to acknowledge the role of mental illness in criminal behavior. The law determines a defendant's psychiatric status by the so-called McNaughten Rule: does the accused know the difference between right and wrong, and can he conform his conduct to the law? By that standard, even those offenders who are flagrantly mentally ill from a medical point of view are nevertheless found sane from a legal perspective. And so they are sent to a prison instead of a psychiatric facility.

The McNaughten Rule was defined by an English judge in 1844, and psychiatry has advanced greatly since then. In most other countries, a more nuanced and sophisticated understanding of mental illness has been incorporated into their legal systems through some version of the Durham Rule: Was the offense the product of a psychiatric condition? This allows courts to make a finding of "diminished capacity," whereby defendants are held partially responsible for their actions and sent to secure mental hospitals for treatment.[53]

Ironically enough, the Durham Rule was originally developed in the U.S., the one industrialized nation that has for the most part failed to adopt it into its criminal code. In this, the putatively most Christian country on earth, love of punishment apparently is so powerful that even the mentally ill are granted no mercy.

Prison Rehabilitates

Nonsense! Prison itself does not rehabilitate anyone; it is the high school equivalency class, the plumbing apprenticeship or the sex offender group that can turn a convict's life around. In Chapter 5 we will learn that, contrary to the "nothing works" naysayers, some educational and therapeutic programs do indeed reduce recidivism. That raises a very interesting question, however: if the objective of prison is the transformation of criminals into law-abiding citizens, should society not concentrate its resources on schooling and treatment? Why spend good money on razor wire and correctional officers?

State prisons devote only 6% of their budgets to rehabilitation; the rest goes to cost factors like guards' wages and capital construction that do nothing to further the ultimate goal of resocialization.[54] Yet my sense is that many, perhaps most inmates would require very little compulsion if offered a *genuine* chance to improve their lives. Like most people, they do not need to be forced to accept a good thing—so long as they believe that it really, truly is a good thing!

The problem, of course, is to persuade felons that attendance at court-ordered classes and counseling sessions will indeed lead to a better future. At present the overwhelming majority of convicts, myself included, are convinced that America has no interest in welcoming us into mainstream society and helping us succeed. If that should ever change—if you ever do decide to invite us in, and if we find the courage to accept your open hand—then U.S. correctional departments could be restructured on the Finnish model.

Security at Hameenilla penitentiary consumes only a small portion of the corrections budget: it consists of ten handguns that remain locked in the warden's safe at all times.[55] Because residents are granted regular home leaves, they have no need to escape or rebel. Called "pupils" or "clients," not prisoners, they return to Hameenilla voluntarily, because they know and believe that their community will take them back once they complete their education and therapy.[56] Their prison is a place of hope, and "hope does not disappoint" (Romans 5:5)—at least not in Finland.

*   *   *

There is not much left of prison, is there? It reduces crime only marginally; it does not teach criminals a lesson; it fails to deter potential offenders; it incapacitates the wrong kinds of felons and cannot stop those already locked up from causing terrible suffering to others, even behind bars; it inflicts punishments like inmate-on-inmate rape on offenders who really belong in mental hospitals; and it wastes money on security measures that, by themselves, cannot change convicts' lives for the better. Our commonly held beliefs about prison have collapsed.

In 1980, when our next interview subject first started to visit a city jail as a prison minister, he too held many of the preconceived notions that we have dispelled in this chapter. Meeting real prisoners not only opened the Reverend Bill Twine's eyes but also led him into his lifelong mission: operating Onesimus House, a faith-based halfway facility for ex-offenders returning to the community. Somewhere near you, there are other men and women like the Reverend Bill who are quietly working to make their neighborhoods safer by reintegrating former inmates into society. As you read the Reverend Bill's story, ask yourself: could I spare a few hours or a few dollars to help men and women like him?

Interview with Reverend Bill Twine

Q: Tell us a little about your background.

A: I was born in 1952. My parents owned a small grocery store in the Norview section of Norfolk, Virginia, which they converted to a snack bar and hot dog stand in 1958. They made it into a kind of hangout for the local kids—not quite like the TV show *Happy Days*, but not too different, either. There were pinball machines and pool tables and signs on the wall forbidding gambling and cussing. I remember my mother breaking up many a fight with a dose of cold water! Looking back, I may not have continued the family business, but I have been able to carry on the family legacy.

Q: How did you do that?

A: Because my parents' restaurant was a place of safety, a refuge, and that's what we provide at Onesimus House, too. We aid ex-offenders in making a transition from prison to the community by providing them with a place where they will not feel threatened, where they can feel the love of God and the care of other people.

Q: But you didn't jump straight from your parents' hangout to running a halfway house for newly released prison inmates, did you?

A: Oh, no! I went to college, graduated in 1974, and planned to go into teaching. When that didn't work out, I sold insurance from 1976 to 1982. Also, I started working with kids from difficult backgrounds in my spare time, when I became a deacon at Norview Baptist Church in the late 1970s. These weren't abused children, you understand, but they came from homes with neglect, substance abuse and alcoholism. We took them camping, to baseball games and to the beach.

Q: How did this lead to prison ministry?

A: In 1980, I started volunteering at the Norfolk City Jail with the Gideon Ministry. At first, I just handed out New Testaments in the cellblocks, but then the jail chaplain asked me to teach a Bible study class. The response from the inmates, who were mostly younger men, was really encouraging to me. And, having worked with eleven- and twelve-year-olds at my church, I couldn't help but see that many of the prisoners at Norfolk City Jail were not much older—eighteen or nineteen—and from the same neighborhood. It was a kind of an epiphany for me: I saw the connection between the younger and the older kids.

Q: Did you experience this insight in connection with any particular inmate?

A: Yes, actually. There was an eighteen-year-old accused murderer in the jail at that time by the name of Billy, and in his expresssion I could just *see* the face of an eleven-year-old boy named Jeff who came to our church. And Billy also happened to come from a neighborhood near Norview Baptist Church. So I couldn't look at him as someone to be feared and ostracized, because the connection between that eighteen-year-old felon and the children from our neighborhood was so clear, so visible to me. That recognition melted the fear away.

Q: And it also got you hooked on prison ministry?

A: Yes. I began with one Bible study class per week, then did two, and finally taught four or five classes per week—still as a deacon at my church. But that set up a conflict for me: I just loved what I was doing at the jail, yet I also felt I ought to be out selling insurance. So by 1981 or so, I knew I had to make a decision, and I started talking to my pastor and my wife and the manager of my insurance company. In fact, that manager was the one who had led me to the Lord and had discipled me; he was a very devout Christian businessman. Everyone agreed, so in 1982 I became ordained as a Baptist minister, and we incorporated Onesimus Ministries.

Q: Onesimus wasn't originally intended to be a halfway house, was it?

A: No. Initially, Onesimus was meant to facilitate the ministry to the inmates in Norfolk City Jail, at the invitation of the sheriff. That's what we did from 1982 until 1984, until I got fired.

Q: You can get fired from being a prison minister?

A: Oh, yes—if you give an interview to the local TV station without asking the sheriff's permission! Well, it all worked out for the best. For the last six months or so before I was invited to leave, I had begun to see the need for some place for released inmates to go to when they left jail or prison. All we had at this time in Norfolk was a homeless shelter! When the sheriff kicked Onesimus out of his jail, my organization was out of a job, in a way, and this was an area where we could do useful work.

Q: How did you get started?

A: In the summer of 1984, I got a call from an Onesimus board member whose church had a piece of property in the country that was vacant and that could be used for housing. We were able to use it rent-free, but we had to maintain it and pay property tax. That's how we operated for just about ten years, until we bought the property in the mid-1990s.

Q: You mentioned a board of directors. Who funds Onesimus Ministries?

A: We have maybe two hundred individuals and forty or so churches who have supported us financially for the last twenty-five years. Initially, we were completely funded by donations, but once we started actually housing ex-offenders, we could charge them a fee. That was $35 per week at first, and now it's $85 per week. The fees meet about two-thirds of our budget, which is now roughly $125,000 per year. Sometimes we also get grants for specific projects, like a new roof or a used van. But we accept no federal or state money at all. I'm an old-fashioned Virginia Baptist, I believe in the separation of church and state.

Q: What does it cost to house one man for one year at Onesimus?

A: Just over $3,000 per resident. That same offender who would cost the taxpayer over $20,000 per year if he were incarcerated in a state penitentiary. Plus, our guys are gainfully employed, paying taxes, restitution, court costs, and contributing to the local economy.

Q: Give me a sense of the growth of Onesimus Ministries over the last quarter-century.

A: We began with one resident, a man named Al who was a non-violent alcoholic convicted of theft. We had only the one house at that time, with room for eight to ten men. By 1994, the main house had been expanded to hold fourteen or fifteen men, and we had a townhouse in Virginia Beach with three or four more residents. In 1999, we acquired a second townhouse, adjacent to the first. Today the main house holds about eighteen men, the two townhouses hold about seven, and we are moving into a new house in Norfolk that will hold four more.

Q: Give us an overview of what you do at Onesimus House.

A: We provide room and board and transportation, as well as assistance in reintegrating into the community. When I say "we," I primarily mean Bob Crown, who is the on-site house manager. He works with the new arrivals until they are employed and manages the day-to-day activities, like transporting residents to and from work, Alcoholics Anonymous meetings, church, and appointments with Probation and Parole Officers.

Q: You mentioned AA; do you provide any treatment for substance abuse at Onesimus House?

A: Not treatment, per se, but during the last ten, fifteen years we have moved into doing on-site testing for alcohol and drugs. That protects the integrity of the program and helps residents maintain their sobriety. During our community meetings at Onesimus House, we talk about drug addiction and alcoholism, of course, but we rely on local social services and the community for counseling and therapy.

Q: Roughly 80% of prison inmates have substance abuse problems, so you must see a lot of that in your residents, too.

A: Yes. So many of them struggle with freeing themselves from drug and alcohol addiction. They stand on the threshold of freedom, but they're unable to walk through. For some reason, there's a fear of living clean and sober.

Q: Why do you think that is?

A: The years of addiction foster a lifestyle—a destructive lifestyle, but a lifestyle nevertheless. With this lifestyle comes a sense of community, and a purpose in life: to score drugs and get high. Punishment and the lack of parole are not real issues, which is why the abolition of parole in 1995 was such a useless idea.

Q: What do you mean?

A: Well, let me tell you a story. In 1994, the recently elected governor of Virginia, George Allen, came to Portsmouth, to conduct public hearings with his committee to abolish parole. I attended one of those hearings, and while I was sitting there, listening to the governor, I received a message on my pager to call Onesimus House.

Q: That must have been a really urgent message, to interrupt you at that hearing.

A: It sure was. I got word that one of our residents, who has a long history of drug addiction, had not come home. And I remember thinking about the futility of the whole process: here was the governor advocating abolishing parole and enacting mandatory sentences in order to deter crime, and somewhere in the area, there was one of my residents relapsing, fully aware that a relapse would terminate him from the program and ultimately place him back before the judge.

Q: Did this man risk returning to prison?

A: Of course. At his sentencing, the judge had suspended a twelve-year term on the condition that this man complete the Onesimus House program. But even with these inevitable consequences, it was not enough to deter him from relapsing, which is indeed what happened. I doubt seriously if the outcome would have been any different if his sentence had excluded the possibility of parole.

Q: Some would say that this man merely got what he deserved. He knowingly broke the law, so he and others like him don't deserve parole.

A: That's basically what Governor Allen told the General Assembly in 1994. He said that the legislators had to make a choice: to have compassion for the victims of crime, or the criminal. He implied that one cannot do both, but that is the exact opposite of what Jesus taught! When the Pharisees discovered Christ consorting with sinners and other less desirable individuals, he responded to his critics by saying, "Go and learn what this means, 'I desire compassion, and not sacrifice,' for I did not come to call the righteous, but sinners" (Matthew 9:13). Everybody on this planet is eligible to receive God's mercy and compassion.

Q: They might be eligible to receive *God's* mercy, but not necessarily *society's*.

A: Why should we be any less merciful and compassionate than God? Is that what we, as Christians, really want to do—to be *less* than God? But even if you do not want to be a Christian, you still have to temper justice with mercy for practical reasons.

Q: Please explain that further.

A: The number one priority of the Department of Corrections is to maintain public safety. This includes maintaining secure facilities, as well as providing community supervision of released inmates. Obviously, an ex-prisoner's success in the community will depend heavily on the preparation he has received while incarcerated—things like drug therapy, education, and job training. And his success also depends on the support that is available once he is released—support like that which we provide at Onesimus House. We make a great contribution to public safety by making sure released inmates stay alcohol- and drug-free, and by finding work for them.

Q: That is indeed one of your strong suits, isn't it—finding jobs for your residents?

A: Oh, yes. All of our guys are employed within ten days of arriving at Onesimus House. We have a large support base through our churches, and we have a reputation with local businesses. If it's one of our guys, he's okay—he'll show up for work! And some of our graduates have formed their own businesses and now hire our people regularly.

Q: What kind of work do Onesimus residents perform?

A: Oh, just about everything. They have laid utility lines and storm drains throughout Tidewater, installed ceilings in Harbor Park, finished the interior of the Norfolk Southern office building, salvaged aircraft hangars at the Naval Air Station, built bulkheads in some of the finest Virginia Beach neighborhoods, built and painted custom homes, repaired tug boats and welded in local shipyards, laid the foundation of Larkspur Middle School, and even laid the foundation of Indian Creek Correctional Center, ironically enough. One of our former residents even crafted and installed a spiral staircase in the home of a Virginia Beach judge. He had spent time in the state penitentiary and the local jail, most of his problems stemming from his drug addiction.

Q: How do you find candidates for Onesimus House?

A: I go to jails and prisons and interview them. Then I look at their institutional records and listen to what other inmates, counselors, in-prison job supervisors, and chaplains say about them.

Q: What else do you do at Onesimus House, apart from researching potential residents?

A: In the beginning, I did everything: I was at the house every day, all day, and most evenings, too! I was the one who found the men jobs, took them to work, and drove them to AA at night. Then, in 1986, we hired our first on-site resident, Dan Berrios. He attended Regent University during the day and handled a lot of the day-to-day stuff in the evenings. That allowed me to take a part-time job at St. Bride's Correctional Center.

Q: How did that come about?

A: In 1987, I got a call from Reverend George Ricketts, the executive director of Chaplain Services of the Churches of Virginia, which provides prison chaplains for the Virginia Department of Corrections. He had been given my name by Dr. John Craven, who had been my mentor; he had brought me through the ordination process at my church. Reverend Ricketts invited me to work part-time at St. Bride's as a chaplain, which I still do. And in 1997, I also became Chaplain Supervisor of Chaplain Services.

Q: What do you do with Onesimus nowadays?

A: I do a lot of fundraising, talking to men's and women's groups at our churches, trying to get help for the House and the prison ministry.

Q: That can't be easy work!

A: That's true. For the most part, the Church today does not seem interested in prison reform, as organizations like the Christian

Coalition have endeavored to steer Christians to supporting candidates with strong anti-crime platforms. Unfortunately, America's war on crime has evolved into a war on human dignity.

Q: What do you mean by "a war on human dignity"?

A: Let me give you an example: recently, a father mailed his incarcerated son a letter written inside a blank church bulletin. Along with
the letter, he enclosed a bookmark and gospel tract. These items
were sent back undelivered because they violated a new directive
governing inmate mail! Or take the cutbacks in food budgets: the
state is now spending *less* than $2.00 per inmate per day on food.
That's *less* than $2.00, for three meals!

Q: Why do you think there is so little sympathy even from Christians
when they hear of things like this?

A: Because it's so easy to hate someone who is different and unlike
us. We tolerate inhumane prison conditions because we think that
those convicted of serious crimes are not like us, but different. That's
why I always tell those church groups to whom I speak, "There is
someone present in this room today who has a loved one in prison!"
I remember that after one of these presentations, the president of
the Women's Missionary Union shared with me that her son was
in a Texas penitentiary. The truth is that prisoners are no different
from us. They are our children and our neighbors. They are us.

Q: Actually, colonial Virginia was in large part settled by released convicts who had come here from England, wasn't it?

A: That's right! In 1641, Governor William Berkeley of Virginia even
wrote a letter to officials in London, complaining about the large
number of ex-prisoners immigrating to Virginia. He warned that if
it didn't stop, Virginia would become a penal colony. Some things
never change!

Q: Well, even if Virginia hasn't changed much from 365 years ago, have
you noticed a difference in the type of residents who have come to
Onesimus House over the last twenty-five years?

A: Oh, yes. In the early years, they were all nonviolent offenders. Today,
we have about 60% substance abusers and 40% sex offenders. We
took the first sex offender in the late 1980s, a young man named
Rusty J. who came to Virginia from Arkansas by way of the U.S.
Navy in Virginia Beach.

Q: What was he like?

A: His main issue was paranoia. This was before the days of internet sex offender registries, you understand, but he still thought that everyone knew about his past. One day, he saw another resident whittling a stick, and Rusty thought the guy was implying that he was a "tree-jumper"—prison slang for rapist.

Q: How did he progress at Onesimus House?

A: Well, most of our people stay six months and then transition to one of our less-structured townhouses. There they can stretch themselves a little bit, but they still have the security of knowing that we're there to help them. Rusty, on the other hand, stayed about twelve months at the main house, working construction and doing fine. Then he got his own apartment and quickly relapsed with drugs. He came back to Onesimus for six months and struggled a lot with depression. I'd say Rusty was "high maintenance"—he needed a lot of attention.

Q: Like those kids from dysfunctional families at Norview Baptist Church in the late 1970s?

A: Yes. Or the kids at my parents' restaurant. Rusty was a threshold case for us, our first "high risk" case. That prepared us for taking more sex offenders later.

Q: How do you determine which sex offenders you'll take and which you won't?

A: We look at the nature of the offense, and the type and number of victims. We won't take someone with more than one victim or someone who attacked a stranger, because we don't want a predator re-offending in our community.

Q: How did you develop these criteria for sex offenders?

A: Through careful study of other programs. But, you know, there really were no models for us when we started in the mid-1980s. There was no textbook on how to set up a halfway house! Of course, there were large, sophisticated, very intensive operations like the Delancey Street Restaurant in San Francisco. But I didn't have the resources to what they do at Onesimus House.

Q: How successful are you at preventing new offenses by your residents?

A: Generally speaking, the ones who go back to prison or jail are those who fail a drug test or fail to maintain their sobriety. There have been some new offenses committed, but in almost every instance, we ourselves—Onesimus House—were the victims. For example, a man took one of our vans and used it to go and buy drugs, or another resident came back drunk one night and started a fight. There have been five or six such cases in twenty-five years.

Q: And did you take back any of the men who committed offenses against Onesimus House?

A: (Long pause.) Yes. Some of them we got out of jail ourselves and returned to the House. Others, of course, went back to prison. It all depends on the circumstances.

Q: Do you remember one particular case that sticks in your mind as an especially successful reintegration of an ex-prisoner—a kind of Joseph, who ended up running all of Egypt?

A: Yes—one of the first young men I met at Norfolk City Jail, in fact, in 1980 or '81. Randy was sentenced to eight years for manslaughter. After he arrived in prison, he decided to write a letter to his former employer, from whom he had stolen prior to killing someone else. In the letter, he apologized for stealing, listed everything he had taken, and promised to pay his boss back.

Q: Sort of like the Letter to Philemon, in the New Testament?

A: That's right; in fact, Randy used that as his model, because we'd studied it in one of our Bible study groups. His employer was so impressed with that letter that he visited Randy in jail and then wrote to the parole board, to tell them that he would give Randy his old job back if he were paroled. The parole board granted Randy first parole, and he went to work for his old boss. Over time, he was given more and more responsibility, and when his employer retired, he sold the business to Randy. He is now known in Norfolk as a *very* successful businessman and a very active church member. No one knows his past.

Q: Randy's employer clearly forgave him that theft. Does forgiveness also play a role in your work at Onesimus?

A: Forgiveness is within the domain of the church, so we try to operate Onesimus House as a place where grace and forgiveness can be obtained. After the resurrection, Jesus told his disciples in the upper room, "If you forgive the sins of any, they are forgiven them; if you retain the sins of any, they are retained" (John 20:23). So we try to practice grace in our response to failure, because we understand that there will be failure and relapse.

Q: Tell us more about the place of grace in your work.

A: Grace is the one thing that makes our faith unique, the one thing that can overcome any resistance. And we Christians have the patent on that; we have the market cornered! Yet we fail to implement grace in our dealings with others and even with ourselves. I think this is one of the great failures of Christians today.

Q: What do you mean?

A: God told the apostle Paul, "My grace is sufficient for thee: for my strength is made perfect in weakness" (2 Corinthians 12:9). But we modern-day Christians no longer lead with our weakness; we are no longer cognizant of our wounds. We have become self-righteous, believing that our own hard work and our powerful connections have brought us our achievements. We have become the haves of this world, with little regard for the have-nots for whom Christ died.

Q: Can you think of an incident involving one of these have-nots who obtained God's forgiveness through grace?

A: Yes, a former Onesimus resident named Michael. He was a man tormented by depression, tragic relationships, and alcohol. I had to expel him from Onesimus House because of his failure to stay clean, and some years later he committed a horrendous crime.

Q: What did he do?

A: On his birthday, he and his girlfriend murdered four people in a Virginia Beach bar. These people were their friends and coworkers! A few years later, I visited him on death row, and he wrote me a couple of letters afterward. I remember the gist of his letters was his quest to find forgiveness from God and from the survivors of his crime. Sadly, I was of little help to him. I couldn't provide him the answers he sought because I had too many questions of my own.

Q: What kinds of questions?

A: Was I unable to respond to his letters fully because of my unwillingness to forgive him? Or was it more complicated that that? Was I feeling a sense of guilt or responsibility, since I was the one who had originally made a place for him when he was released from prison? And had I ignored my own practice of grace when I booted him out of Onesimus House for his relapse? Did I dare ask myself what role I had played in these tragic events? As I said already, I was of little or no help to this man who was struggling with his own guilt. Fortunately for Michael, he was able to find some closure.

Q: How?

A: For one thing, he turned down the option of lethal injection, choosing the severity of the electric chair instead. But even more importantly, he realized that the key to his closure involved the forgiveness of the victims' survivors. Miraculously, the authorities agreed to arrange for him to call the wife of one of his victims, the owner of the bar. He was able to communicate to her his deep sorrow and regret, and even more amazingly, she was able to communicate forgiveness.

Q: And did that incident answer some of your own questions?

A: Oh, I don't know. I later toured the death house at Greensville Correctional Center and sat in the electric chair. Michael was the last person who had occupied that chair prior to my sitting in it. Crazy!

Q: Do experiences like this one ever make you feel discouraged in your work?

A: Sometimes, sure. The prison environment can suck the life out of any normal, decent human being. But I try to find strength and courage by connecting with members of my community.

Q: Who are they?

A: Many of them are Department of Corrections staff with whom I work day in and day out, or with whom I have worked in the past and still maintain contact. These are people who trust chaplains and don't mistrust me simply because I befriend inmates. And I find community with my fellow chaplains and fellow members of Virginia CURE. [Interviewer's Note: Virginia CURE, Citizens United for the Rehabilitation of Errants, is a prisoner advocacy group.] But even though I feel a deep connection with them, I also still feel powerless sometimes. Maybe fear and disillusionment can be overcome by community, but there is so much work still to be done.

Q: You named the place where you do most of your work, Onesimus Ministries, after the runaway slave in the Letter to Philemon. Is that Scripture the one that really inspires your work with the half-way house?

A: Sure, but there are so many others, like Matthew 25. And I keep running across new ones! The last lectionary reading our Bible study group in the prison read, for instance, was about Jesus raising Lazarus from the dead—and I noticed something I'd never seen before. When Christ calls Lazarus out of the tomb, Lazarus doesn't have a choice—the Son of God has brought him back to life, so he's going to come out. But then Jesus says to the onlookers, "Take the burial cloths, the wrappings off him!"

Q: So they have a choice—whether or not to unbind Lazarus.

A: That's right! Those onlookers don't *have* to take those burial cloths off Lazarus. And I saw that this is what I've been trying to do for the last twenty-five years or so: to take the wrappings off men coming out of prison, out of the concrete tombs of our jails and penitentiaries.

QUESTIONS FOR REFLECTION AND DISCUSSION

SCRIPTURE—Note that when Joseph escapes Potiphar's wife, only his clothes are left in her hand (Genesis 39:23). This parallels the scene in the Garden of Gethsemane, where a young man flees the scene of Christ's arrest leaving only his cloak (Mark 14:51–52). Is there any significance to this, and what might it be?

CRIMINOLOGY—In this chapter, we learned about several instances of scientists producing wildly inaccurate research results because they were unfamiliar with the realities of penitentiary life. Make a list of all the "facts" about prison that you once believed, but which this chapter revealed to be erroneous.

SELF-EXAM—How does this chapter's examination of prison rape and sex behind bars make you feel? Consider how your aversion mirrors that of policymakers and correctional administrators. What practical effects do such emotions have?

INTERVIEW—How would you feel if Onesimus House bought a house near your own home? Would NIMBY apply? Where should such facilities be located?

INTERNET— Read the Vera Institute's report *Reconsidering Incarceration* at www.vera.org.

IMMERSION—Visit a mental health facility or advocacy group to learn more about the "revolving door" between psychiatric hospitals and correctional centers. If possible, let staff arrange a meeting with someone whose mental health problems led to a term of incarceration.

Chapter 3

MOSES AND TURNING
A BLIND EYE TO PRISON

OF ALL OUR biblical criminals and convicts, Moses is the second-worst: he killed an Egyptian slave driver, a duly appointed government official charged with enforcing Pharaoh's laws (Exodus 2:12). In most U.S. jurisdictions, this constitutes capital murder, making Moses subject to the death penalty. Thus only Samson, who slaughtered three thousand Philistines by pushing down their great hall (Judges 16: 27–30), ranks above Moses on Scripture's "Most Wanted" list.

But, while Samson's body count far exceeds Moses', the latter was arguably a greater threat to the Egyptians' national security than the former was to the Philistines'. Why? Because mass murderers like Samson usually unite society against them, whereas revolutionaries like Moses can turn members of the community against each other and destroy the social fabric itself.

In our twenty-first-century eyes, slavery is an obvious evil, and anyone who combats it is a hero. To the Egyptians, on the other hand, the murder of a slave driver was a serious threat, since it could easily have sparked off a general rebellion by the descendants of Jacob. In fact, the fear that the Israelites might "join our enemies and fight against us" was the primary reason why Pharaoh enslaved them in the first place (Exodus 1:10). Time has not preserved Egyptian records that document mass mutinies by the captive Hebrews, but we know from the much more numerous surviving chronicles of Rome that slave revolts were a constant danger in ancient civilizations.

When Spartacus led an army of escaped slaves through Italy in 73 B.C.E., for instance, "All that opulent society, which had enjoyed every luxury slavery could produce, trembled at the thought of losing every-thing—mastery, property, life," writes Columbia University Professor Will Durant. "[N]o man could tell when the revolution would break out in his very home." In the century before the Spartacist uprising, Roman legions also had to fight the First and Second Servile Wars against armies of slaves and quell at least four other major insurrections.[1]

This kind of conflagration is what the biblical murder of the slave driver threatened to ignite in Egypt. Moses was a very dangerous fellow—and he knew it. As Professor Terrence Fretheim of the Luther Seminary has pointed out, the fact that he hid the slave driver's body in the sand (Exodus 2:12) indicates a consciousness of guilt.[2] Moses was quite aware that he had done a great wrong.

What modern readers may not fully appreciate is that even Moses' fellow Israelites would have viewed the killing of a slave driver as profoundly reprehensible. While they did not enjoy being slaves, they never questioned the institution of slavery itself. All of "antiquity took slavery for granted, and would have contemplated with horror the economic and social effects of wholesale emancipation," Durant says.[3]

Not even Moses sought to end the general practice of treating human beings as property. After he returned from Mt. Sinai's summit with the Ten Commandments, he taught God's people how to build an altar using only uncut stones (Exodus 20:24-26). Then, as his very first piece of specific legislation, Moses laid down the law on how to purchase a Hebrew slave, whose property a slave's child becomes (the master's, not the parents'), and how to sell one's own daughter as a slave (Exodus 21:1–11).

Thirteen hundred years and one Messiah later, the apostle Paul still did not see slavery as fundamentally wrong. He understood that "for freedom Christ set us free" and that "we are all baptized into one body, whether Jews or Greeks, slaves or free persons" (Galatians 5:1; 1 Corinthians 12:13). But to Paul this only meant that slaves and masters should treat each other respectfully—advice he repeated with surprising frequency (Galatians 6:5–9; Colossians 3:22–25; 1 Timothy 6:1–2; Philemon). So consistent is the apostle's unquestioning acceptance of slavery that for most of Christian history the notorious twenty-first verse of 1 Corinthians 7 has been interpreted as advising slaves not to seek their freedom but to remain in servitude.

The notion that one person should not own another only gained wider currency in the early nineteenth century in England. As late as 1861, residents of this nation's Southern states went to war to protect their "peculiar institution," as they called it. Many Northerners—including Abraham Lincoln—had no principled objection to slavery initially but fought secession to preserve the Union. For the majority of American Christians of that relatively recent era, slavery did not appear to be the obvious evil that we now perceive it to be.

This raises the interesting question of whether our society, our age, engages in a social practice that will seem as obscenely immoral and unchristian to future generations as slavery does to us. What "peculiar institution" goes unquestioned by Americans across the religious and political spectrum today? Some have suggested: punishment by incarceration.

The Birth of the Penitentiary

As we will see in Chapter 7, correctional facilities are, to say the very least, highly unpleasant places. Keeping a human being confined in such conditions for years or even decades on end would be considered a monstrous crime if this were done by one civilian to another. By committing this act collectively, through our government—by draping this act with all the solemnity of black-robed judges and uniformed guards—by justifying this act with the evil acts committed by inmates before their incarceration—do we thereby make the act of imprisoning more moral, more Christian? Or is locking people into cages in and of itself an evil act?

Of course, there are occasions when it may be necessary or appropriate to commit an act that we would normally consider wrong: killing in self-defense and in wartime are obvious examples. Unfortunately, the definition of "necessary" has proved itself to be endlessly flexible.

Can we say that it is really, truly *necessary* to confine a criminal in prison, when in most cases the public could be equally well protected by GPS-monitored home detention, for instance?

We should note in this context that humanity managed to survive quite well without long-term incarceration for almost its entire history. Until the eighteenth century, prisons held only insolvent debtors, defendants pending trial, and convicts awaiting execution or banishment: just nineteen felons were punished with incarceration in the British colony of New York between 1691 and 1776, for instance.[4] The first modern correctional center, the Eastern State Penitentiary in Cherry Hill, Pennsylvania, was not built until 1829 under the direction of the Quakers.

By keeping an offender in absolute solitude and silence, the Quakers hoped to bring him to repentance. Many of the convicts were driven insane by their isolation, however, so this approach was soon dropped. But by that time, visitors from other U.S. states and Europe had already exported this marvelous new invention, the long-term prison, to their home jurisdictions.[5]

All those freshly built penitentiaries could not be left empty just because they failed to make their residents penitent, of course. So, like any other government boondoggle, the prison was reformed and redesigned, improved and expanded, made bigger and better. And thus the correctional cancer metastasized from the first cell at Cherry Hill to the roughly 1,200 penitentiaries America has today.[6]

By now, to paraphrase Will Durant, modernity takes long-term incarceration for granted "and would contemplate with horror the economic and social effects of wholesale emancipation." But it was not always thus, as we have just seen. So are penitentiaries really, truly *necessary*?

To answer that question, we need to become conscious of the conceptual filters that hide the reality of prison from us. The remainder of this chapter will examine three of these filters: racism, the media, and the law. Obviously, there are also other factors at work here besides these three, but we have to start somewhere.

RACISM

Since this is a book about prisons in the United States, the last Western nation to abandon slavery, racism is a good place to begin our study. Just how bad are racial disparities in the criminal justice system today, forty to fifty years after the civil rights era? Let us examine more closely the overall incarceration rate of 737 prisoners per 100,000 civilians.

When we break this down by gender and race, we find that 681 Caucasian-American men out of 100,000 are behind bars, compared to 4,834 African-American men—a ratio of one to seven. This disparity is even greater in the especially crime-prone age bracket of twenty-five- to twenty-nine-year-olds: 1,607 whites versus 12,809 blacks. By contrast, South Africa locked up only 851 black men out of 100,000 in the last year of apartheid.[7]

An African-American male now has a 32.1% chance of going to prison at some point in his life. Today, 16.6% of all adult black men are either current or former convicts, versus 2.6% of adult white men.[8] While the average prison sentence for Caucasian-Americans is four years, the average sentence for African-Americans is six years.[9]

The American Bar Association's *Justice Kennedy Commission Report* provides a detailed examination of the factors that lead to the shameful numbers above:[10]

- *Over-offending by blacks*: Because African-Americans are more likely to be poor, they are overrepresented in those crime categories that are associated with poverty. Other crime categories, however, do not show disproportionate rates of offending.
- *Unconscious discrimination in discretionary decision-making by police, prosecutors, and judges*: If a suspect or defendant is of the same class and culture as a law enforcement official, he or she is more likely to be let off with a warning, be offered a lenient plea bargain, or have a prison sentence suspended in favor of getting treatment.

- *The War on Drugs*: According to the report, "No single policy has done more to contribute to the current racial disparity in the criminal justice system than the War on Drugs."[11] African-Americans comprise 12% of the general population, 13% of drug users, 35% of drug arrests, 53% of drug convictions, and 58% of those inmates incarcerated for drug offenses.

- *Unintended discriminatory effects of anti-drug legislation*: Connecticut, for example, mandates a three-year sentence enhancement for anyone selling narcotics within 1,500 feet of a school, public housing project, or day-care center. Because this turns virtually all of downtown New Haven into a targeted crime zone, the mostly black drug dealers who live there get longer sentences on average than their white suburban counterparts.

Of course, the four factors reviewed above are not the only reasons why African-Americans are incarcerated at far higher rates than Caucasian-Americans; we have not even touched upon the role of underfunded public defender programs, for instance. But, as the *Justice Kennedy Commission Report* notes, "Whatever the causes, this cannot be permitted to continue."[12]

The American Bar Association's otherwise laudable report unfortunately fails to explain one puzzling fact: racial inequalities in the criminal justice system have grown far worse even as racism in society generally has declined. In 1930, 77% of prison admissions were Caucasian-Americans, 22% were African-Americans, and 1% were of other ethnic backgrounds.[13] As recently as 1984, whites still comprised nearly 60% of all inmates.[14] But by 2003, the racial makeup of U.S. jails and penitentiaries had practically reversed: 68% of prisoners now belonged to minority groups.[15]

What happened in the roughly two decades between 1984 and 2003 to cause this great shift? Viewed from another angle, these could certainly be seen as years of accomplishment for blacks in America, as African-Americans achieved leadership roles in the U.S. Supreme Court, the Joint Chiefs of Staff, and the Department of State, among many other advances. Could it be that, despite these appearances, racism did not in fact diminish between 1984 and 2003, but instead found a new focused outlet?

At its core, racism is fear of what is different or "other." As blacks became further and further integrated into the mainstream of American life during the 1980s and '90s, whites learned that this fear was largely unjustified. Dr. Huxtable on *The Cosby Show* was really just another nice, middle-class fellow with a mortgage to worry about. Neither Clarence Thomas nor Colin Powell was truly different or "other."

However, the late 1980s also introduced white America to another kind of black man who definitely was different, "other," and frightening: the crack cocaine dealer. Criminologists have studied in great detail the impact of the crack epidemic on this country's judicial and correctional systems.[16] But perhaps the role of the crack dealer in America's collective psyche, as a kind of national bogeyman, should be considered as well.

Recall those years, if you will: every evening, both local and national TV news broadcasts were filled with reports of young African-American males machine-gunning each other and innocent bystanders as they battled for turf to distribute narcotics. Some sections of major U.S. cities seemed to have become enclaves of lawlessness where even the police feared to tread. In the eyes of white America, the black drug dealer thus became the agent of civilization's self-destruction, an icon of evil incarnate.

All the fear and hatred that once was projected onto African-Americans generally now was redirected onto the African-American criminal in particular. Psychologically, this had the advantage of appearing to legitimize these ugly, atavistic emotions: while Dr. Huxtable had obviously done nothing to earn whites' malice, a black crack dealer really deserved to be loathed! Hating criminals was downright respectable; the fact that these criminals were also dark-skinned was merely a coincidence.

Yet white America's seemingly righteous wrath at drug dealers (who just happened to be black) is easily exposed as disguised racism.

How? By recalling the fact that 72% of narcotics *consumers* are *Caucasian*.[17] Whites, not blacks, are the primary source of the dollars that keep the drug trade and the turf wars going. If suburban homemakers and BMW-driving lawyers and their privately schooled kids were not so eager to snort, smoke, and inject illegal substances, those inner-city "gangstas" would have no customers and no reason to "pop a cap" in each other.

It goes without saying that the law of supply and demand does not relieve African-American entrepreneurs of the duty to obey laws that prohibit narcotics distribution. By assigning all of the blame for the War on Drugs to that scary black crack dealer on the evening news broadcast, however, white America is very conveniently ignoring its own partial responsibility for the social scourge of narcotics. Pushing unacknowledged guilt off onto others is one of the hallmarks of addiction, of course.

This racial blame-shifting, in turn, has helped hide the reality of prison from us. Over the last twenty to thirty years, this country blinded itself to what was happening inside its jails and penitentiaries: the social destruction of an entire ethnic group. Try, just *try* to imagine what America would look like if one in three *white* men were either locked up or unemployed, barred from many professions, ineligible to vote, infected with prison-borne diseases like HIV and hepatitis C, traumatized by prison rape, and psychologically damaged by supermax-style isolation. Any nation foolish enough to attempt to impose that fate on one-third of its male population would soon erupt into violent revolution. Yet this is precisely what the U.S. did to the African-American community, thanks to the unadmitted racism of its criminal justice policies.

THE MEDIA

Many of the racially biased misperceptions of crime and correctional issues are the responsibility of the media, the second of the three conceptual filters that distort our understanding of prison. In our discussion of the crack cocaine dealer, above, we saw how sensationalistic accounts of ghetto gun-battles ignored the crucial fact that white addicts, not black ones, funded these turf wars through their narcotics purchases. But the media does no better when it comes to reporting crime stories that have no racial angle.

Take the paroxysms of journalistic outrage that froth across the airwaves whenever a molester abducts and kills a child.* Of course, each individual case is an unspeakable tragedy for the unfortunate young victim and his or her family. But the intensity of TV coverage for these crimes presents a skewed picture of the threat they present to our society in comparison to other crimes.

In reality, the number of substantiated sexual abuse cases in America *fell* by 39% between 1993 and 2003. Of all the sex crimes committed against children annually, forty to fifty end in murder—or less than one per state per year.[18] By contrast, *hundreds* of kids and teens are killed annually by drunk or reckless motorists.

The media's failure to present the true relative risk posed by crimes is no less egregious when it comes to garden-variety homicides: between 1990 and 1995, for instance, murder reports on TV network news rose by 336% while the actual homicide rate fell by 13% during that period.[19] Not surprisingly, this distortion of reality has a powerful impact on public opinion: 71% of those surveyed thought there was more crime in 1996 than in 1995, even though index crimes (those tracked by the FBI) had in fact declined 5.1% during that year.[20]

Why does TV feature child abductions, gruesome killings and other lawlessness out of all proportion to the actual incidence of crime? Because such stories are especially cheap to produce, according to former NBC News President Lawrence Grossman.[21] And since the economics of TV production are unlikely to change, the networks will continue to give us only a funhouse-mirror view of criminal justice issues.

The distorting effect of the sheer number of crime stories on the news is exacerbated by the emotional tone of news-entertainment programs like *Nancy Grace*. Here again money plays a role: Grace's nightly

---

* Note that these stories nearly always feature white children. Presumably, black kids are almost never abducted and killed in America!

prime-time show gets the second-highest ratings in CNN's lineup.[22] What is the secret to her success? Holding up felons as public punching bags, so her viewers can vent their pent-up anger after a long, frustrating day at the office.

Grace lends an air of social respectability to her orgies of cathartic hatred by continually reminding her audience that she once served as a district attorney in Georgia. What she does not disclose is that, "On three occasions, involving three separate cases, appellate courts have cited [her] for unethical behavior while she was a Fulton County prosecutor," according to media expert Tim Rutten. Her transgressions were not minor: the U.S. Court of Appeals for the Eleventh Circuit, for example, chastised Grace for "knowingly allowing a police detective to testify falsely." And, in a 1997 ruling by the Georgia Supreme Court, Chief Justice Robert Benham wrote that Grace's courtroom conduct "demonstrated her disregard of the notions of due process and fairness and was inexcusable."[23]

The same "disregard of ... fairness" inspires her TV show, according to TV critic Matt Zoller Seitz: Grace "throw[s] journalistic objectivity in the dumpster,... declaring defendants guilty because, well, they just seem guilty." While she proudly responds, "I don't care what [critics] say," the rest of us should.[24] Encouraging her viewers to execrate criminals may be profitable for her personally, but it makes a sane and humane solution to criminality ever more difficult.

The Law

Our third conceptual filter, after racism and the media, is the law. Here the full authority of government is brought in to support the idea that prisoners are second-class citizens who are not entitled to the same rights as others. In the Prison Litigation Reform Act of 1996 (PLRA), this principle became enshrined in statutory form.

Ostensibly designed to limit "frivolous" lawsuits by inmates, this law has cut the number of prisoner-filed civil rights cases nearly in half, once the growth of the correctional population is taken into account.[25] But how many of these conditions-of-confinement suits are truly "frivolous"?

Take the eighteen Louisiana inmates who sued their parish jail because the cells had no toilet or running water—only a grate-covered hole in the middle of the floor and a one-gallon jug of water for drinking and washing feces off the grate. Under the PLRA, both federal and state courts dismissed their case because the prisoners "had not identified a single human need of which they were deprived."[26]

Even the mistreatment inflicted on Iraqi detainees at Abu Ghraib would not necessarily qualify as actionable under the PLRA, according to Stephen Bright of the Southern Center for Human Rights.[27] Unless there is "a prior showing of physical injury"—the key legal test of the PLRA—prisoners can now be subjected to just about anything. "As the law stands today, the standards permit inhumane treatment of inmates," a federal judge in Texas noted.[28] A federal judge in Illinois pointed out that, thanks to the PLRA, "Rare is the prisoner who succeeds in winning a case at all, much less winning more than a nominal sum."[29]

This approach to prisoners' rights extends to medical treatment, a subject we will examine in Chapter 7. While civilians can sue their doctors and nurses for malpractice if they fail to adhere to the American Medical Association's standards of care, convicts' lawsuits must meet the much higher "deliberate indifference" standard. This legal test requires evidence that medical staff *intended* to deny proper care; mere negligence or incompetence is not enough.

Thus, when a Texas inmate was refused therapy for his hepatitis B and C on the grounds that he was mentally ill, the U.S. Court of Appeals for the Fifth Circuit dismissed his suit as "frivolous."[30] No *civilian* doctor could get away with refusing to treat a patient for no other reason than his or her psychological disability, of course. But a *prison* doctor can—so long as there is no positive proof of having "*intentionally* treated [a patient] incorrectly."

But is it really, objectively true that one group of human beings has fewer rights than other groups? Are there in fact legal *Untermenschen*?

In our discussion of the first conceptual filter that hides the reality of prison from us, we saw that racism is fear of what is different or "other." Arguably, our other two conceptual filters, the media and the law, induce the same kind of fear, not on the basis of ethnicity, but on the basis of past actions. Instead of using dark skin as the distinguishing feature, the mark of Cain, Nancy Grace and the PLRA use felony records. The fact that criminals and convicts have at some point committed bad acts supposedly makes members of this group entirely unlike and fundamentally dissimilar to all other human beings.

"No One Just, Not One"

If we are Christians, that last sentence should make us cringe, of course. The basis of our faith is that "there is no one just, not one" (Romans 3:10), and that I personally need Jesus to save me from my sins. To regard a fellow sinner as less than myself *based on his or her sin* is just about the most unchristian thought imaginable.

Thus the Gospel is actually our most powerful tool for freeing ourselves of the misperceptions caused by racism, the media, and the law. So long as we remember that we are all sinners in need of salvation, we will see prisoners as our brothers and sisters, and today's correctional facilities as unworthy of a civilized and Christian nation. This is what Jesus tried to show us at the very moment of his death, as Ronald Nikkel of Prison Fellowship International explains in this meditation on the thief crucified next to our Savior:

> As a condemned man stripped of dignity and life itself, he had nothing to give to Jesus except his horrible past and ironically nothing left to lose except the same horrible past. Only moments before turning to Jesus, he and the other crucified bandit were deriding, insulting, and cursing Jesus along with a mob of gawking, bloodthirsty spectators. But then at the very last moment, with his dying breath, he deliberately turned to Jesus and thereupon found himself in the embrace of a heavenly grace—no conditions and no questions asked.

It is a story that unsettles me because if God doesn't require any deposit or guarantee of goodness from the most heinous of scoundrels who turn to Him when there is nothing left of their lives, it means that my accumulated goodness is absolutely meaningless and worthless, counting for nothing. If Jesus welcomes those who have squandered their lives and who come to the dead end of human life totally destitute of everything, even of time itself, you and I are no more fit or deserving of grace than scoundrels.

It is at this point that a realization sinks in—what makes me think that I am any better than the condemned bandit on the cross? Are you and I any less the scoundrels for thinking that our goodness is actually good and that it merits grace? Isn't grace always for the undeserving? Whether we are hanging helpless on the cross next to Jesus, or languishing in a miserably stinking and overcrowded prison cell, or kneeling in the cavernous silence of a magnificent cathedral, or looking up at the suffering of the Lord from the foot of the cross—the bottom line is that we can only turn to Him as scoundrels in the company of scoundrels, stripped of all spiritual trophies and any sense of goodness. Jesus Christ lived and died only for the salvation of scoundrels.[31]

In a Calvinist liturgy of the late sixteenth century, written for the return of an offender to the community, we find a historical expression of this same understanding of our common human bond as scoundrels and sinners:

We in the sin of this, our brother, accuse and condemn our own sins; in his fall we all lament and consider our sinful nature; also, we shall join repentance, tears and prayers with him and his, knowing that no flesh can be justified before God's presence, if judgment proceeds without mercy....

We all here present join our sins with your sins; we all repute and esteem your fall to be our own; we all accuse ourselves no less than you; and now, finally, we join our prayers with yours, that we may obtain mercy, and that by the means of our Lord Jesus Christ.[32]

"We all accuse ourselves no less than you"—try to imagine Nancy Grace making that statement on her TV show, and you will have some idea of how far America is removed from a Christian view of crime and prison.

Eventually, all great injustices come to an end; that is Jesus' promise and the testimony of history. The captive Hebrews escaped Egypt, African slaves were emancipated in the Deep South, and the vast majority of this country's convicts will also return home. Not *all* inmates can or should be released, of course; judging by the past, 300,000 to 400,000 (out of 2.3 million) need to be confined to protect the public. Even they are not truly different or "other," however, and must be treated with charity.

When the great Exodus from America's penitentiaries begins, it will need people like Moses and Aaron and Miriam. Our next interview subject will be one of these spiritual leaders, I believe: in the penitentiary where we are both housed, he is already acting as a shepherd to his faith community. Like Moses, who could not imagine himself as a leader when God challenged him at the burning bush, my friend Carlton would surely also object to my vision of his future. But he and men and women like him are this nation's best hope of freeing itself of its bloated correctional system. As Prison Fellowship Ministries' Mark L. Earley puts it, "God is going to raise up the next generation of leadership for His Church outside the wall from his people behind prison bars!"[33]

A final note: nowhere in the following interview will you find Carlton mentioning the fact that he is black. But since we examined racism in this chapter, it is only appropriate for us to ask whether he would have been treated quite so harshly if he had been of the same race as his judge. Carlton's case illustrates well what the *Justice Kennedy Commission Report* means by unconscious discrimination in discretionary decision-making.

Had he chosen to do so, Carlton's judge could have sentenced him to three *concurrent* ten-year terms instead of three *consecutive* sentences.

That small change would have reduced Carlton's actual time served from roughly twenty-seven years to approximately nine. If the judge had seen someone resembling his own son in the dock, would he not have used his discretion differently?

INTERVIEW WITH "CARLTON L."

Carlton L. was sentenced to thirty years for three counts of
aggravated involuntary manslaughter in 1997.

Q: Tell us a little about your life before you were arrested for your current offense.

A: I was born in 1969. My father worked in construction, my mother in the textile industry. We were a very religious family and went to a Baptist church every Sunday as I was growing up. I was never in any trouble with the law. At parties, I would drink a little, but I never did drugs. I graduated from high school in 1987, worked at a TV shop for two years, and then joined a major multinational manufacturer of power equipment, specifically large transformers. I worked there from 1989 until 1996 in a variety of different positions, manufacturing different parts of huge transformers. In the end I was working as a support team technician, which was considered a good assignment. My work evaluations were always good. But I should say that I only went to church occasionally between 1987 and 1996.

Q: What happened in 1996?

A: I was involved in an automobile accident that resulted in the deaths of three people in another car. I was driving home from a relative's house, and I was under the influence of alcohol.

Q: Tell us about this accident.

A: I don't actually remember any of it because I was severely injured. An ambulance took me from the scene to a local hospital, and then I was flown by helicopter to Duke University Medical Center in Durham, North Carolina. There I was placed on life support for roughly two weeks. Along with several other injuries, the main artery to my heart had been ruptured, and my spleen had to be removed. I was unconscious throughout all of this, so I don't even know how many operations they did on me.

Q: How long did you stay in the hospital?

A: About two months, after which I was released in North Carolina. I had some family there who wanted me to stay with them,
but I returned back to Virginia. Two weeks later, the Virginia
State Police came to question me, and another month later I was
indicted for three counts of aggravated involuntary manslaughter.
I was released on bond until my trial in 1997.

Q: Tell us about your trial.

A: It lasted two days. The prosecution's main argument was that I'd
been reckless because I was drunk and speeding. I didn't deny
that, and I agree that I was partially at fault. But my lawyer's
argument was that the victims had also shown reckless behavior.
There were two eyewitnesses to the accident who testified at my
trial as part of my defense. They had seen the victims horseplay-
ing with their car and almost getting hit by a tractor-trailer a
few moments before the accident. Shortly after that, they came
speeding from a side road and turned into the main road without
stopping. That's where we collided. Of course, I didn't see any of
this myself; this was eyewitness testimony from the couple living
across the street.

Q: How did you feel about those three people dying in this accident?

A: I was very sorry to have the whole thing occur. I hate to see anyone lose their life under any circumstances, especially when I
played some part in it. When the family members of the other car's
occupants gave their victim impact statements at my sentencing,
I understood their feelings completely; I probably would have felt
the same way. That's why I apologized to those families as well as
to the community.

Q: Tell us about your sentencing.

A: The jury recommended a sentence of ten years for each count,
which was not the maximum. Normally, because the charges stem
from a single event, these sentences would be served concurrently,
and that would have meant eight-and-a-half to nine years actually
behind bars. After the jury made its recommendation, the judge
ordered a pre-sentence report, which recommended a four-and-a-
half-year sentence. But in the end, the judge followed the jury's
recommendation of three ten-year terms—except, he ordered

those three ten-year terms to be served consecutively. So I now have to serve twenty-five-and-a-half to twenty-seven years.

Q: Did the judge give any reason for doing that?

A: Not that I can recall. But I do remember him saying that he felt he would probably never see me again, if I walked out of his courtroom that day.

Q: Did you try to appeal the sentence?

A: Yes, with my family's help. They had paid for my trial lawyer, and they paid for years and years of appeals, too. But all the appeals were rejected. And under the "no parole" law, there is no other way for me to be released early—no time off for good behavior, nothing.

Q: Was the shock of that very long sentence what made you turn to Jesus?

A: No. There are many inmates who turn to the Lord in prison, but for me it happened in the hospital. On numerous occasions, doctors and nurses would look at my medical charts and say, "I don't know how you survived." And they would say, "The Lord must have saved you for some purpose." That got me thinking. Also, one day, after all my other visitors left, the chaplain came by and shared with me my mother's faith throughout the many surgeries. All the doctors had told her that they expected me to die within twenty-four hours. The chaplain encouraged me to turn my life over to God, and he let me know that I was about to embark on the journey of a lifetime. So I started reading the Bible in my hospital bed.

Q: Were you facing criminal charges at this time?

A: No, not then. But I knew that charges might be brought against me in future. And I didn't try to hide from that. Duke University Medical Center released me, and I could have just stayed in North Carolina instead of returning to Virginia, where the accident had happened. But I went back, because I knew I had to face what I had done.

Q: Did you continue to read the Bible after you left the hospital and went home to Virginia?

A: Yes, and I started going to church regularly again. Also, I went to church after I made bond, after I was arrested. I received overwhelming support from churches in the surrounding community—

not just my own, but others, too. They visited me, gave me money because I couldn't work, and even gave me money for lawyers. So I really felt the love of Jesus in its practical form. This helped me to see that there was more to the Christian faith than just words in a book. It was love in action.

Q: Did you continue to walk with Jesus after you entered the prison system?

A: Yes. I attended church services as often as they had them, twice a week as I recall. I also got pastoral visits from my home church's minister every six months or so, and he continues to come to visit me occasionally. He also stays in touch through cards and with my family. He's a wonderful man.

Q: Did you take any classes after you came to prison?

A: Well, I'm fortunate, I guess, in that I have more education than most inmates. Most educational programs in here are more geared to them: remedial reading, high school equivalency, and so forth. But the prison in which we are now, Brunswick Correctional Center, is unusual in that it has a computer course. I graduated from both parts of that, the introductory one and the advanced. In my work prior to my arrest, I had worked with computers a lot, and I wanted to maintain my skills. [Interviewer's Note: The size of this class has meanwhile been cut in half.]

Q: What kind of job did you get at Brunswick?

A: I began working as a chaplain's clerk pretty soon after I arrived here, and I've held that job continuously since then, under three different chaplains.

Q: What do you do as a chaplain's clerk?

A: My work consists of aiding in scheduling services for all different denominations and faiths. We have about twenty-five prison ministers and other religious volunteers who come here regularly for Protestant, Catholic, Jehovah's Witness, Buddhist, and Islamic inmates. I liaise between the volunteers and program sponsors and the chaplain as well as the other staff here. Distributing religious literature, setting up the musical equipment and lecterns used at different services, and scheduling appointments for other inmates to see the chaplain are some of the other things I do, too.

Q: Apart from the office work, what do you do?

A: At the Protestant services, I am the worship leader. That means I conduct the service from beginning to end—leading the congregation in prayer, calling on the choir to sing, inviting congregation members up for the Bible reading, introducing the volunteer or sponsor if he or she is preaching the sermon, or preaching the sermon myself. Protestants have services twice a week, and I usually give a mini-sermon at each one. Depending on the volunteer or sponsor, I may also give a longer sermon.

Q: Before I became a Catholic, I attended Protestant services that you led, and I remember some of the sermons you preached. Tell us about the one called "Fight Night at BWCC."

A: Well, "BWCC" is "Brunswick Correctional Center." The sermon is based on Psalm 42 as a starting point, and it talks about David's struggle within himself. He is exiled at this point because his son Absalom has taken over the kingdom. David is wrestling with his faith and his current situation: if I love God as much as I say I do, why does it seem that my circumstances are getting the best of me? If I am a man after God's own heart, how come I am in exile? Each time his situation gets worse, his faith speaks up to quiet his heart and to comfort his soul. He realizes that God has not forgotten him, and some day he will rise again.

Q: How did you come to choose Psalm 42 as the topic of that sermon?

A: I think that this psalm speaks to men who are incarcerated and are trying to do the right thing. I see my role as helping the men in here keep faith and keep doing the right thing, even though their circumstances get very unpleasant at times—just like David's. They find themselves with a battle raging inside. Has God forgotten them? And the answer is that God has not forgotten us, any more than he forgot David. God spoke to David's heart, and he will send a comforting word into our own hearts. It's not in vain that we keep doing the right thing, even though we're incarcerated.

Q: Have you ever thought about becoming a minister when you are released?

A: Well, first I would have to get a job to provide some financial stability. But yes, I would like to attend a seminary and become a pastor eventually. I believe my experience as a prisoner could help others turn from a life of crime and bring out undeveloped talents, so I would like to go into prison ministry especially.

Q: Apart from leading worship services and preaching sermons here at Brunswick Correctional Center, what else do you do to help prisoners keep faith?

A: I also counsel some men one-on-one, if they want it. Many inmates are more comfortable speaking with me than with a staff member. Some of the issues they bring to me are thoughts of suicide, the death of a family member, other family problems—such as disobedient children or a wife who wants a divorce—or disputes with other prisoners. Sometimes we'll talk on the rec yard, or in the lobby of a housing unit, or even in the man's cell.

Q: What is the most common problem that inmates bring to you?

A: Many men are very lonely and despairing because they are cut off from their families. Many families cannot afford to come to visit their incarcerated relatives or pay the surcharges on the prison's collect-call system. Also, hardly anyone in the free world writes letters any more—it's all instant communication, e-mail and cell phones. Prisons are the last place on earth where pen and paper is the primary means of communication!

Q: And, of course, many inmates have no connection at all anymore with their families in the free world.

A: That's right. Many prisoners feel abandoned, and they really have been.

Q: Do you and the inmates who seek your help ever talk about their crimes?

A: Certainly. You know, despite the overwhelming propaganda out there, most offenders that I have come in contact with are first-timers who came in here when they were a lot younger than even I was. They are very, very regretful that they made their mistake—but there is no one to tell that to, no one to listen. Who can you turn to, to say that you're sorry?

Q: Do you think that most of these men would re-offend if released?

A: I don't know if they would re-offend; that depends on a lot of things, like if they find a job and have gotten some help with their drug addiction. But I know that most of them don't *want* to re-offend. They don't sit in here planning how they're going to terrorize people when they get released. They dream of going straight, but they don't know how. They tell me, "I'm sorry I made the mistake I made—but where do I go from here?" They feel despair, because they know there's no second chance for them.

Q: And how do you answer that question, "Where do I go from here?"

A: I tell them that you have to continue to be patient and take one day at a time. Also, I instruct them that they first must forgive themselves. That's important, because you cannot continue to harp on your past mistakes—you cannot change them. What has happened, has happened. I tell these men: now you know what can happen to you, *if you allow it to happen.* This gives the individual the opportunity not to excuse his mistake, but to accept it. And then I point out the positive aspects I see in the man before me: he might be good at helping others with their education, or he might be a good listener, or he might know how to comfort others in a crisis through his own experience.

Q: How do you know what a particular prisoner might be good at?

A: I observe people, and I listen. Many people in prison discover talents and abilities that they did not know they had within them. That can happen through their faith—they might learn how to sing in the church choir. Or they might write poetry. A lot of men around here have picked up crocheting and make all kinds of things with their hands. It all depends on what opportunities they are given. If there is no choir, no English class, no arts and crafts program, men can't discover their abilities. But these men really need these opportunities to discover their talents, so they can stop hating themselves and start forgiving themselves.

Q: Is self-hatred a big problem among prisoners?

A: Yes. A lot of inmates have very low expectations of themselves. They figure that nobody cares if they can do something besides getting high and doing crime.

Q: I noticed that you didn't mention Christ in this discussion of forgiveness; you only talked about prisoners learning to forgive themselves. Why is that?

A: I don't always bring up Jesus in the one-on-one counseling sessions because you have to feed men what they can digest. Some of them aren't ready for Christ yet. We are a vast culture of many faiths, and so I have to be ready to help regardless of whether I have the same faith as that person or not. Jesus summed that up in one word: love. If you give these men love and forgiveness, you have already brought Christ to them, even though you might not have used the word "Jesus" in your conversation.

Q: But what about those occasions when you do mention Christ explicitly?

A: When I talk about Jesus in counseling sessions, I talk about how he has made it possible for us to endure these circumstances and go through the trials and tribulations of life that we face day in and day out. To the person who has to deal with sickness, I talk about Jesus the Healer. To the individual who is dealing with legal problems, I introduce Christ as the Lawyer, the advocate who speaks up for us. To the man who is restless and weary of mind, I introduce Jesus as the Master of Peace who comforts all hearts. To the person who is struggling with finances, I introduce Christ as the Great Provider.

Q: And do you find that your one-on-one counseling sessions are successful in helping inmates with their problems?

A: Most of the time they are. A lot of people don't know what strength they have inside until they are put to the test. We are often stronger than we look. These situations we face, they can bring out not just our best side, but our true being.

Q: "Our true being" is a problematic phrase in this context. A lot of people in the free world, and even many inmates themselves, think that everyone in prison is a born criminal, beyond salvation and rehabilitation. We're supposed to be beyond hope.

A: That's right, many people do think that way. But no one in here is *born* bad. Some time in the early stages of our lives, we get our lives clouded up with bad things, which lead to really bad choices, which land us in here. But this does not have to be the end. The brighter, better side is capable of rising again. And the key to that better side rising again is experiencing the love and forgiveness of Jesus.

Q: Do you believe that Christ has forgiven you?

A: Certainly. I believe he forgave me long ago, when I first asked him to come into my life, in Duke University Medical Center. But I certainly understand that society often requires more of others than they are willing to give themselves.

Q: Explain that further, please.

A: I think we find it very hard to forgive others. For example, the judge who sentenced me: if that had been his very own son in the courtroom instead of me, I daresay that he would have pled for mercy—and he would have granted it. Or a female guard who talked to me just a few days ago. She has been holding a twenty-year grudge against a man who promised to give her husband some wood to make a piece of furniture. Her husband forgave the man a long, long time ago, but she continues to harbor hatred on her husband's behalf and says she can't ever forgive him.

Q: What did you tell this female guard?

A: I told her that bitterness can ruin us all, if we let it. If we fail to administer love and forgiveness to those individuals who have harmed us, we are the ones who will suffer in the long run. Jesus told the disciples, "For if ye forgive men their trespasses, your heavenly Father will also forgive you; but if ye forgive not men their trespasses, neither will your Father forgive your trespasses." Certainly Jesus would have forgiven this man long ago, just as her husband did—and welcomed him with open arms. It's Jesus that we ought to try to follow, not our own bitterness.

QUESTIONS FOR REFLECTION AND DISCUSSION

SCRIPTURE—Professor Fretheim makes the point that the Bible uses the same verb—*nakah*, to strike—when the slave driver beats the Israelite, when Moses kills the slave-driver, and when God punishes the nation of Egypt. Does the use of the same verb indicate some sort of equivalence between these actions? Does it suggest a tacit approval or endorsement of violence?

CRIMINOLOGY—Do you think that prison inmates should have the same legal rights as civilians? The same rights, but to a lesser degree? Or should they be denied some rights altogether? Which ones, and why? What are some of the long-term implications of enshrining the principle that some people have fewer legal rights than others?

Self-exam—Do you ever watch "true crime" TV shows or read legal thrillers? Examine how frequently the electronic and print media are sending you messages about the criminal justice system. How have these messages shaped your attitudes and opinions?

Interview—Carlton said that "society often requires more of others than they are willing to give themselves." This is a frequent theme in Christ's preaching; see Matthew 7:12, for instance. Why is this? What can you do to change it?

Internet—Visit the Prison Legal News Web site (www.prisonlegalnews.org). Familiarize yourself with the unfamiliar terms and then read some articles and court decisions. See especially Margo Schlanger, "The Political Economy of Prison and Jail Litigation," *Prison Legal News*, June 2007.

Immersion—Have a real talk with a black friend about the criminal justice system. Ask your friend to put you in touch with the associate pastor at his/her church who helps inmates and their families.

Chapter 4

SAMSON AND VICTIMS' RIGHTS

I F ONLY I had enough time, I could write an entire book on criminal psychology based just on the story of Samson (Judges 13–16). An FBI profiler would note that he has all the hallmarks of a narcissist with Oedipal issues who grew up to be a juvenile delinquent and ultimately a killer.

- A single child, Samson was conceived after an angel visited his previously barren mother (Judges 13:3). No doubt she told him that story many times as he grew up, reminding him that he was "consecrated to God" as a Nazirite, or Nazorean (Judges 13:5).
- As if that were not enough to swell a little boy's head, Samson's parents clearly did not know how to say "no" to him: later, they even allowed him to break the Mosaic code by marrying a non-Israelite woman (Judges 14:1–3).
- Samsom grew up to be a very nasty young man: he killed thirty men and robbed them of their clothes simply to pay off a gambling debt; he burned down the Philistines' fields by tying three hundred foxes' tails together in pairs and setting them on fire; and he "killed a thousand men" who had come to arrest him for his various felonies (Judges 14:19, 15:4–5, 15:15).

In the end Samson got his comeuppance, of course: Delilah played on his vanity to wheedle the secret of his strength out of him. After she cut off his hair, the pledge of God's special favor, Samson was "bound...with bronze fetters [and] put to grinding in the prison. But the hair on his head began to grow as soon as it was shaved off" (Judges 16:21, 22).

To me, as a fellow prisoner, that is one of the most beautiful verses in all of Scripture: God does not abandon his beloved, even in the penitentiary! He always gives us that second chance, another shot at redemption.

Society, on the other hand, does not grant second chances to notorious felons like Samson and me. Instead, he was brought to the Philistines' great hall and forced to "play the buffoon before…about three thousand men and women" (Judges 16:23, 27). But even in the depths of his ordeal, a stranger showed Samson some kindness. In the Philistines' hall, a "boy" held the blind prisoner's hand and led him to the relative safety of the columns (Judges 16:26, NIV).

What mystifies and troubles me about Samson is that, even after that boy's kind gesture, he "grasped the two middle columns [and] pushed hard," destroying the hall and killing "more [people] at his death…than those he killed during his lifetime" (Judges 16:29, 30). Of course, I understand that, in the much rougher times in which he lived, the deaths of so many Philistines was considered a blessing from God. But was it only for this act of extreme vengeance that "the hair on [Samson's] head began to grow" in his captivity? Could he not have used his second chance to a better purpose?

Professor J. Clinton McCann of Eden Theological Seminary calls Samson a "flawed hero" because he killed Philistines out of personal revenge, not to liberate Israel.[1] While this is true, I see a deeper problem in the destruction of the great hall: the nature of Samson's three thousand victims. Who, after all, were the people who had assembled there? Surely they were all relatives of Samson's *previous* victims! Every one of the more than one thousand men he had slaughtered during his rampage through Philistia had had a family that loved him. More than likely, it was those relatives who now wanted to take a closer look at the captured Israelite champion—and, no doubt, to hurl some curses at him.

If this is true, then we cannot accept Samson's murder of the three thousand men and women in the great hall as a Godly act. Significantly, the Book of Judges itself does not explicitly endorse his final slaughter of civilians, in contrast with his earlier killings in battle. When Samson slew one thousand Philistine militiamen with the jawbone of an ass, for instance, the Lord ratified this military victory by splitting a rock to provide the warrior with water (Judges 15:19). No such divine seal of approval follows the destruction of the great hall, however.

Thus Samson should be seen as one of the Bible's great tragic figures, much like King Saul. Although Saul violated the rules of priestly sacrifice (1 Samuel 13:8–14), God continued to grant him great military successes (1 Samuel 14:22–23, 47–48). But his repeated disobedience (1 Samuel 15:4–23) led Yahweh to abandon him and put David in his place. While our Father does give us second chances, we are obligated to make use of them in a way that is pleasing to him—and in that regard, Samson's suicide–mass murder was a terrible failure and a warning.

In the rest of this chapter, we will take a closer look at the people he killed in the great hall. They were, most likely, the survivors of crime victims and thus highly germane to the subject of this book. But this raises a difficult question for me as an author and you as a reader: Do I, a convicted criminal and victimizer, have any right to discuss the victim's perspective?

The only possible answer is that I have no such *right*—but I do have an *obligation* to try to give victims a voice in these pages. What I hope to do below is to encourage a new public conversation about how victims fit into the criminal justice process. Such a discussion is necessary, I believe, because the role victims play during trials, in the legislatures and at parole hearings has changed greatly over the last three decades. During that same period, the U.S. correctional population rose from 300,000 to 2.3 million, thanks in part to the three factors we examined in the previous chapter: racism, the media and the law. But the victims' rights movement also contributed to the vast overexpansion of prison systems, as criminologists tell us.

Justice for All

"From the mid-1980s to the early 1990s, prison growth was driven most forcefully by the war on drugs," according to a recent study. "But in the 1990s, the primary cause of prison growth ... became longer sentences."[2] Professor Todd R. Clear of the John Jay College of Criminal Justice

(SUNY) concurs: in recent years, the leading cause of correctional expansion has been the "large number of people [who] are now being sentenced to very long or life sentences."[3] These longer terms of incarceration came about mainly through the abolition of parole in the federal system and nearly all states, a general trend toward tougher punishment, and the passage of "mandatory minimum" laws. Thus, between 1984 and 2004, the length of the average term of incarceration *doubled*.[4]

What led to this revolutionary policy change? Public outrage following a series of high-profile cases like the abduction-murder of Polly Klaas in 1993, for instance. Actual crime rates had already begun their long and still ongoing decline in that year; but every other month, it seemed, some parolee committed another mind-bogglingly gruesome homicide. And CNN milked each case for every ratings point possible.

The same year, 1993, also saw the founding of Justice For All by a group of Texas women who had themselves fallen victim to crime. Describing itself as "an advocate for change in a criminal justice system that is inadequate in protecting the lives and property of law-abiding citizens," Justice For All has grown into a 3,500-member organization with a long list of accomplishments:

> Justice For All is responsible for important victims' rights legislation that has passed in Texas. Justice For All members were responsible for a new Department of Corrections policy allowing victims' families to view executions, habeas corpus reform law, curtailment of Texas's "good time" policies for inmates, averting a policy to allow inmates access to telephones, curtailing inmates' lawsuits against victims. Victims are now allowed to address their perpetrators after sentencing in many Texas courts.[5]

Justice For All also actively promotes the death penalty, organizes protest petitions for parole hearings, and endorses political candidates based on their toughness on crime.[6] Judged by its own standards, this group and others like it have been enormously successful; indeed, they have transformed the landscape of American justice.

But, while some of the reforms initiated by the victims' rights movement have been very helpful, others may not have been the best means to its ultimate ends: healing pain and achieving justice. This is not to suggest that organizations like Justice For All are in any way insincere. However, to reach their objectives, victims' groups have in large part focused on two methods—executing offenders and creating the world's largest prison system—that have proved to be ineffective and unchristian. The concerns of victims must be addressed, but there may be more appropriate ways of doing so.

What is it that victims ultimately need? According to the Reverend Dr. Marie M. Fortune, a widely published author and advisor on domestic violence to both the Department of Justice and the Pentagon,

> Justice requires that the victim have an opportunity to tell her/his story, to have that telling heard and acknowledged by people (or institutions) who matter to the victim, to receive compassion (a willingness to suffer with) from her/his community, to have protection of others from harm, to have the perpetrator held accountable by the community, to receive material restitution from the perpetrator (where there has been material cost due to the victimization), and to be vindicated (set free from the memories) by the community.[7]

These goals can be grouped under the two general headings mentioned above: healing pain and achieving justice. So let us examine each set of needs in turn and inquire how best to meet them.

HEALING PAIN

Certain of the Reverend Dr. Fortune's goals are beyond the scope of this book since they do not involve the courts or prisons. But we must note here that some of the crime-victim movement's greatest achievements have come precisely in the area of improving the community's caring response to victims.

Without the advocacy of victims and their supporters, Congress might never have authorized the creation of the Office for the Victims of Crime in 1983, for instance. This agency organizes training programs for victim services providers, acts as an information clearinghouse, and administers the Crime Victims Fund (CVF). Financed through fines and penalties paid by federal offenders, the CVF has distributed over $3 billion since 1988 to more than 4,000 domestic violence shelters, rape treatment clinics, and reimbursement programs that cover victims' medical costs and lost wages. Many of these organizations are staffed by crime victims who have found healing and meaning in helping others who have been harmed.[8]

When it comes to providing "an opportunity to tell [one's] story [and] to have that telling heard," groups like Justice For All (JFA) have done great work in promoting the use of victim-impact statements in court. My only wish here is that this approach be expanded to include post-trial, in-prison programs: many inmates "long for the meaningful accountability that comes from having formal and legitimate avenues for expressing their desire to make amends to the victims," according to Barb Toews of the Pennsylvania Prison Society.[9]

MURDER VICTIMS' FAMILIES FOR RECONCILIATION

If the healing of pain is the ultimate purpose of telling one's story, then the experience of Murder Victims' Families for Reconciliation (MVFR) must at least be mentioned here. This organization was founded in 1976 by relatives of murder victims who came to believe that "reconciliation within ourselves, within communities, or with the offenders can be a positive act moving society toward transformative justice and paving the way for the ultimate abolition of the death penalty."[10] They tell their stories in Not in Our Name—Murder Victims' Families Speak Out Against the Death Penalty:

> ... opposition to the death penalty is not just about the offender.
> It is about how we choose to respond in the aftermath of a

devastating trauma and loss. It is about who we all want to be. It is about believing that the way to honor a loved one is to work for the prevention of violence, rather than to replicate it [through execution].[11]

According to MVFR member Marietta Jaeger, whose seven-year-old daughter was abducted and killed in 1973, she experienced the same emotions as any other murder victim's relative: "Initially, I would have been happy to take [the killer's] life with my own hands." But she "finally c[a]me to understand that God's idea of justice is not punishment but restoration" and asked the FBI to offer the perpetrator life imprisonment and psychiatric care instead of capital punishment. Jaeger believes that "family members who maintain a 'vindictive mindset' allow themselves to become in a sense the killer's next victim... they remain bitter and tormented, filled with hatred and unhappiness."[12]

But who can blame murder victims' relatives for experiencing "bitter[ness] and hatred," given the depth of suffering that has been forced upon them? A typical victim impact statement gives voice to the feelings of a mother whose daughter was killed:

Chrissie was our future, our legacy to the world. The days of joyful, whole family reunion are over. The home, a place of refuge from the world has been invaded by violence. We go thru the motions of living, but there is no joy, peace, rest or closure. Now all we have are years of accumulated photos....[13]

The brother of another murder victim wrote in his victim-impact statement,

One challenge each of us had to deal with as Bill's survivors is the anger that such a heinous crime leaves behind. What do you do with it? On the one hand, we want Larry to experience all the pain he created for Billy, our family and friends. But, Larry's murder was so heinous and depraved, that to inflict it or even wish it on anyone would entail crossing over to the cruel-heartedness Larry lives by.[14]

That is the terrible emotional trap into which offenders force their victims. If some, like Marietta Jaeger, can slip this snare through forgiveness, they are blessed indeed; if others cannot escape the cruel grip of anger, then we must respect their feelings. Certainly we should pray for them all.

"Be Angry, but Do Not Sin"

Respecting the feelings of those who have been victimized by crime does not necessarily mean that we should make their emotions our own, however. By analogy, we may sympathize deeply with a childless couple that experiences wrenching envy in the presence of our own offspring, but we would not feel obligated to share their jealousy. Especially in the case of anger, we must carefully distinguish between compassion for and approval of this dangerous sentiment.

Christians base their judgment in such matters on the Bible, which wisely acknowledges that anger has its place—but also cautions that it must end. In his Letter to the Ephesians, Paul makes this point by quoting Psalm 4:5 (LXX): "Be angry, but do not sin; do not let the sun go down on your anger" (4:26; cf. Romans 12:14, 17, 19–21). According to James, the brother of the Lord, "the wrath of a man does not accomplish the righteousness of God" (James 1:20). And while Jesus himself felt "anger" at the Pharisees' "hardness of heart" (Mark 3:5), he never *acted* in anger and warned the disciples against doing so (Luke 9:54; cf. Matthew 5:22).

Since we are now on the subject of Scripture, let us examine which biblical passages the two victims' rights groups above see as their respective inspirations. Bill Pelke, founding board member of Murder Victims' Families for Reconciliation and president of Journey of Hope ...From Violence to Healing, declares on his Web page, "The answer is love and compassion for all humanity. I am a Christian, and Jesus said, 'Whosoever has no sin, cast the first stone.' Under that criteria, none of us can cast the stone of death."[15] Pelke joined MVFR while fighting to overturn the death sentence imposed on his grandmother's killer, a ninth-grade girl.[16]

On Justice For All's homepage, the following appears immediately below the American-flagged banner: "Justice will only be achieved when those who are not injured by crime feel as indignant as those who are. —King Solomon"[17] Here we should reflect on the possible significance of the fact that, while MVFR leads off with the words of Jesus, JFA prefers an Old Testament figure like Solomon. Second, we must take note that the Justice for All motto asks us to feel "indignant," or righteously angry—a feeling not encouraged in the New Testament. And, third, it is surely important that the lines JFA attributes to King Solomon were never actually said by him. In fact, they are nowhere to be found in the Bible; to confirm this, use an exhaustive concordance. Not everything that sounds like justice is in fact God's idea of justice.

I do not bring up the subject of Justice for All's misattributed "scriptural" slogan to discredit this organization; as I hope I have made clear, I applaud much of what it and similar groups have done, and I sympathize with its members' suffering. However, as our study of victims' needs moves from *healing pain* to *achieving justice*, we must remember that crime victims are human too—and thus prone to error.

Achieving Justice—Capital Punishment

To return to the Reverend Dr. Fortune's statement, achieving justice should certainly include the protection of others from harm, accountability for the perpetrator, and material restitution for the victim. But there are many different ways in which these policy objectives may be put into practice. Below, we shall see that the two policy implementations favored by the victims' rights movement—the death penalty and extremely long prison sentences—are neither effective nor Christian. They may sound good at first, much like the putative Solomon quotation, but ultimately they do not serve the interests of victims or society.

Without engaging in a long review of "pro" and "con" capital punishment studies, we can at least all agree that those U.S. states that use the death penalty have significantly *higher* homicide rates than those that do not.[18] New York has not executed anyone since 1963, and still the number of murders is at a forty-four-year low.[19] Even Justice For All's review of the evidence admits that "the general deterrent effect [of executions] may remain statistically elusive"; most criminologists would prefer the word nonexistent.[20] It is not surprising, then, that the great majority of capital punishment proponents no longer claim any practical crime-reducing benefits from execution and instead rely on Scripture to make their case.

What is peculiar about many Christian pro–death penalty arguments is that they are based on the Old Testament: the covenant with Noah set down in Genesis 9 and the covenant with Moses made on Mt. Sinai. Why is Christian reliance on passages like these so strange? Because with our faith in Jesus "we are released from the law, ... the obsolete letter," and instead placed under "the new covenant in [our Savior's] blood" (Romans 7:6; Luke 22:20), as we saw in Chapter 1. Those interested in "The Bible and Capital Punishment" can turn to the Appendix.

Meanwhile, let us examine another possible argument for the death penalty: that it imparts a great emotional benefit to relatives of murder victims. But that is questionable, according to Jim Willett, a Texas prison warden who supervised an astonishing eighty-nine executions between 1998 and 2001:

> I don't think those victims' families got everything they thought they'd get when they came to see [criminals] die. It's like at Christmas when you're expecting something and then you actually get it and it isn't as neat as you thought it was when you were waiting for it. They have the same kind of thing happen to them. It doesn't do for them what they thought it would do.[21]

And the questions go deeper. Even if executions gave satisfaction or pleasure to victims' relatives, is it truly good for them and society generally to indulge the urge to watch another human being die? Most of us desire things or experiences that are enjoyable in the short term but ultimately harmful to our psyches and souls; the emotional "high" of alcohol or drugs comes to mind. Do executions fall into this category? Are they the equivalent of a snort of cocaine or an all-night drinking binge?

ACHIEVING JUSTICE—LONG PRISON SENTENCES

Those who would answer the questions above in the affirmative often suggest very long prison sentences, including life without the possibility of parole, as an alternative to the death penalty. For non-capital crimes, victims' rights groups have also advocated ever-lengthier terms of incarceration. But, as with capital punishment, very long prison sentences turn out to be ineffective, unchristian, and of dubious emotional benefit to victims.

Other chapters of this book look at this policy alternative from several different angles. Here I will offer only a few salient facts to lay the groundwork:

- As we saw earlier in this chapter, longer sentences were the primary cause of prison growth during the 1990s, a decade that saw the number of inmates rise 51.6%. But this vast expansion of the correctional system lowered the crime rate by only 4.4 to 7.9%, as we learned in Chapter 2. Given those poor results, one could reasonably argue that the tens of billions of dollars spent on extra prisons might have been more wisely invested elsewhere: in crime victims' compensation programs or individual therapy, for instance. A survivor of a shooting may benefit more from fully paid-for medical and psychological treatment than from having the offender's sentence lengthened from five years to ten. Did anyone actually give victims this option?
- Longer prison sentences lead to greater numbers of older inmates. Thanks to age-related medical problems, these convicts cost up to three times as much to house behind bars as younger felons.[22] But

incarcerating the elderly does not make the streets any safer: crime is overwhelmingly a young man's game, and "most men age out of committing violent crimes in their thirties," says former New York Corrections Commissioner Michael Jacobson.[23]

• Even older ex-inmates are likely to re-offend, however, if they are not provided educational and therapeutic programs while incarcerated. According to the American Bar Association, warehousing convicts will "increase the chances that prisoners, once released, will be neither equipped nor inclined to conform their conduct to the law," while rehabilitating them and providing reentry assistance provably reduces crime.[24] One simple example: in the state in which I am incarcerated, 49.1% of those inmates who get no education while serving time are re-incarcerated after release, but only 19.1% of those who do complete educational programming end up behind bars again.[25] That means roughly two-thirds fewer *future* victims! To achieve such results on a wider scale, however, America will have to pay a price: it will have to say good-bye to no-hope, no-frills penitentiaries.

This is, of course, a very difficult idea for crime victims to accept. In one of the victim-impact statements quoted earlier, for instance, we read that

> If the murderer walks free—EVER—the survivor's anger is heightened by fear of revenge, by fear of re-victimization, by anger at the double injustice of a murderer living freely while the loved one is still just as dead as the day [he or she was] murdered.... Possibility of parole, after even 25 years means that every 2 years Billy's family and friends will be dragged through this horror and anxiety again and again and again. This is not how any of us deserve to spend our retirement or last years here on Earth, traveling to parole hearings. It is simply not fair to give this depraved excuse of a human being this kind of undeserved power over the lives of innocent people.[26]

Feelings like this neither can nor should be dismissed easily; they are real, and they must be heard and respected. But even—or perhaps especially—from the victims' point of view, some context might be helpful.

RECIDIVISM

Having read the entire victim-impact statement from which the passage above was excerpted, I agree that in this particular case, there is some real justification for the fear that the offender could pursue the victim's family if released. Generally, however, the exact opposite is true: while the national average recidivism rate is 67.5%, paroled lifers only re-offend at a rate of 20.6%, the lowest of any category of felons. Moreover, only 18% of these new crimes are violent, making the violent recidivism rate of lifers on parole just 3.7%. That is by far the lowest percentage of any category of offenders.[27]

A 1999 Department of Justice study of 11,000 sex offenders, another highly feared group of criminals, was equally encouraging: even if they receive no treatment behind bars, rapists and molesters recidivate at a rate of just 17.6%; and if they do get therapy, that rate drops to 7.2%. Those results are duplicated in a 2002 study of 9,454 sex offenders in forty-three states by Canadian psychologist Dr. Karl Hanson.[28] And it must be remembered that the majority of new crimes committed by released sex offenders are not sexual in nature: of those rapists who recidivate after being discharged from prison, only 2.5% commit another rape.[29]

If murderers and sex offenders are not as dangerous as one might think, then who should be feared? The approximately 1.1 million felons currently serving time for *nonviolent* crimes.[30] *All* of them will leave prison eventually, and their violent recidivism rates are bad news indeed.[31]

Category of Offender	Overall Recidivism Rate	Of New Crimes, Percentage that Is Violent	Violent Recidivism Rate
Property:	73.8	21.9	16.2
Drug:	66.7	18.4	12.3
Public Order:	62.2	18.5	11.5

What do those numbers mean to you and your family? Roughly 146,000 assaults, malicious woundings, molestations, rapes, robberies, kidnappings, and murders that *will* happen, thanks to the inevitable release of those 1.1 million nonviolent offenders. By contrast, if every single one of America's 127,677 lifers were to be freed today, only 4,734 would commit another crime of violence, given the above-referenced violent recidivism rate of 3.7%.[32]

What this suggests is that—with the important exception of those cases where a particular offender poses a specific threat to victims or their relatives—much of the fear that victims have of their perpetrators is not reasonable. Again: this does *not* mean those emotions are not sincerely felt, nor that they should not be treated compassionately! But if the goal is to provide *real* help to victims, then *real* dangers should be addressed.

"The Suffering of Another Person"

There is another factor to be considered here, a simple truth of morality, psychology, and ultimately common sense. Because I am a convicted criminal, I arguably have no right to state this truth, so I will yield to Barry Holman, former Research and Public Policy Director at the National Center on Institutions and Alternatives, and now Director of Research and Quality Assurance at the Washington, D.C., Department of Youth Rehabilitation Services. This is how he phrased this central principle of human life in an interview about the effects of excessively long terms of incarceration: "Causing someone else to suffer doesn't make up for suffering that was caused to someone in the past. It just can't. There aren't simple ways to just end people's pain. *Healing doesn't come from the suffering of another person.*"[33]

If that last sentence is indeed objectively true, then over-sentencing ultimately harms *victims*, because they are living a lie. All the effort and money spent on constructing ever more prisons will not heal their pain. In the end, it is all a waste and a self-deception.

Crime traumatizes victims, and the simple truth is that trauma can distort one's perception of reality. For instance, when the U.S. Supreme Court forbade capital punishment for juveniles in 2005, the mother of a young woman murdered by a sixteen-year-old expressed the concern that "the decision sends a disturbing message to would-be criminals—they can order teens and children to commit violent crimes, and no one will be seriously punished." The victim's husband said, "It's a shame that a person can commit a crime in this country and not be held accountable."[34]

What sentence did the killer receive in lieu of execution? Life without the possibility of parole. Imagine an entire lifetime, from age sixteen until death, spent in a cage. No one was "seriously punished"? No one was "held accountable"?

What should be noted in this context is that the mother in the above case is a victims' rights advocate who was appointed to Virginia's three-member parole board in 2002. For the victims' rights movement, this was a great achievement. For prisoners, it led to the lowest parole rate in the country.[35] And, for Virginia's taxpayers, this crime victim's appointment to the parole board meant having to pay for the continued incarceration of approximately 6,000 parole-eligible inmates.[36]

Parole was abolished for all felons who entered the Virginia system after 1995, so all of these men and women have served well over ten years behind bars; not a few have served over thirty. If each of them costs no more to incarcerate than an average convict, as opposed to an elderly one with medical problems, then Virginia is spending $135,900,000 per year to imprison them.[37] That may make victims *feel* safer, but, given the low recidivism rates of older ex-inmates, it will not actually *make* them safer.

Is there a better way to achieve justice for victims and address their needs? Perhaps the following interview with Dr. Linda L. White, of Sam Houston State University, points toward a radically different option: not retribution but reconciliation. While her story is indeed an amazing one, however, I do think it carries two risks for those of us who have not lived through a tragedy like hers.

The first is that we may be tempted to dismiss Dr. White as a saint: "Maybe she can forgive her daughter's killer, but I could never do that." To counter this objection, we should develop the courage and imagination to "love your enemies . . . for if you love those who love you, what recompense will you have?" (Matthew 5:44, 46). We are, after all, called to "be perfect, just as your heavenly Father is perfect" (Matthew 5:48).

The second temptation we may encounter when we hear Dr. White's story is to dismiss her kind of justice as impractical: "How could one possibly make this work in a court system that processes tens of thousands of criminal cases per year?" Jesus encountered the same kind of objection when he proposed feeding the five thousand with five loaves and two fishes. Yet "all ate and were satisfied" (Matthew 14:20), and I suspect the same would happen if America decided to make the "impossible" possible in its criminal justice system.

Are miracles possible after all?

Interview with Linda White

Q: Tell us about your background.

A: I was born in 1940. Before 1986, I was a homemaker, raising two sons and a daughter while my husband worked in the oilfield service industry. Throughout my twenties and thirties, I was very active in our local Presbyterian church: I taught Sunday School, worked with women's groups, and conducted Bible studies. I did no prison ministry, though; I was absolutely oblivious to the issue.

Q: Your spiritual life changed dramatically in 1971, I understand.

A: Yes. We moved back to the Houston area, and for about six years I did not get involved in anything except playing bridge. Then one of our kids began to have some problems growing up, and in 1977 I began to attend the Palmer Drug Abuse Program and, later, Al-Anon. They became my church: I found more love and acceptance there than in most churches. They also gave me a level of acceptance of other people, because they reminded me that I am just as flawed as anyone else. I continued to attend those groups for several years after 1986, too.

Q: What happened in 1986?

A: Our twenty-six-year-old daughter Cathy was abducted, raped, and murdered by two fifteen-year-old boys who were high on drugs and wanted her car.

Q: How did you respond?

A: My husband and I were devastated. My biggest sensation was emptiness. I remember sitting at my table in the breakfast room, having almost an out-of-body experience. It just was not real.

Q: Did you feel angry at the perpetrators?

A: Both of my sons did, but my husband and I never went through that. We went straight from disbelief to devastation. We did not have the energy to feel angry.

Q: Did you later feel any anger or frustration during the investigation and trial?

A: No, we were very fortunate because the two boys were arrested immediately and then took plea bargains. That was very good for us.

Q: What happened to the perpetrators?

A: They were certified as adults, but because you had to be seventeen to be eligible for the death penalty at that time, the maximum sentence they could receive was sixty years. One boy got fifty-five years, the other fifty-four. I felt great about that.

Q: Did you begin your work in the criminal justice field at that point?

A: In a way. My husband and I attended meetings of a murder victim families' support group because I wanted to learn more about the court and legal system. But I grew disenchanted with that group over time.

Q: Why was that?

A: Because the level of anger and bitterness at those meetings seemed to grow and grow, whereas I was attempting to move in a positive direction. There were several little incidents where I felt out of place.

Q: Describe some, please.

A: We had a guest speaker come to talk to us about grief, a professional counselor. She was really very, very good, but after she left, the group members badmouthed her terribly. They said that she could not possibly understand unless she had had a child murdered. But I had just gone through that, and I had started reading books on grief counseling, and I liked what she had said. So I realized that the group members had really put up a lot of barriers to healing.

Q: Talk more about that, please.

A: For some people, the idea of healing is just unthinkable. "If I find a way to go forward in a healing direction, I am being disloyal to my murdered loved one." Life no longer makes sense, so you have to find new meaning. A lot of the people in that group, and others like it, find meaning by dedicating themselves to closing legal loopholes, making sentences longer, having the death penalty applied more widely, making prison tougher. But none of those things can heal your own pain.

Q: You mentioned that there were some other things about this group that bothered you.

A: Yes. We would all sign petitions to block paroles: they would be lying on tables in the back, it was like a part of the process, part of the spirit of the meeting. And I began to feel really uncomfortable with that, because I did not know anything about this person and whether he deserved parole. I only knew that someone was still devastated by the crime, and this was their way of coping with their pain. For many of those people in that group, parole was never going to be appropriate, no matter what. It never would be.

Q: So you left that group?

A: Yes. I did find some comfort there early on, because they were fellow victims. But then the group became like a sweater I had put on that did not fit, and I took it off.

Q: So what did you do next?

A: I started going to church again. At first, I went to take Cathy's daughter, Ami, but it became a sanctuary for me, too. We would sit there and tear up during services; I became known as the lady who cried. Then I became really involved again, teaching Sunday School, doing committee work, singing in the choir, being elected elder. If something interests me, I do not want to be on the side-lines. That lasted until, oh, 2001, at which time I gradually with-drew from church attendance.

Q: What happened then?

A: I became really uncomfortable with some of my denomination's and my church's judgmentalism around the homosexual issue. It seemed to be the main conversation in and around church. Here in East Texas, a lot of religion is only about being washed in the blood and about your own salvation. My view is that the pre-Easter Jesus is just as important as the post-Easter Jesus. What he said and taught was important, too.

Q: Some examples?

A: My favorite New Testament verse is Matthew 25:40: "Inasmuch as ye have done it unto one of the least of these, ye have done it unto me." And in the Old Testament, something Jesus could have said himself: "He hath shewed thee, O man, what is good, and what the Lord doth require of thee: to do justly, and to love mercy, and to walk humbly with thy God" (Micah 6:8). To return to your earlier question, I do feel the lack of a church in my life now.

Q: You said earlier that many members of the support group you attended found meaning by trying to make the criminal justice system tougher. How did you find meaning?

A: By deciding to go back to college and study psychology, so I could become a death educator and grief counselor. That was in 1987. I wanted to help others who had lost a loved one through murder. As it turned out, though, I did not end up getting a license and practicing as a counselor, except informally.

Q: Why was that?

A: Because in 1992, halfway through my master's in Clinical Psychology, I taught some freshman classes in psychology and, in 1993, a senior-level class on death and dying. That hooked me completely! I have continued to teach here at Sam Houston State University ever since, even while getting my doctorate in Educational Human Resource Development at Texas A&M in 2001. I am now an adjunct professor of philosophy and psychology—and lately criminal justice, too.

who will let us come to talk about nonviolent alternatives to the death penalty, based on our own experiences as murder victims' relatives.

Q: Do you ever counsel newly bereaved relatives of murder victims?

A: No, because we do not go out and solicit, like the other groups do. This is a very touchy issue. With the other groups, the prosecutor often sends their materials to the relatives. But we do not support the usual prosecutor's agenda of seeking the death penalty, so we are not welcome in most jurisdictions.

Q: When did you decide to pursue your Ph.D.?

A: In 1997, and that led to another great turning point. I decided to do my dissertation on the new Victim–Offender Mediated Dialogue program that had recently been started by David Doerfler for the Victims Services Division of the Texas Division of Criminal Justice. This program arranged for supervised and mediated meetings between offenders who had committed crimes of extreme violence, and their victims or relatives of their victims.

Q: So what did you do?

A: In the summer of 1999, I took the training to be a mediator. That in itself was a very spiritual experience. And then, in the fall, I interviewed four sets of victims, offenders, and mediators after they had gone through one of these sessions. I looked for themes that explained what made this program so successful—because they all agreed that it was very, very successful indeed.

Q: After you finished your research for the Ph.D., did you arrange for a mediated dialogue with the boys—now men—who had killed your daughter Cathy in 1986?

A: Yes. On April 28, 2001, Cathy's daughter Ami and I met with Grant and a mediator. We only met with one of the two perpetrators; the other was not deemed suitable by the staff of the prison.

Q: What was that meeting like?

A: We were taken to the prison chapel and then Grant was brought in. There were three sessions in one day, totaling about five hours. The whole thing was videotaped, so we and Grant could review it later—separately, of course. The whole experience is so intense that you miss things, so you have to go back later to look at it again.

Q: How would you describe the meeting from your perspective?

A: Oh, very liberating! I had worked hard over the years not to carry around the negative energy of the crime; but, of course, there was some. This meeting completely freed me of that. And this is what I had come for: I wanted the empowerment that I had seen in the four victims I had interviewed for my Ph.D. dissertation.

Q: Did it bring you closure?

A: No. Many of us who have had a loved one murdered hate that word "closure." But the meeting helped me get to know myself better. I wanted to know if I was who I thought I was: I could be compassionate about all those guys I taught in my prison classes, but could I be compassionate about *this* guy? Could I see him as a human being, too?

Q: And could you?

A: Yes. But you know, by my definition of forgiveness—letting go of the negative power that the crime holds over you—I had probably forgiven Grant years ago without even realizing it. If anyone had asked me if I had forgiven him, I would have looked at the person blankly! Grant and the other boy had been complete nonentities for me during all those years. But I think the process of forgiving them began when I started teaching in prison.

Q: And the mediated dialogue deepened that process?

A: Yes, it completed it. Maybe that is the real closure—and a new beginning, as well. I can never think of Grant the same way again. Forgiveness is a gift that you allow yourself to have, and you get it through grace—the Spirit of God in our lives. We get a lot of things we do not know we need, and the power to forgive is one.

Q: Can you tell us anything about what happened at the meeting with Grant?

A: Oh, he was so remorseful from the start! Over and over, he kept saying how he would do anything to change the past. He told us how he had tried to be a tough guy during his first few years in prison, but then came to feel the need to apologize to his victim's family because of another prisoner. This man saw something in Grant and took him into his own family during visits. That allowed Grant to get in touch with his own feelings. When this family informally adopted him, it really transformed him.

Q: Did he tell you anything else?

A: Yes, he told Ami and me Cathy's last words. She looked at the guy with the gun and said, "I forgive you, and God will forgive you, too." The way Grant told us this was not like, "She forgave me so you have to forgive me, too." It was more of a self-indictment: "She said that, and yet we *still* killed her." So he was not asking us to forgive him but accusing himself.

Q: And what did you say to him in response?

A: I did not tell him that I forgave him at the meeting, but I think he knew it anyway. At the end, the mediator took a photograph of Grant and Ami and me, and I put my arm around Grant's shoulder. Later, in a letter, I wrote him that I forgave him.

Q: How did Ami feel about the mediated dialogue?

A: She also felt very empowered personally, and she felt closer to her birth mother.

Q: How do you think Cathy would feel about your journey, from death and dying expert, to prison teacher, to participant in this kind of meeting?

A: Oh, I know without any question that if there is anything Cathy would want me to do, it is this.

Q: How about your sons and your husband?

A: Over the years, my sons' anger has died away, but they have not made my journey. My husband supports what I do.

Q: And your other family members?

A: My niece, for example, watched the videotape of the five-hour meeting with Grant, and she said, "Every day of her life, Cathy knew she was loved, but this young man never knew that." Grant is a very wounded person: he grew up in foster care, with a lot of abuse and abandonment. He had no concept of what it meant to be loved until that other prisoner's family befriended him.

Q: Did you ever use your training to conduct a mediated dialogue for another victim and offender?

A: Only once so far. It was a surrogate mediation. A prisoner who had already done a mediated dialogue with his own victim agreed to stand in for an offender who was not willing to participate. That went very well.

Q: Why did you mediate only one such dialogue?

A: Because my schedule went crazy! I teach full-time at Sam Houston, do board work for Murder Victims' Families for Reconciliation, go to conferences and seminars, and now I am returning to teach in prison.

Q: Why do you think that members of other murder victims' families groups have dealt with their suffering in a way so very different from yours?

A: The majority of those who become involved in the victims' rights movement after the murder of a loved one are white, middle- or upper-middle-class folks. They have a view already about the criminal justice system, and it is not necessarily reflective of reality. They think that crime is increasing monumentally every year; they do not realize that the most common *victim* of crime is a young black male; they believe that there is so much rehabilitation offered in prison that anybody who gets out without being rehabilitated is to blame for that themselves. The politicians take advantage of these mythological ideas and, in all fairness, often get caught up in the myths themselves. When I meet with such people, I often ask myself: How can someone who knows so little about the system and about what is effective in fighting crime be so active and have a voice that is so loud, so important?

Q: Do you see any prospect of change?

A: Yes, through education. We have to get accurate information into the hands of policymakers. My great value in this is that I am a crime victim's survivor, but I looked deeper and did not just accept superficial ideas.

Q: Do you think Victim–Offender Mediated Dialogues should become a formal part of trials or sentencing hearings?

A: No, I think it is important in America to maintain due process; I do not trust the system! But maybe we could offer the restorative justice model side by side with the regular model of judicial procedure.

Q: That in itself would require an enormous transformation of the court system.

A: Yes, but we need to start looking at this not just in terms of what crime has been committed. We have to look at what harm has been done, and how to address that harm without more harm being done. What our courts are doing now just is not working in many respects.

QUESTIONS FOR REFLECTION AND DISCUSSION

SCRIPTURE—Samson killed both himself and "about three thousand men and women" by pushing down "two ... columns" (Judges 16:27, 29). This parallels eerily Mohammed Atta's mass murder-suicide and the destruction of the Twin Towers in New York on 9/11. Can you imagine that one day he might be remembered as a "flawed hero," like Samson? What does this say about Samson? About America? About you?

CRIMINOLOGY—Why do you think no one has told you that released lifers and sex offenders are much *less* dangerous than released drug and property offenders? Make a note to reconsider this question after reading Chapter 6.

SELF-EXAM—California psychologist Paul Berg thinks that reconciliation between killers and their victims' families is pathological. "Some psychiatrists will tell you forgiveness is healing," says Berg. "I don't believe it. I think it's overrated."[40] Is there some truth to what he says? Why or why not?

INTERVIEW—Try to put yourself in Dr. White's position after her Victim–Offender Mediated Dialogue. Would you support Grant's release? Why or why not? And what about the other perpetrator? As a practical matter, can one release only one of the two, based merely on the fact that one of them participated in a restorative justice program? What if Grant had agreed to participate, but Dr. White had pulled out at the last moment?

INTERNET—Visit both www.jfa.net *and* www.mvfr.org to read more about Justice For All and Murder Victims' Families for Reconciliation.

IMMERSION—Volunteer one afternoon at a battered women's shelter or a crime victims' services bureau.

Chapter 5

DAVID AND REHABILITATION

DAVID GOT AWAY with murder! By any reasonable standard of justice, having Uriah the Hittite killed to cover up his adultery with Bathsheba was a crime of the first order. Yet David not only received no official punishment for this offense, but he continued to reign over Israel in all honor even after the prophet Nathan exposed his wrongdoing. In America, by contrast, Richard Nixon faced indictment and incarceration for felonies considerably less serious than murder.

Let us review David's crimes. After he saw Bathsheba bathing on the roof of her house, he "sent messengers and took her" (2 Samuel 4:11). Professor Walter Brueggemann of Columbia Theological Seminary points out that this turn of phrase implies force and thus rape.[1] Certainly there is no indication in the biblical text that Bathsheba was given the option of saying no when a group of the king's men showed up on her doorstep and informed her that she was about to be "taken" by his royal highness.

Having impregnated the object of his illicit passion, David realized that his crime would soon be exposed. Bathsheba's husband was off campaigning in the war against Ammon, so he could not have fathered the child growing in his wife's womb (2 Samuel 11:5, 1). What in the world is a king to do when he breaks the sixth commandment?

Clever fellow that he was, David immediately recalled Uriah the Hittite from the front, pretending to seek a report on "how the war was going" (2 Samuel 11:7). He ordered Uriah, "Go down to your house," hoping the soldier would sleep again with his wife, which would explain her pregnancy (2 Samuel 11:10, 11). Uriah was so loyal to his fellow soldiers, however, that he refused that pleasure even for one night, so long as his comrades were "encamped in the open field" (2 Samuel 11:11).

Undeterred, David "made him drunk" the next evening, but even alcohol could not overcome Uriah's virtue (2 Samuel 11:13). That sealed his fate: David instructed his general Joab: "Place Uriah up front, where the fighting is fierce. Then pull back and leave him to be struck down" (2 Samuel 11:15).

When Nathan confronted David with this crime, he characterized it with brutal accuracy: "You have cut down Uriah the Hittite with the sword; you took his wife as your own, and you killed him with the sword of the Ammonites" (2 Samuel 12:9). Even though David did not physically wield the weapon that took Uriah's life, he was no less guilty of murder.

Yet there was no punishment for this offense! No impeachment and removal from office, no indictment and trial, no jail time, and certainly no execution—no justice at all. Under our current understanding of law and order, Israelite society should have erupted into a conflagration of violence when a high-profile felon like David failed to get his just deserts. But, strangely enough, the Bible does not record any sudden increase in the Hebrew crime rate.

How can this be? Could Scripture be trying to tell us that justice can be achieved without judicial punishments like execution or imprisonment? Might we perhaps redefine justice as the profound transformation of the offender?

To explore this idea further, let us examine precisely what happened after Nathan pointed out David's crime to him. Those of us who can remember our Sunday School lessons will find the following to be familiar territory: this is the process of repenting. Note, however, that the structure of the story required the order of the first two items to be reversed.

- Confession—As soon as Nathan confronted him, David admitted, "I have sinned against the Lord" (2 Samuel 2:13). He neither quibbled about "what the meaning of 'is' is," nor did he try to discredit

Nathan by having an underling leak damaging information to the *Jerusalem Post*.

- Perfect Contrition—According to the theologians, imperfect contrition consists of sorrow for one's sins that arises from a quasi-selfish motive like fear of losing heaven, whereas perfect contrition is sorrow motivated purely by love of God and regret at having offended him. The latter is what David expressed in the *Miserere*: "Against you alone have I sinned...my sin is always before me" (Psalm 51:6, 5).

- Repentance—Not only did David ask God, "Have mercy on me," but he also acknowledged his total dependence on the Lord for his own restoration: "A clean heart create for me, God; renew in me a steadfast spirit" (Psalm 51:3, 12).

- Atonement—Theologians tell us that this takes two forms, interior and exterior. In David's case, there was the famous internal sacrifice of "a contrite spirit,... a broken, humble heart," which surpasses the standard "burnt offering" (Psalm 51:19, 18). Externally, he accepted the obligation to bring others to the same well of divine mercy that had just saved him: "Rescue me from death, God, my saving God, that my tongue may praise your healing power.... I will teach the wicked your ways, that sinners may return to you" (Psalm 51:16, 15). As we saw in the Introduction, the same dynamic can be found in Paul's First Letter to Timothy: "For that reason I was mercifully treated,... as an example for those who would come to believe" in Christ (1:16).

- Punishment/Consequences—This is not normally part of the Christian process of seeking and obtaining forgiveness, of course. However, it is the aspect of David's case that is perhaps most relevant to our present inquiry: although he was indeed punished for Uriah's murder, the penalty David received was greatly reduced, and was imposed by the Lord instead of a human judge.

Originally David was to have been publicly humiliated and killed (2 Samuel 12:11–13). After he confessed his guilt and God forgave him, however, Nathan told him that not he but the child

Bathsheba bore him would die (2 Samuel 12:13,14). If that strikes us as utterly barbaric, we must recall that "punishing children and grandchildren to the third and fourth generation for their fathers' wickedness" was considered just in ancient Israel (Exodus 34:7). David "besought God for the child" and fasted for the seven days of his son's illness (2 Samuel 12:16–18). He undoubtedly felt the loss as a blow—but not as a cruel and unusual punishment. By the standards of his own age and culture, he was let off relatively lightly.

Nor was he subjected to a formal judicial process before a human judge. In any society, ancient or modern, part of the penalty for any crime is the embarrassing and humiliating ordeal of standing in the dock and listening to witnesses testify about one's bad character. As anyone who has undergone a public trial will confirm, David was very fortunate to be spared this experience.

Overall, then, we can fairly question whether the term "punishment" is even appropriate for what happened to David. It might be more accurate to say that he had to suffer the consequences of his crime, as opposed to suffering a judicial penalty.

So far, David's response to Nathan's "indictment" seems to follow the standard format of Christian penance. In one respect, however, it is unusual: the whole royal court was made aware of the five elements reviewed above.

- Scripture does not state explicitly that Nathan's initial confrontation with David occurred in a public place, like a throne room. However, someone else must have been present to record the prophet's speech and the king's response.
- David himself added an explanatory note to the *Miserere* to ensure that all of his readers understood the biographical background: "A psalm of David, when Nathan the prophet came to him after his affair with Bathsheba" (Psalms 51:2).
- Finally the king made no secret of his penitential fast, since "The elders of his house stood beside him, urging him to rise from the ground...[and] take food with them" (2 Samuel 12:16, 17).

In our current context, the fact that the process of David's penance was so very public must surely be considered crucial. Because his confession, contrition, repentance, atonement, and punishment/consequences took place completely openly, the citizens of Jerusalem were unlikely to feel that their king had gotten away with anything. Justice was affirmed and satisfied without executing or imprisoning Uriah's killer. What really mattered was not that the criminal was punished, but that he had truly changed.

The kind of change that David underwent was spiritual in nature—hardly a surprise, since the Bible is a spiritual book. And certainly criminals today need spiritual transformation no less than David did. Given the educational, medical, and psychological deficits of our society's offenders, however, we can safely say that spiritual change is not enough: some this-worldly intervention is necessary, too. So let us take a closer look at rehabilitative programs behind bars and examine whether they can transform prisoners' lives.

REHABILITATION AND ITS ENEMIES

After nearly three decades of focusing almost exclusively on punishment and incapacitation, criminologists have recently begun urging a return to rehabilitation in corrections. "We're seeing a sea change now away from the lock-'em-up-and-throw-away-the-key approach," says Professor Debbie A. Mukamal of the John Jay College of Criminal Justice.[2] Not just academics, but even the general public have come around to favoring treatment and education over warehousing: in 2006 a Zogby poll found that 87% of Americans want prisons to provide rehabilitative programs for inmates, while only 11% support a punishment-only system. Similarly large percentages favor federal funding of reentry services for released convicts. According to Dr. Barry Krisberg, President of the National Council on Crime and Delinquency, "These survey results tell us that Americans have looked at the thirty-year experiment on getting tough with offenders and decided that it is no longer working."[3]

This is very bad news for private prison corporations and guards unions, as we shall see in our next chapter. Because both big business and organized labor are financially dependent on America's massive correctional complex, they routinely resist any suggestion that criminals can be reformed into law-abiding citizens. That is why, throughout this chapter, you will read about educational and therapeutic programs being cut back in state and federal prisons.

To counter the objections of those with a vested interest in the status quo, advocates of rehabilitation behind bars need quick, commonsense arguments like the following:

- *Rehabilitation is crime prevention.* Reginald Wilkinson, the reform-minded director of the Ohio Department of Corrections, asks people to consider, "Who would you rather sit next to on a bus? A person who is very, very angry about their prison experience and untrained and uneducated? Or a person who obtained a GED and vocational training in prison and is on his or her way to work?"[4]

  According to another enlightened law enforcement official, Sheriff C. T. Woody of Richmond, Virginia, "Cracking down on crime is crucial, [but] it will not fix the problem.... Without meaningful in-house programs to educate inmates, incarceration is tantamount to a criminal training center.... Ultimately, our community pays the cost."[5]

- *Rehabilitation has not been given a chance.* As we learned in Chapter 2, state prisons devote only an average of 6% of their budgets to rehabilitation; the rest goes to guards' wages, capital construction, and other cost factors. Louisiana, the state with the highest per capita incarceration rate, spends less than 1% of its "correctional" budget on treatment and education.[6]

- *Rehabilitation saves money.* The average annual cost for a truly effective therapeutic or educational program is $12,000 to $14,000.[7] While that sounds like a lot at first, it is actually well in line with a typical state college tuition or a year's worth of intensive substance abuse treatment. And it certainly is less than the average annual per capita cost of incarceration: $22,650.[8]

In 2001, Steve Aos and his colleagues at the Washington State Institute for Public Policy (WSIPP) published a groundbreaking meta-analysis of 400 studies on the effectiveness of rehabilitative programs of all types, both in and outside of prison:

» Juvenile offender programs with a prescribed curriculum were found to save taxpayers $5,720 to $31,661 per participant per year when compared to incarceration[9]

» For adult criminals, "moral reconation therapy" and "reasoning and rehabilitation" programs saved taxpayers $2,202 to $2,471 per participant per year, while basic education and vocational training saved $1,852 to $2,835[10]

These figures do not include crime victim costs; if those are factored in, savings range from $9,176 (adult basic education) to $131,918 (multisystemic therapy for juveniles).[11]

In 2006, Aos and other researchers at the WSIPP released an examination of the fiscal impact of so-called evidence-based programs—those that can demonstrate their effectiveness. This study determined that every $1 invested in such programs saved taxpayers $2.59 to $2.75 by lowering crime and thus making new prison construction unnecessary. If Washington State increased its annual expenditure on "evidence-based" programs from $41 million to $85 million, the state would save $2.4 *billion*.[12]

• *Rehabilitation works.* According to Aos and his colleagues, good programs can produce 20 to 30% reductions in recidivism rates.[13] Dr. Thomas O'Connor of the Oregon Department of Corrections supports the figure of 30% for in-custody programs and cites a 40% drop in re-offending for community-based initiatives.[14] In the federal Bureau of Prisons, multiple studies have demonstrated the positive impact of treatment programs on recidivism rates.[15]

The San Francisco County Jail lowers the re-offense rates of violent criminals by an amazing 42 to 80% through its RSVP, Resolve to Stop the Violence Program. (The wide range, 42 to 80%, reflects the varying lengths of time inmates spent in the program—the longer, the better.) According to founder Sunny Schwartz, program manager George Jurand, and Sheriff Michael Hennessey, RSVP saves the city $4 for every $1 spent on incarceration.[16] Some of the keys to the program's success are the active involvement of crime victims in empathy education sessions and the use of stress management techniques like yoga and acupuncture.

- *Objections to rehabilitation are hypocritical.* When it comes to their own families, all middle-class Americans believe strongly in the power of education, substance-abuse treatment, and mental-health care to improve their loved ones' lives. Private schools, Betty Ford Clinics, individual sessions with compassionate therapists— we know these work well for "our kind of people." So why on earth should they be any less effective in helping "those kinds of people"?

EDUCATION

In Chapter 2 we saw that, in Virginia, completing an educational program produces a 61% drop in the re-incarceration rate: while 49.1% of ex-prisoners who took no academic or vocational classes return to the penitentiary after release, only 19.1% of those who do get a degree of some type come back. Other studies have found that educational programs reduce recidivism anywhere from 20 to 60%.[17]

Why is there such a very wide range of results, from 20 to 60%? Because different researchers use different yardsticks: recidivism vs. re-incarceration, program participation vs. program completion. The general consensus seems to be that merely *taking part* in academic or vocational classes lowers *re-incarceration* by 29 to 33%.[18] In addition, participation in educational programs has been shown to lead to higher levels of employment and higher wages after release.[19]

If a one-third reduction in re-incarceration does not seem like a lot, recall that 672,000 inmates are released every year, of whom 67.5% (or 438,750) recidivate and 51.8% (or 336,700) are actually sent back to the penitentiary.[20] Cutting the latter number—the re-incarceration rate—by 30% not only means 101,010 fewer prisoners, but also roughly 101,010 fewer crime victims. Not worth the effort?

Because the educational deficiencies of the convict population are so extreme, even modest improvements in their skill levels would yield significant results. In Chapter 2 we saw that 19% of prisoners are completely illiterate, and another 40% are functionally illiterate; 68.2% of state inmates did not graduate from high school.[21] Raising these hundreds of thousands of men, women, and juveniles from near-total benightedness to the basic proficiency of a GED would dramatically increase their chances of living crime-free upon release. If you cannot fill out a job application form, how can you find legal work?

Sadly, correctional departments are not taking advantage of this obvious and relatively easy way to reduce re-offending and transform lives. Only 51.9% of state inmates and 56.4% of federal prisoners participate in some sort of educational program during their entire period of incarceration.[22] And according to the Reentry Policy Council, "at any given time, however, the actual percentage of prisoners engaged in educational and vocational [classes] is far lower."[23]

It is not as if inmates are not anxious to learn. In some states, waiting lists for educational programs can run into the thousands.[24] But instead of increasing course offerings, prison systems are actually trimming back academic and vocational classes. Between 1991 and 1997, educational participation levels fell 12% among state inmates and 6% among federal prisoners.[25] The Florida Department of Corrections has decreased its treatment and educational budget by 47% since 2001, according to a report by the Ex-Offender Task Force commissioned by former Governor Jeb Bush.[26] Kansas has cut its high school equivalency program in half in recent years, and Oregon has virtually eliminated GED classes.[27] "Today at the [Oregon State Penitentiary], out of twenty-four programs, only three remain," says veteran correctional Sergeant Gary Harkins.[28]

When it comes to in-custody college programs, the situation is even more dire. Researchers have found post-secondary-level education to be especially effective in reducing recidivism:

- In 2005, a fifty-state study by the Institute for Higher Education Policy found that correctional college classes cut re-offending nearly in half [29]
- Psychiatrist James Gilligan of Harvard Medical School, an expert on violence prevention, cites studies in Michigan, Indiana and California that all demonstrate the same thing: earning a college degree while incarcerated is the single best predictor of a crime-free future [30]
- According to Rudy Cypser of CURE-NY, a program conducted by Burlington County College at one New Jersey prison cut the recidivism rate of discharged inmates from 80 to 10%, and a program by Alexander City State Junior College at an Alabama correctional center lowered levels of re-offending from 70 to 75% to 16% [31]
- A Texas report showed that earning an associate's degree behind bars produced a 13.7% recidivism rate; a bachelor's degree, a 5.6% rate; and a master's degree, a 0% rate [32]

What is especially important to note is that many of these studies were conducted and/or published in the late 1980s and early 1990s. How did policymakers respond to these findings? By abolishing Pell Grants for convicts in 1994, which led most states to eliminate their in-prison college tuition assistance soon thereafter.

Thus full college programs behind bars fell from 350 in 1982 to just twelve in 2001.[33] Nationwide, less than 5% of prisoners now are enrolled in any kind of college class, never mind a degree program.[34] In Utah, to cite but one example, the state legislature eliminated funding for Utah State University's distance-learning program for prisoners in 2007, even though not a single graduate was ever re-incarcerated.[35] All that remains today is the occasional community college course or two for those few inmates whose families can afford to pay for them privately.

Why were in-prison college programs cut back so dramatically? Because politicians claimed that Pell Grants to convicts reduced the availability of tuition assistance to the children of law-abiding citizens.

But only 1% of Pell Grants went to inmates—as these politicians knew very well.[36]

Ask yourself why politicians were so eager to torpedo an effective and relatively low-cost educational program that they went so far to deceive voters. *Cui bono?*

SUBSTANCE ABUSE TREATMENT

In Chapter 2 we saw that 37% of state prisoners were under the influence of alcohol when they committed their crimes, while another 33% were high on drugs. The Department of Justice reports that 76.2% of state inmates and 82.1% of federal prisoners were "alcohol- or drug-involved" prior to their incarceration.[37] Not surprisingly, 19% of state and 16% of federal inmates committed their current offense specifically in order to obtain money for narcotics.[38]

Is there no balm in Gilead, no effective response to the enormous role that drugs and alcohol play in criminal behavior? Of course, there is: substance abuse treatment.

According to the National Association of State Alcohol and Drug Abuse Directors, the recidivism rate of drug-involved state prisoners drops from 75 to 27% if they receive proper, intensive therapeutic services during their incarceration.[39] Only 7% of those convicts who completed Texas's substance abuse program returned to the penitentiary within two years.[40]

Not only does substance abuse treatment behind bars significantly reduce future offenses, but it also saves money. Connecticut, for instance, calculates that every $1 invested in prison-based drug therapy saves $6 in other corrections-related costs, or $37,000 for each participating inmate.[41] In the WSIPP meta-analysis cited earlier, Steve Aos and his colleagues found that adult in-custody substance abuse treatment produces little or no savings if only direct financial benefits to taxpayers are considered. But experts generally acknowledge that most of the cost of narcotics offenses actually arises far "downstream," in the form of higher health care expenditures. When those factors are taken into account, drug therapy saves $2,365 to $15,836 per participant.[42]

So-called diversion programs, which send addicts to community-based facilities instead of prison, are even more cost-effective, of course. According to the Campaign for Treatment Not Incarceration, it costs $22,650 to house an offender in a correctional center for one year *without* addressing his or her substance abuse issues, but only $4,000 to $9,000 to actually *treat* the person's addiction outside penitentiary walls.[43] Our subject is rehabilitation *in* prison, however, so we will focus on what is currently being done behind bars to end the scourge of narcotics.

Perhaps not so surprisingly, in-custody drug therapy is rare and getting rarer. In 1991, 41% of state inmates and 39.4% of federal prisoners who were drunk or high at the time of their offenses received substance abuse treatment during their subsequent incarceration. By 1997, however, those figures had dropped to 18 and 18.9% respectively.[44] The Substance Abuse Policy Research Program estimates that today less than 5% of correctional budgets goes to drug and alcohol programs.[45]

In Oregon, substance abuse treatment receives only half of one percent of total prison spending.[46] Thanks to statewide budget cuts in 2003, Texas virtually eliminated its in-custody addiction therapy,[47] and in Chapter 8 we will learn that Florida and Kansas have done so as well. Only the tiny faith-based facilities in those states now offer some hope to inmates—and to those citizens who will be victimized by released but untreated substance abusers.

Especially insidious is the drift from effective but expensive treatment programs to cheaper self-help groups or classes. Just like the anti-smoking ads sponsored by the tobacco industry, groups and classes *appear* to be sincere attempts to help addicts but in fact are very nearly useless. Nevertheless, these sham programs are slowly replacing genuine therapy.

In 1991, 24.5% of state prisoners and 15.7% of federal inmates received drug treatment; but by 1997 those figures had dropped to 9.7 and 9.2% respectively. During that same time period, however, so-called other drug-abuse programs were expanded from 15.5 to 20.3% for state prisoners and 10.1 to 20.0% for federal inmates. These "other" programs consist of the aforementioned "self-help or peer groups" and "drug-abuse education classes," the Department of Justice informs us.[48]

In 2000, I had the dubious honor of participating in one of the latter. The Virginia Department of Corrections requires all of its prisoners—including those who, like me, have no history of alcohol or drug problems—to take "Substance Abuse Services Orientation," a course of four one-hour classes. After (then) fourteen years of incarceration, my turn had finally come.

The classes were conducted by a so-called counselor, a staff member whose primary job consists of reviewing and updating the security levels of the one hundred or so inmates on his case load, to determine if they need to be transferred. (The job title is a leftover from the 1980s, when this position still involved counseling.) After his regular eight-hour shift, this person had to spend an additional hour in a small, hot room with a dozen sullen convicts—a chore he performed with obvious reluctance. We prisoners, of course, had no intention of opening our hearts to a "cop" whose job it was to determine our "dangerousness." So we silently accepted the photocopied handouts, mutely listened to his mumbled remarks, and quietly filed out when he ended the class early.

As far as "peer groups" like Narcotics Anonymous or Alcoholics Anonymous are concerned, I cannot offer firsthand reportage but can point out some obvious problems. To begin with, these groups are not intensive enough and reach too few inmates: the AA group at my facility meets just once a week and draws only seven to ten convicts out of 700. Perhaps more importantly, inmates are not "peers" but competitors in a Darwinian struggle for survival. We simply dare not trust each other completely, and thus the effectiveness of self-help recovery groups plummets.

In a few Midwestern and Western states, some policy makers have come to understand that classes and groups are no substitute for genuine drug treatment. Illinois, Montana, and Indiana have each constructed special prison units for narcotics offenders and are achieving impressive reductions in recidivism rates. "Just being in jail isn't going to fix this," says Montana's Republican Governor Brian Schweitzer. "Jail doesn't get the demons out."[49]

While it is heartening to hear such words of wisdom, we should consider that the size of these narcotics units ranges from forty to two hundred participants. That leaves *tens of thousands* of incarcerated addicts in those three states without treatment. As I suggested earlier in reference to cutbacks in educational programs, you should ask yourself, *cui bono?*

Mental Health / Sex Offender Treatment

Just as there are diversion programs that send substance abusers to community-based treatment facilities instead of prison, so too have some jurisdictions begun to handle mentally ill offenders outside the formal criminal justice machinery. Housing these unfortunate men, women, and juveniles in penitentiaries not only fails to address their problems but also wastes money: while it costs the Pennsylvania Department of Corrections $80 per day to house a regular convict, a psychologically disabled inmate costs $140 per day.[50] But again, since our focus here is *in*-prison rehabilitation, let us turn to therapeutic programs for incarcerated rapists and child molesters.

The current political climate makes rational discussion of sex offenders almost impossible. If facts actually mattered, there would be great grounds for hope:

- In Chapter 3 we saw that substantiated cases of sexual abuse fell by 39% between 1993 and 2003. The number of sex crimes against children that end in murder is less than fifty per year nationwide.
- In Chapter 4 we learned that only 17.6% of sex offenders commit new crimes even if they receive no treatment while incarcerated. When they do receive therapy, the recidivism rate drops to just 7.2%

- According to the Center for Sex Offender Management, one-fifth of all rapes and one-half of all cases of child molestation each year are committed by adolescents (ages thirteen to seventeen). Up to 80% of these underage perpetrators have a diagnosable psychiatric disorder, and 40 to 80% have a history of being sexually abused themselves.[51] Lock 'em up and throw away the key?

- Professor John Q. LaFond of the University of Missouri-Kansas City cites research that online sex offender registries and notification laws neither reduce the number of sex crimes nor make them easier to solve.[52] On the other hand, Internet listings of offenders' addresses have led to the vigilante-style murders of four molesters in Washington and Maine.[53]

- GPS bracelets are obviously a good idea for certain high-risk categories of sex offenders. Given the fact that more than three-quarters of rapists and molesters never recidivate, however, mandating GPS devices for *all* of them is a waste of taxpayers' money.

- Dr. Fred Berlin of Johns Hopkins University told Ted Koppel on ABC's *Nightline*, "[It] is a failure of the criminal justice system [to] think they can punish [sexual deviancy] away.... As a physician and as a citizen, I feel a moral and professional obligation to provide treatment to people who..., absent that treatment, might pose a risk to the community."[54]

At the facility in which I am incarcerated, there is a one-of-a-kind, federally funded sex offender residential treatment (SORT) unit, where roughly one hundred of these men are housed together and receive intensive therapy. Over the years, some of them have become acquaintances of mine, even friends. While that may strike you as strange, it has allowed me to gain some insights into these "monsters."

One particular child molester whom I made a point of befriending was a middle-aged, middle-class man who was clearly lost in and frightened by "the big house." What I learned during the hours we spent together on the rec yard is that fear had been the dominant emotion of his life; absolutely everything, including adult sexual relationships, scared him profoundly. So instead of anger or disgust,

I found myself experiencing a vague sort of pity for him: "Boy, this guy needs *help*!"

He was one of the very few sex offenders who actually received real help during his incarceration, unlike the overwhelming majority of rapists and molesters. The next time some politician attempts to appeal to your worst instincts, you may wish to recall this man and where he is today: in *your* community, not in *my* prison. So the primary beneficiary of the therapeutic help he received is...*you* and your family.

Reentry Programs

Assisting ex-convicts in their reentry into society is all the rage among lawmakers. As we saw in Chapter 2, prisoners face many hurdles when they return to society:

- Former drug offenders are often barred from public housing and food stamps,[55] and 15 to 27% of all released inmates end up in homeless shelters.[56]
- Most ex-convicts no longer have driver's licenses, Social Security cards, or birth certificates—essential prerequisites for finding a job, renting an apartment or applying for public assistance.[57]
- Roughly 85% of addicts return to drug use within one year of gaining their freedom; 95% do so within three years of release.[58]
- Those prisoners who have children find that they owe an average of $20,000 in child support debt upon discharge.[59]
- Others face old court fines that accumulated interest charges during their incarceration. As one former convict said when he found a $10,000 debt of this type awaiting him, "Now I see why there's recidivism. I'm willing to do almost anything, especially working with my hands. But I can't deal with this fine."[60]
- In Chapter 2 we saw that many states bar released inmates from any profession requiring a state license. Texas, for instance, excludes ex-prisoners from over one hundred job categories, including plumbing, electrical systems, and heating/air conditioning repair.[61] Ironically, those are the very skills that some

highly motivated convicts acquired in their prisons' maintenance departments.

- Thus 60% of former inmates remain unemployed one year after discharge. Those who do find work earn half as much as comparable employees without criminal records.[62]

- According to the Urban Institute, many ex-prisoners return to a very small number of inner-city neighborhoods that are neither economically nor socially able to absorb them. In Ohio, for instance, 20% of all of the state's released convicts return to just 3% of the so-called block groups, or neighborhoods, in Cleveland's Cuyahoga County.[63] Urban areas with high "coercive mobility"—a constant flux of removing and returning residents due to incarceration—become so destabilized that crime rates actually rise, even though law enforcement *appears* to be cracking down on crime.[64]

- In Oregon, sex offenders have such a hard time finding a place to live that Polk County District Attorney John Fisher sought permission to house fifteen of them in his own home. "Some means need to be found to transition these people back to society," he says. "Rightly or wrongly, they are seen as inhuman monsters, but mostly they're pathetic human beings."[65]

Some federal and state officials, as well as many secular and religious charities, have begun to address these problems with a variety of small reentry programs. But, while it is encouraging to know that such initiatives exist, it is important to note that they benefit only a tiny minority of the 672,000 inmates discharged from correctional centers each year. Thus the examples below actually demonstrate the enormous opportunities missed, the hundreds of thousands of lives wasted by not fully funding reentry programs.

Passage of the Second Chance Act will not substantially improve matters, unfortunately: the bill's appropriations request is only $100 million per year, which amounts to just 41 cents a day for each of those 672,000 ex-convicts. By contrast, this country spends an average of $62.04 per inmate per day to incarcerate America's 2.3 million prisoners.[66]

Why are jails and penitentiaries well supplied with tax dollars while reentry is done on the cheap, if at all? One last time, ask yourself: *cui bono?*

If this nation wanted to, it could have really effective reentry for free: simply release convicts twelve months early and use the entire $22,650 cost of incarceration for that final year as each ex-inmate's individual reentry budget! The savings to taxpayers would come in the form of dramatically reduced rates of re-offending. As the following examples show, we already know what to do; all we lack is the will (and the funding) to do it.

- In Virginia, the state's Department of Corrections and the federal Department of Justice are jointly operating the Virginia Serious and Violent Offender Reentry Initiative (VASAVOR). Six months before their scheduled release dates, prisoners are transferred from state facilities to special cellblocks in one of three major city jails. There they get ID documents; anger management, substance abuse, and job interview counseling; mental health assessment and services transition; and help with locating an apartment. In the program's second phase, after release into the community, participating ex-convicts are intensively supervised by a Transition Team comprised of probation and parole officers, social workers, and faith-based volunteers.[67] Norfolk Sheriff's Major Mike O'Toole points out, "Until this program, they just dropped [released inmates] off and told [them] to contact probation and parole."[68]

- A similar state-sponsored pilot program in Shawnee County, Kansas, has managed to lower the recidivism rate of participating high-risk prisoners from the expected 80% to just 13.7%.[69] Significantly, this initiative focuses on building a one-on-one relationship between each convict and a specially trained correctional staff member—the human touch.

- In the Montgomery County, Maryland, jail, Warden Robert Green has set up a one-stop career center that teaches inmates basic computer skills and allows them access to job-related Internet sites. Craig Dowd, the program's manager, tells of one former prisoner "who came back to me and said, 'I have a townhouse. I got my family back together. And I owe it all to having been in jail.' "[70]

- Many of the smaller faith-based reentry organizations, such as the Rochester Network for Reentry and Exodus Transitional Communities, Inc. (ETC), were founded by and/or employ former convicts.[71] Because they have walked in their clients' shoes, these groups' staff members can provide uniquely useful assistance to newly released inmates. ETC notes, for instance, that "the most difficult element of successful reintegration is not finding, but rather maintaining employment."[72]

- One small secular charity, Project Return, Inc., of Middle Tennessee, achieves a re-incarceration rate of just 13%, compared to the statewide average of 43%. That saves the taxpayers $4.7 million per year in correctional costs alone, for a program serving only 800-odd returnees—roughly 0.12% of the annual total number of discharged prisoners.[73]

What all of these programs and organizations have in common is a strong emphasis on the role of volunteer mentors. In his Congressional testimony on behalf of the Second Chance Act, Justice Fellowship President Pat Nolan emphasized that ex-convicts "need relationships with caring, moral adults." The key is to mentor inmates "both while they are still incarcerated and after they return to their community." By befriending prisoners before their discharge, "mentors show a commitment to the inmates that many have never experienced before in their lives."[74]

Of course, some ex-convicts will re-offend despite their mentors' best efforts, as Les Kimlee explains.

> I took this as some sort of personal failure, by not keeping him on the "straight and narrow."... I didn't want to set myself up for another fall.... [But s]ubsequently I agreed[, and] I really have come away with much more than I give in this relationship. I've learned that mentoring doesn't mean I need to be all wise and powerful. After all, that's God's job.

> I believe a good synonym for "mentor" is friend.... Typically we get together for coffee about once a week and simply share what's going on in our lives.... Tim [the ex-convict] has helped me with several household projects and taught me a few things along the way. By sharing our lives, we build each other up.[75]

As inspiring as Les Kimlee and Tim's experience is, we must note that neither mentoring nor even sophisticated reentry programs like VASAVOR can succeed by themselves. One of the major deficiencies of all the initiatives reviewed above is that they do not engage prisoners until the last few months of their sentences. If inmates have spent the last ten or twenty years *not* dealing with their emotional problems, addictions, and educational deficiencies—because "old-fashioned" in-custody rehabilitation programs have been eliminated—is it realistic to think they can turn their lives around in the last six months before release? "Saying we don't have to address these issues on the inside but [can] address them when [convicts] come out is ridiculous," says Glenn Martin of the National HIRE Network.[76]

And some so-called reentry programs are mere charades that set participants up for failure. New York's Project Greenlight, for instance, lacked a community aftercare component, which experts consider essential; inmate attendance in some classes was as low as 15%; and funding cuts led to the program being terminated two years early. As a result, those offenders who took part in Project Greenlight actually recidivated at a *higher* rate than a statistically matched control group of non-participants.[77]

For those interested in exploring reentry issues further, the Urban Institute offers a small library of excellent studies.[78] The Institute also collaborated with the Council of State Governments to produce the *Report of the Re-entry Policy Council*, whose thirty-five "policy statements" are in fact detailed, step-by-step blueprints for setting up a variety of local and statewide reentry initiatives.[79] Since reintegrating ex-prisoners really is the key to overcoming America's addiction to jails and penitentiaries, this report is perhaps the single most important resource for reformers of all stripes.

Nobody can say they were not told how to fix the problem.

THE FUTURE

For those who take up the challenge of reforming and reintegrating prisoners, here are some possible guiding principles:

Conversion of the Community—All rehabilitation and reentry efforts must fail unless society learns to welcome released convicts, says Richmond, Virginia, Sheriff C. T. Woody:

> Fixing the problem [of recidivism] requires more than a change in inmates' attitudes. It requires a change in our community's attitude—one that allows ex-inmates to find jobs and re-connect with their families so they can become productive citizens.... [A] first step is for our local businesses and other community organizations to reconsider their policies on hiring ex-offenders and give them a real chance at succeeding once they are released.[80]

In his Congressional testimony, Pat Nolan stressed this point in terms that should resonate strongly with people of faith:

> Dr. Martin Luther King Jr. said, "To change someone, you must first love them, and they must know you love them." While many people would never associate the word "love" with prisoners, love is precisely what has been lacking in the lives of these men and women.... A loving mentor lets the inmates know that the community is invested in their success.[81]

Incentivizing Prisoners—Under current conditions, convicts have little reason to participate in educational or therapeutic programs. Nothing they do can shorten their sentences, so they give in to despair. Even the American Bar Association recognizes this as a major impediment to rehabilitating criminals; in its *Justice Kennedy Commission Report*, it recommended that "participation in [rehabilitative] programs... be encouraged by giving credit toward release."[82]

Former Republican Governor of California George Deukmejian reached much the same conclusion in 2004, when he chaired a prison reform commission at the request of Governor Arnold Schwarzenegger. If inmates meet specific educational and drug treatment goals, the commission said, then they should be granted supplemental sentence reduction credits. Convicts newly entering the correctional system should be given a flexible sentence and a detailed, individualized rehabilitative plan, with early release being contingent upon completion of that plan.[83] Unfortunately, the "action governor" chose not to take action on this proposal.

Incentivizing Correctional Staff—According to the *Justice Kennedy Commission Report*, "Correctional officials need to have a stake in the success of prisoners returning to the community, not a vested interest in their returning to prison."[84] The ABA recommends: "Performance measures for probation officers should be based upon the number of probationers or parolees who successfully complete their community supervision rather than by the number of revocations or disciplinary measures."[85] But, while that sounds good in theory, it cannot be made to work in practice: probation officers know very well that the more ex-inmates stay out of trouble, the sooner they themselves will be out of a job!

Justice Reinvestment—Justice reinvestment is reentry on steroids: instead of spending money on prisons, state funds are redirected to those communities that "produce" the most inmates, thus giving local leaders the freedom to respond to crime as they see fit. This may mean "investing" the money in a prison sentence, if a particular offender warrants that. But in many cases it can mean community service for the criminal, which costs less than incarceration and thus frees up funds for crime prevention.

For example, in Deschutes County, Oregon, Dennis Mahoney of the Department of Corrections developed a pilot program for juveniles who otherwise would have been sent to prison, instead putting them to work landscaping parks, constructing bunk beds for needy families, and building Habitat for Humanity homes. The community benefited by the tasks accomplished, a 72% reduction in the locality's youth incarceration rate, and a savings of $17,000 per case.

"We can point to their work and say, 'Look what they can do...if given the opportunity,'" says Mahoney. "Service is honorable. The public recognizes the contribution and supports them."

So successful was this program that Deschutes County officials expanded it to adult offenders, who built a child advocacy center and a homeless shelter in record time. No doubt you can guess how this story ends: with state funding for this program being eliminated in July 2003.[86]

Connecticut state Representatives Michael P. Lawlor and William Dyson have not had the financial rug pulled out from under their feet yet. In 2004, their legislation transferred $13.4 million from the Department of Corrections budget to local crime prevention efforts.[87] New mental health clinics and drug treatment centers essentially paid for themselves, by lowering crime and thus reducing the need for prisons.[88]

Criminal Justice Corps (CJC)—If you dare to dream big, picture the expansion of Dennis Mahoney's Deschutes County, Oregon, program nationwide through a Criminal Justice Corps. His inspiration for this concept is the Civilian Conservation Corps (CCC), generally regarded as one of the most successful government initiatives of all time. During the 1940s, the CCC's 900,000 members built billions of dollars worth of bridges, national parks, hatcheries, and municipal auditoriums.

Now imagine what two million convicts could do! "If prison w[ere] a service learning experience, and parole and probation were service action ventures," Mahoney says, then a Criminal Justice Corps "could contribute more to contemporary society than the CCC did sixty years ago."[89]

Too much to hope for?

*   *   *

Our next interview subject, Kent I., has not allowed himself to be deterred by the lack of effective educational and therapeutic programs in today's warehouse-style prisons. Thanks to the financial support of his family, he was able to earn advanced college degrees by correspondence; and in his spare time he conducts a painting class for his fellow inmates. But his class is hampered by a lack of funds and, truth be told, a lack of support and encouragement from the community. With an outside volunteer and just a little money, Kent I. and other inmate leaders could accomplish so much more....

Interview with "Kent I."

*Kent I. was sentenced to life in prison and two years
for murder and the use of a firearm in 1990.*

Q: Tell us a little about your life before you were arrested for your current offense.

A: I was born in 1966. My father was a fireman and my mother a homemaker. Our family was pretty religious, but from the age of twelve onward I started getting rebellious and began messing around with girls, alcohol, and drugs. After I turned thirteen, I started working with my uncle as an electrician and went through the apprenticeship program to become a certified electrician. I went into business with my brother-in-law in 1989. Throughout this time, I continued to use alcohol and drugs—the whole range, from pot to cocaine—but I was never arrested for that. It did affect my job performance, though.

Q: Tell us about your crime.

A: In 1990, I got into a fight with my brother-in-law in my condominium, and I ended up shooting and killing him. There were guns all over my house because I was a collector. At the time of the crime, he was high on drugs, but I wasn't. I didn't call the police after I shot him because I panicked; my only thought was to get out of the condo. I headed straight for a cocaine party at another house, got blasted, and went on the run for about a month and a half.

Q: Where did you go?

A: I didn't go anywhere! I stayed right in the same area, going from one drug party to the next, staying high the whole time. Then someone saw me on *America's Most Wanted* and turned me in for $2,000. The police came to arrest me at his house with a SWAT team, because I was known to have a lot of guns. But I didn't have any weapon with me when I was arrested.

Q: What happened after you were brought to the police station?

A: I gave a statement to the detectives. I explained to them that this wasn't the first time my brother-in-law and I had fought, but it was the first time we had fought over a gun. The detectives believed me, they were nice to me. About three weeks later, after the arraignment, I made bond and went home.

Q: But then you were put back into jail, right?

A: Yes. At the arraignment, it had come out that there was an insurance policy on my brother-in-law that named another family member as the beneficiary. So after the arraignment, the prosecutor upped my charges to capital murder, murder-for-hire. He was going to go for the death penalty, so the court had to revoke my bond and put me in jail.

Q: But at your trial, you didn't get the death penalty, or we wouldn't be talking now.

A: That's right. At the trial, the charges were reduced back down to first degree murder, because there was no conspiracy between me and the family member named in the insurance policy. The prosecutor was even going to offer me a plea bargain. But I refused the deal, because I felt I had shot my brother-in-law in a fight, more or less in self-defense.

Q: But the jury convicted you anyway.

A: Yes. After I refused the plea bargain, the trial went forward, and the jury convicted me of first degree murder, under the theory that my sister had hired me to kill my brother-in-law. But *she* was never charged! I guess I must have been in a conspiracy with myself.

Q: How do you feel about the trial and the verdict now?

A: I believe I definitely should have gone to prison, because I took a man's life. But I still don't think I should have been convicted of first degree murder.

Q: Did you feel any remorse at the time of the trial?

A: Oh, before then. I got high immediately after I killed my brother-in-law because I couldn't stand what I had done. Then, after I made bond, I did more drugs than I had ever done in my life because of the guilt. That's how I coped with all my problems back then: with drugs.

Q: After your bond was revoked and you were sitting in jail, waiting for your trial *without* drugs to help you cope, did you think about what you had done?

A: A lot! There's nothing else to do in jail. I kept thinking about "what if...," wishing I'd done things differently. I wanted to explain to the family of the victim, to apologize to them. But because of the loss they wouldn't have been able to listen to me—I'd killed their flesh and blood. I understand those feelings. And there's no room in the legal process later on to talk to the victim's family either.

Q: How do you imagine there could be an opportunity for someone convicted of a very serious crime, like murder, to talk to a victim or the victim's family?

A: Maybe after you've been convicted. I think it would help the victim—or in my case the victim's family—understand what had happened. But it would have to take place in a mild setting.

Q: What do you mean by a "mild" setting?

A: It's like looking at a dog in a dog pound. He looks vicious and barks a lot, and you fear him because you don't know what's inside that dog. But then, if you open the gate to the dog pound, you're able to experience the personality of the dog, and he might not be threatening at all.

Q: But some dogs *are* dangerous!

A: Sure. But you can never know unless you open the gate and meet him. Even if the dog is vicious, at least then you know that he is dangerous, and you can put that issue to rest. You'll never know until you give him a chance, though.

Q: I suppose some dogs might also change over time.

A: That's right. It's funny: so many people believe that a man cannot change from being a bad person to being a good person while he's in prison. But it's a fact that people can and do change from being good to being bad! Most people in prison now were good at one point and then turned bad. So why not the reverse?

Q: Do you regret not having had an opportunity to meet the family members of your victim—in a "mild" setting, a setting that's not like a dog pound? What would you say to them if you could talk to them now?

A: Yes, I regret that a lot. If I could meet the victim's family now, I would ask them for forgiveness. Nothing I can say can ever change what happened. But I would like to tell them the sorrow of my heart. If I could tell them that, they would know that there is compassion in my heart.

Q: Why didn't you tell the family members of the victim about your remorse at your trial?

A: Because I never got to tell my side of the story on the stand. All the court heard was the statement I had given the detectives after my arrest. So the victim's family didn't get a chance to look me in the eyes, and I wish they had. I know that most things can be faked, but I think it's really hard to fake or mask the eyes. They could have seen how sorry I felt.

Q: Have your feelings changed in the years since the trial?

A: Sure, because I turned my life over to the Lord. I know he has forgiven me, even if the victim's family hasn't.

Q: So that has comforted you?

A: Yes, but you have to look at the context. The hardest thing about being a Christian is not that you know Jesus has forgiven you; it's forgiving yourself. That's incredibly hard, because guilt is so strong within us. And in some ways, being a Christian has made forgiving myself even harder.

Q: Why is that?

A: Well, I know I shouldn't have taken my brother-in-law's life. But what really bothers me now, as a Christian, is that *he* has no more opportunity to be saved. I took that opportunity away from him. At the time he died, my brother-in-law was a man with a lot of problems, like drugs and alcohol—a lot of the same problems I had. He did not have a relationship with Jesus, so chances are that he died unsaved. That really, really bothers me a lot. It's devastating. And I was close to him! That's where my remorse is centered now—the life he's missed out on with his family, of course, but especially his soul and where he's spending eternity.

Q: When did you turn your life over to Christ?

A: It began in jail, after my bond was revoked, but really only in 1992 or so. I played a lot of games with the Lord at first. But in 1992, I was sitting in isolation—that's the punitive segregation unit—and I was contemplating my life in prison. Somehow, I started talking to Jesus, and I asked God to show me his way, since my way wasn't working out too well. My parents and other church members gave me a lot of encouragement. I started reading the Bible, and I started drawing and writing poems.

Q: What were your drawings of?

A: A lot of them were Christian in nature, or they showed the beauty of God's creation—all the things you lose in prison. Smelling the fresh air, hearing the birds, the sunrises and sunsets.

Q: How did you learn that Jesus had forgiven you?

A: From the Bible and other religious books, such as those by Chaplain Ray. [Interviewer's Note: Chaplain Ray is the author of numerous Christian tracts and books about his ministry to well-known criminals, such as the *Catch Me Killer* and *Murf the Surf*. These books are widely distributed by prison chaplains.] I learned from the Bible and these books that God had turned other people's lives around—people like me, drug users and criminals.

Q: So how did that make you feel?

A: Experiencing Christ's forgiveness wasn't like a bolt of lightning or anything like that. It took time and effort to come to the realization of God's love and mercy—that even someone like me could truly be forgiven.

Q: What does Jesus' forgiveness mean to you?

A: It means that I am no longer guilty of anything. I have been pardoned. I have been justified by his blood, the work of the cross. But that's no different from what Christ has done for every other sinner. My sins are bigger, but it's the same forgiveness.

Q: How does the feeling of being forgiven by Jesus relate to your feelings about the victim's family?

A: Oh, I still long for forgiveness from them. That hasn't changed at all. Remorse will always be there. If I could give my own life to bring their loved one back, I would. I'm not afraid of death anymore, ever since I turned my life over to the Lord.

Q: How did your new life in Christ affect your behavior behind bars after 1992?

A: Well, I started trying to do right. I took the courses and programs I was asked to take, and I took another apprenticeship program with the facility's maintenance department. Also, I took two computer courses offered by the prison, and I did Bible correspondence studies on my own. Later, in 1998, I took mainstream college courses from the local community college. [Interviewer's Note: Kent's parents had to pay for these courses, because Kent's life sentence and age disqualify him from free education.] The community college granted me an associate's degree in liberal arts in 2002. Then I took correspondence courses with a Christian seminary in Missouri and earned my bachelor's degree in Christian counseling in 2003. In 2004, I got my master's, and in 2005 my doctorate.

Q: Why did you choose Christian counseling as your major?

A: Because I want to help people. There are so many people here with backgrounds similar to mine—drug users, you know. I can relate to them, and they can relate to me.

Q: Have you been able to help other inmates here, in this prison?

A: Sure. I worked as a teacher's aide for many years, which allowed me to help others and also furthered my own education. God has given me his favor throughout these years. It's nothing I've done, it's all God's doing.

Q: But you no longer work as a teacher's aide now, right?

A: Right. I work for the maintenance department as an electrician. I still teach painting in my spare time, though.

Q: We want to hear about that. First, however, tell us about your job, because that involves an important part of prison life that civilians may not be familiar with.

A: Well, I do regular electrical work on the prison grounds. But I also maintain and repair the master antenna TV (MATV) system, which provides the compound with a basic cable package.

Q: What would you say to those civilians who are outraged when they think of prisoners lying around all day, watching TV, having a great time?

A: I would say that TV is an essential element of institutional security. Just like parents in the outside world, correctional staff use TV as an electronic babysitter. There are nowhere near enough jobs or programs, so inmates would be fighting or rioting out of sheer boredom if they didn't have TV.

Q: And the choice of channels offered on prison TV reflects the fact that it is a pacification device, right?

A: Yes. I really care about education, as you know, so I believe the institution's cable system should offer things like the Learning Channel, National Geographic, and the History Channel. I would also like to see religious stations like TBN, INSP, and the Angel Network. A lot of inmates could really benefit from these kinds of programs, because we're all spiritual beings. We are body, mind, and soul.

Q: So what does the prison TV system offer instead of those channels?

A: Basically, the networks plus ESPN, BET, and VH1. There is only one educational station: Discovery Channel. But on the dayroom TV, "majority rules," so they stay tuned to sports and music videos. All the guys are hollering at the screen or singing—it's mayhem! The guards love it, though, because it keeps the inmates occupied. But watching that junk for hours a day, year after year, does not exactly improve their minds. It feeds their carnal nature.

Q: Tell us about the art classes you're teaching now.

A: I organized those with the help of two other prisoners here. I and one other man did all the paperwork the administration required, got the supplies together, and had the easels made—all that stuff. For the actual teaching, all three of us work together as a team. The classes started in the fall of 2004, with one group of twelve inmates meeting three times a week.

Q: And how did that work out?

A: After other inmates saw the progress those twelve were making, we had a huge rush of requests from others to get involved. I even had a guard who wanted to participate; she wanted to stay late after work to do this. Anyway, the program was so popular that we ended up having three separate classes of twelve men each. If we had more room, more time, more teachers, we could sign up even more. There's an incredible demand for this!

Q: Why do you think painting is so popular with prisoners?

A: They look on it as a hobby, but really it's therapy. It gives them a feeling of accomplishment and builds their self-esteem. It gives them hope and puts them in touch with their creative side—and that comes from the Creator.

Q: Explain more about the therapeutic aspect of art classes.

A: At this particular prison, we have a mental health unit, for inmates with psychological problems. One of the men from that unit participated in the first class, and a staff member told me that his attitude changed dramatically. Someone finally took an interest in him and let him express himself! He felt empowered. This in turn helped him to focus better on the psychological counseling he was receiving in the mental health unit, and they were able to reduce his medication.

Q: All right, that is a striking example, but it's only one man. Is anyone else benefiting from the classes?

A: Sure, especially the older prisoners. Everything in prison is geared toward younger men: in sports, it's all basketball, and in education, it's mostly remedial reading and high school equivalency classes. So older men are crowded out. They're isolated, don't fit in. But the art classes give them hope, a sense of well-being, something to be proud of. Plus they can send their paintings out to their families, and that strengthens their ties with their community.

Q: What sorts of things do the prisoners paint?

A: Simple things, like sunsets. Things that accentuate the beauty of God's creation. As you become an artist, you develop an appreciation of God's creation—the skies, the birds, the colors—everything becomes more intense.

Q: Do you use the art classes to talk about your religious faith?

A: When I teach these guys, I always throw in that God is allowing me to do this, but I don't browbeat them with the Bible. I let them know that God has given me this ability, and I want him to get the glory for it. That will register in their subconscious, I believe. The Bible says, "My word will not return void; it will go out and accomplish what I please." I really believe that.

Q: What do you think that art does in these men's lives?

A: There's a lot of depression in prison, and painting takes inmates out of this place for a while. Also, most people in here cannot express what they're feeling with words; but with painting, they don't need words.

Q: And then there is the self-esteem, as you mentioned.

A: That's right. The world says that we're worthless and useless—lock 'em up and throw away the key! But, according to God, we all have worth. In fact, he loved us so much that he sent his son to die for us. Painting puts us in touch with the worth that we have in God's eyes, because we can see the gift he gave us. All you have to do is to accept it.

Q: Do you think the work you are doing with prisoners in your art classes somehow makes up for the harm you caused in your crime?

A: No. I am not earning my forgiveness by teaching painting. This is a *fruit* of the forgiveness. I am giving back some of what God has given me. He said to the disciples, "Freely have you received, freely shall you give."

Q: So you're saying the forgiveness came first?

A: That's right. God offered David forgiveness before he even asked, and he did the same with the Sinful Woman. He saw their hearts, who they were inside. He forgave them, and as a result of that, David and the Sinful Woman felt endless gratitude.

Q: What hopes do you have for your own future?

A: I'm going to keep doing the will of the Father. What I've been given is the same message and confirmation that Christ heard at his baptism and at the transfiguration: "You are my beloved son, in you I am well pleased." That means me, too, because of the obedience to his word. Jesus said, "If you love me, obey me." That's what I'm trying to do.

Q: Do you hope to get out one day?

A: Sure. I was sentenced under the expectation of being released one day, since I was not given life without parole. The judge said that, even though he was sentencing me to a lot of time, there was light at the end of the tunnel. The light at the end of the tunnel is Christ.

Q: What would you do if you were released?

A: I would like to work as a Christian counselor and evangelist, because I have a testimony to give. It's my responsibility to bring people to Christ. But it's a love-responsibility, as opposed to an obligation. I *want* to do this.

Q: Would you come back into prison to continue teaching your art classes?

A: Oh, yes. Both through my art classes and in other ways, my witness can encourage these men in here.

Q: What would you say to people who might say that art classes for prisoners amounts to coddling them?

A: I would tell them that people in here can and do change. And they need the opportunity to *show* the change! One of the problems with the system is that educational programs—academic, vocational, even artistic—are minimal or nonexistent. So there's no opportunity to better oneself. Almost everyone in here is going to get out one day, so you need to take that person while he's still inside and educate him, give him an opportunity to become a better person.

Q: And when that prisoner gets out—what then?

A: Then he needs to do more than just be functional, hold down a steady job. Every prisoner needs to give back something to the community that he's hurt by breaking the law. That's what I want to do, if I ever get out. I want to give back some of what I've been given.

QUESTIONS FOR REFLECTION AND DISCUSSION

SCRIPTURE—In the "genealogy of Jesus Christ" that begins Matthew's Gospel, the evangelist refers to "the wife of Uriah" without even mentioning Bathsheba's name (1:16). If the purpose of the genealogy is to establish Christ's bona fides as "the son of David," why include such an explicit reference to David's murder-by-proxy of Uriah? Why not just call her Bathsheba? What is the Bible trying to tell us about Jesus and about us?

CRIMINOLOGY—Consider more closely what you have been told about sex offenders in the media and what the reality actually is. Then consider some of the currently popular "solutions" to the "problem" of released sex offenders. Are they potentially counterproductive, even increasing the risk of re-offending?

One example: eighteen states now have "exclusion zones," laws that ban sex offenders from living within 1,000 to 2,500 feet of schools, playgrounds, etc. Iowa has been pursuing this policy with particular rigor: 90% of the land area in its major cities is now off-limits to released rapists and molesters. As a result, the number of sex offenders who have given up the attempt to live law-abiding lives and have gone underground has doubled.

The Iowa County Attorneys Association has listed fourteen problems with the state's exclusion zone law and has urged the legislature to repeal the statute. Research has shown that exclusion zones do not reduce the number of sex offenses against children, in large part because the great majority of such crimes occur within the family. By creating a false sense of security, experts believe, exclusion zones may actually facilitate the commission of sex offenses.

According to *Governing Magazine*, "these well-intentioned residency rules may ultimately do more harm than good."[90] What do you think should be done instead?

Self-exam—The San Francisco County Jail uses acupuncture and yoga to reduce re-offending. Are there programs or techniques to which you would object? Which ones, and why? Or is any program legitimate so long as it reduces crime?

Interview—Kent mentioned that a female guard wanted to stay late after work to join his art class. What he did not mention is that she would not have been allowed to do so because the Department of Corrections recently issued a rule forbidding this kind of "fraternization" between staff and inmates. Thanks to this new policy, inmate leaders like Kent find it much more difficult to organize programs for other prisoners; someone has to supervise such activities, after all. Thus we see here yet another example of one of the structural problems of incarceration: prisons are supposed to reduce crime, but the real or imagined exigencies of "institutional security" constantly undermine programs that might actually reform criminals. Is there any way to resolve this inherent conflict? Or would it be more honest to admit that cages can never be good learning environments?

INTERNET—Obtain the Report of the Re-entry Policy Council at www.reentrypolicy.org and get to work.

IMMERSION—Visit a halfway house or reentry initiative operating in your town. If there is none, visit a homeless shelter; many former prisoners (especially sex offenders) end up there.

Chapter 6

DANIEL AND CORRECTIONAL MAMMON

JESUS LIKED DANIEL a lot. How do we know? Because it was the Book of Daniel that Christ turned to on the worst night of his life, the night he was arrested and cross-examined by the Sanhedrin. At times like that, all of us seek counsel and comfort from what we know best.

When the high priest asked him over and over again, "Are you the Messiah, the son of the Blessed One," Jesus finally answered, "I am; and you will see the Son of Man seated at the right hand of the Power and coming with the clouds of heaven" (Mark 14:61, 62). That was a paraphrase of Daniel 7:13—the first passage of Scripture that came to Christ's mind as he tried to explain who he really was. Perhaps he had memorized it as a youth, since Daniel's persecution foreshadowed his own fate and the prophet's visions told of his coming reign.

As the high priest peppered him with questions on the night of his arrest, Jesus surely recognized his interrogator as a spiritual cousin of King Nebuchadnezzar, another corrupt and merciless leader who valued only the external forms of piety and used religion to maintain social order. Nebuchadnezzar, you will recall, had ordered all citizens of the Babylonian empire to worship a golden statue. When three of Daniel's friends—Mesach, Shadrach, and Abednego—refused to join this idolatry, the king had them "cast into a white-hot furnace" (Daniel 3:20). Men like Nebuchadnezzar and the high priest who interrogated Jesus consider true believers like Mesach, Shadrach, and Abednego—and, of course, Christ—as a challenge to their own power. Thus, Daniel's three friends *had* to be burned alive, just as surely as a troublemaking country preacher named Jesus *had* to be crucified (Daniel 3:8–12; cf. John 11:47, 48).

We should in all fairness acknowledge that, by the standards of their societies, each of these men was a "criminal" (the priests' term for Christ, see John 18:30). Mesach, Shadrach, and Abednego broke a properly promulgated law or "decree" whose objective was not at all unreasonable: unifying the ethnically diverse Babylonian empire through a common religion (Daniel 3:7, 10). We fool ourselves—and, more importantly, misunderstand the Gospel—if we think that our society would treat Daniel's three friends or Jesus any better than the Babylonian and Roman empires did.

In standard scriptural exegesis, the turning point of Daniel 3 is considered to be Mesach, Shadrach, and Abednego's decision to resist the "exigencies of empire": to go to the flames rather than commit idolatry. This is what makes them "immortal figures"; according to Professor W. Sibley Towner of Yale Divinity School, "they are not so sure God can save them from such a hopeless situation, but they know what he demands in any case."[1] If we focus solely on the spiritual heroism of Daniel's three friends, however, we risk overlooking some very interesting lessons on *why* empires always end up sending innocents to the gallows.

Just now we noted that Mesach, Shadrach, and Abednego were handed over for execution because they violated a royal edict commanding all Babylonians to worship a golden statue of King Nebuchadnezzar. We also noted that, superficially at least, this royal edict had a legitimate purpose: to unite a heterogeneous, multicultural empire around a single focus for public worship. But why were Daniel's three friends singled out for the very first prosecution under this new law?

Those not familiar with the ways of empire might suspect that great reasons of state were the king's motive: to ensure that every citizen obeyed the new decree, perhaps, Nebuchadnezzar decided to publicly sacrifice a few close aides. That guess would be mistaken, however. In reality, the rulers of empires are mere human beings who are frequently motivated by their own petty desires, not weighty political considerations. Thus it was in Daniel's day, and so it is in ours.

In ancient Babylon, it was the Chaldeans' hunger for power and money that nearly cost Mesach, Shadrach, and Abednego their lives.

Because only Daniel, but not the Chaldeans, had been able to interpret King Nebuchadnezzar's dream, the Jewish deportees were in the ascendancy at the royal court: they received "many generous presents" and were made "administrators of the province of Babylon" (Daniel 2:1–30, 48, 49). The Chaldeans quite understandably looked for an opportunity to recoup their influence and wealth, so as soon as the royal decree was passed they "accused the Jews to King Nebuchadnezzar" (Daniel 3:8, 9).

In the ancient Roman province of Judea, the Sanhedrin's motive for doing away with Jesus was just as prosaic: "If we leave him alone, all will believe him, and the Romans will come and take away both our land and our nation" (John 11:48). Note that "our"; truly "the love of money is the root of all evils" (1 Timothy 6:10).

Interestingly enough, both the Chaldeans and the Sanhedrin used their respective empires' legal systems to eliminate threats to their power and maintain their access to wealth. When we turn to the richest, most powerful empire in the history of the world, modern-day America, we find a similar nexus between the criminal-justice machinery and concrete financial considerations. Close observers of the correctional system have even given this phenomenon a name: the prison-industrial complex, or PIC.

But the ruling elites of Babylon and Rome used their laws and courts only as defensive weapons, to protect their positions and their fortunes. America's ruling elites, by contrast, have managed to turn the criminal justice system into a moneymaking operation in its own right. For big business, organized labor and politicians, this country's annual correctional budget of $63 billion is not primarily an investment in public safety, but an enormous trough at which they can gorge themselves without restraint.

If that sounds extreme, recall what we learned in this book's Introduction: the crime rate today is the same as in the early 1970s. So there must be some reason *other than public safety* why seven times as many Americans languish behind bars. Or, to be precise, 63 billion reasons.

The "Rising" Crime Rate

Close observers of the national scene will raise an immediate objection to the analysis above: in late 2006, the media widely reported an upsurge in violent offenses. Therefore, the relationship between crime, incarceration, and money must be more complex than suggested here—or so one might think.

But a closer look at the FBI's Semiannual Uniform Crime Report of December 18, 2006, reveals a startling fact: the crime rate is actually *falling*. While the number of violent offenses did indeed rise by 3.7%, the number of nonviolent property crimes dropped by 2.6%.[2] And since there are roughly 7.5 nonviolent offenses committed for every violent one,[3] the decrease in the former more than offsets the increase in the latter. America will experience over 200,000 *fewer* crimes in 2006 compared with 2005, if the preliminary figures of 3.7% and 2.6% hold for the whole year.[4] According to Brian Roehrkasse of the Justice Department, the overall crime rate—combining violent and property crimes—"was the lowest crime rate measured…in more than thirty years."[5]

The bad news: of the total number of offenses committed, a greater proportion will be violent. However, even the latter statement is subject to a major qualification: nearly the entire rise in violent crime was due to a 9.7% increase in armed robberies. The number of murders, assaults, and rapes, on the other hand, remained nearly unchanged.[6]

"[B]efore this speculation gets out of hand, as it did with the juvenile superpredator frenzy in the mid-1990s, let us look more closely at what we know—at what the data actually say," recommends the American Correctional Association's journal, *Corrections Today*. "The increase in [the violent crime rate of] 2005 was so small that the 2005 rate was still 1 percent below the 2003 rate…. In all, there is little statistical support for an upcoming crime wave."[7]

So why did publications like *Time* hyperventilate about "the next crime wave" in late 2006?[8] In part to sell magazines, of course—but also because the law enforcement community had just launched a major campaign to improve its cash flow.

According to the *Washington Post*, federal grants to local and state police "have been cut by more than $2 billion since 2002." This led "many police chiefs and law enforcement officials [to] complain that the Bush administration has retreated from fighting traditional crime in favor of combating terrorism."[9] As *USA Today* explained, "The International Association of Chiefs of Police ... has been pushing for more crime-fighting funds."[10]

What the story of the "rising" crime rate of 2006 illustrates, then, is the powerful role of financial interests in determining criminal justice policies. As we turn now to our primary subject, prisons, let us continue to ask the question we raised repeatedly in our last chapter, on rehabilitation: *cui bono?* Who profits?

"CRIME MAY NOT PAY, BUT PRISONS SURE DO"

So says Bill Deener, financial writer for the *Dallas Morning News*, but even he may not realize just how true that statement is.[11] The figure of $63 billion mentioned above refers only to local, state, and federal governments' annual expenditure on corrections. It does not include the profits from prison labor and the financial exploitation of inmates' families.

What makes correctional capitalism so enormously rewarding is that none of the usual rules of free enterprise apply:

- consumers are not allowed to choose between competing vendors
- there are no negative consequences for breaches of contract
- prison profiteers are allowed to manipulate the legal and regulatory framework governing operations, thanks to the generous distribution of political donations

For taxpayers it is important to realize that the three principles above apply not only when the consumer is an inmate using an overpriced correctional telephone system, say, but also when the customer is the government being bilked by a private prison operator. *Everyone* gets ripped off.

Best of all, the incarcerated consumer base keeps on expanding regardless of actual market conditions. The fact that the crime rate continues to decline *should* lead to a contraction of the corrections industry; as demand falls, so *should* supply.[12] But instead the nation's convict population has grown by an average of 3.3% a year since 1995;[13] the state in which I am incarcerated is currently increasing its prison department's bed capacity by over 10%;[14] and Prince George's County, bordering Washington, D.C., plans to expand its jail system by 28%.[15] According to the Pew Charitable Trusts, America's penitentiary population will expand 13% by 2011, at an additional annual cost of $27.5 billion.[16]

How does the correctional system manage to defy basic laws of economics and common sense? By the same tried and tested method used by the military-industrial complex against which President Dwight D. Eisenhower issued his famous warning. Back then, big business, labor, and the political elite exploited public fear of communism to steer as much cash into their own pockets as possible. Today that same unholy alliance plays on fear of crime to enrich itself.

But there is one important difference between the military-industrial complex and the prison-industrial complex. While the former actually did some good by protecting the Western world from an aggressive Soviet Union, the latter does little if anything to lower crime, as we saw in previous chapters. In fact, the primary "product" produced by the corrections business is...recidivists, who are then used to justify even more jails and penitentiaries.

To understand the vast range and scale of moneymaking opportunities behind bars, it helps to think of America's 2.3 million inmates as this nation's third-largest city, exceeding Houston by a quarter of a million residents.[17]

- Building the physical infrastructure to house this population earns architects and construction companies $4.3 billion annually [18]
- Operating private prisons is a $2 billion-a-year industry dominated by Correctional Corporation of America (CCA) and the Geo Group [19]

- Feeding convicts is the key to Aramark Correctional Services' success: the world's third largest food services company, it provides a million meals a day to inmates in 1,500 private and government-operated facilities[20]
- Managing prison infirmaries is a business worth $2 billion per annum to Correctional Medical Services (CMS) and Prison Health Services (PHS)[21]

And at every turn correctional capitalists develop new ways to turn a buck behind bars. The anti-immigrant hysteria that swept America in the summer of 2006, for instance, will primarily benefit CCA and Geo, since they will operate detention centers for deportable aliens. According to Wall Street analysts, profit margins for these immigration prisons will exceed 20%, and demand is expected to grow by $200 to $250 million every twelve to eighteen months.[22]

Another corporate stroke of genius is a plan to issue all convicts radio-linked wristbands, so that guards can determine each inmate's precise location within the facility. To anyone with real penitentiary experience, this looks like technical wizardry that serves no useful purpose. But Technology Systems International and Wheels of Zeus, Inc., nevertheless expect to earn $1.5 billion from their gadgets in the coming years.[23]

GOLD COINS

How do corporations persuade government officials to spend taxpayer dollars on their products? Through the judicious use of campaign contributions, of course. After California's Democratic Governor Gray Davis closed four private prisons in 2003, for instance, the Geo Group gave $58,000 to Republican gubernatorial candidate Arnold Schwarzenegger; hired his recall campaign's policy director, Joe Rodata; and donated another $10,000 to an initiative committee tied to the self-proclaimed "action governor." Of course, it was pure coincidence that Geo was awarded a no-bid contract to reopen one of the the shuttered facilities after Schwarzenegger's election.[24]

When Geo had trouble filling its new Reeves County Detention Center in Texas, it hired a gentleman named Randy DeLay to lobby the federal Bureau of Prisons (BOP) to send inmates there. Randy's brother Tom just happened to be the most feared man in Washington, D.C., at that time, so the company got what it wanted: several hundred warm federal bodies. Only cynics would see any connection between the BOP's wise policy decision and the $100,000 check Geo subsequently gave to Representative DeLay's personal charity.[25]

In 2005 the Colorado state auditor released a scathing report on that state's $53 million contract to house 2,800 prisoners in six private penitentiaries, four of them owned by CCA. Not only were none of the commercial correctional centers' medical clinics licensed by the Department of Public Health and Environment, but nine inmates' deaths—including two arguably preventable ones—were not reported to state authorities. According to state Representative Liane McFadyen (D-Pueblo West), "It's clear that the for-profit prison industry has no desire to follow their contracts."[26]

The state auditor found other problems, too: CCA facilities have a high rate of staff turnover, because the corporation's guards are paid less and receive fewer benefits than guards in state correctional centers. As a result, private prisons are frequently short-staffed—so short-staffed, in fact, that Colorado levied $126,000 in fines against CCA in 2006. Critics of prison privatization have calculated, however, that paying fines costs CCA *less* than hiring a full complement of guards.[27]

But, even as the state auditor was bringing to light the hazards of correctional entrepreneurship, Colorado awarded two new contracts to CCA for massive expansions of its facilities, as well as additional contracts to Geo and Cornell Companies.[28] How can this be? Cynics point to the fact that CCA and its executives gave at least $43,000 to Colorado political parties and candidates like Governor Bill Owens.[29]

In the 2005–2006 election cycle, the Geo Group gave a total of $114,157 to Republican candidates nationwide, compared to $74,725 to Democrats. However, the largest single beneficiary of Geo's largesse was Democratic Governor Bill Richardson of New Mexico, who received

$42,750 from the company in 2005 and 2006. Geo currently operates two prisons and one hospital in New Mexico and may soon get a contract for a new correctional center there in Clayton.[30]

From political and charitable donations like these, it is only one small step to outright corruption. In 2005, John G. Rowland, former governor of Connecticut, was sentenced to one year and one day in federal prison for accepting $100,000 in bribes associated with no-bid contracts for the renovation and construction of two juvenile prisons. According to the indictment, part of the bribe was paid in gold coins.[31]

Sometimes the business world's lust for correctional dollars takes on an almost comical aspect. When the Colorado Department of Corrections attempted to lower operating costs by buying less beef and more ground turkey, Terry Fankhouser of the Colorado Cattlemen's Association complained that "this decision sorely disappoints and offends Colorado's beef producers."[32] National newspapers had great fun with ranchers who "cried fowl" and "talked turkey" to "get beef back behind bars." But Republican state Senator Ken Kester, whose district includes Colorado's largest cattle ranches, understood that this was no laughing matter to his constituents. In a press release, the senate communications director celebrated Kester's valorous and eventually successful defense of cattlemen: "I want to know, where's the beef?"[33]

The problem is that the success of narrow commercial interests like Colorado's beef producers inevitably comes at the expense of taxpayers at large. Moreover, even when there is malfeasance, private correctional corporations are not punished. Florida's Inspector General, for instance, found in 2005 that both CCA and Geo had overcharged the state $12.7 million and failed to fulfill their contractual obligations. Yet the two companies were each awarded contracts for additional private prisons only one month after publication of this critical report.[34]

In the correctional health care field, CMS and PHS typically receive $2,700 a year for each inmate in a state's prison system, and their profit depends entirely on providing medical services that are worth *less* than that.[35] Nor do these clever corporations fear lawsuits from mistreated patients, as civilian HMOs do. Thanks to the Prison Litigation Reform Act and other "reforms," inmates simply have no means to make CMS and PHS live up to their medical, ethical, and legal obligations.

Accountability—a term so beloved by "tough on crime" politicians—is nearly impossible in the corrections business because every sector in the industry is now controlled by only a couple of major players. Just as two remaining manufacturers of military aircraft have the Pentagon at their mercy, so too do CCA and Geo, or CMS and PHS, control their respective markets. Why compete, if quiet collusion is so much more profitable?

Prison labor

When we turn to prison factories and service centers, we again find large companies and government agencies setting aside the usual rules of free enterprise to benefit themselves, not the public. Law-abiding citizens lose good jobs because inmates' wages are so low; and convicts lose educational programs because those cost money, whereas work programs generate revenue. Thirty U.S. states now rent out their inmates to private firms that need cheap, compliant, legally powerless workers.[36]

In 2002 U.S. prisoners produced $1.5 billion worth of goods and services. Delco, Dell, TWA,[37] Wal-Mart,[38] Upjohn, Toys "R" Us, Chevron, IBM, Microsoft, Boeing, and Nintendo are only a few of the major corporations that have employed inmate workers.[39] Even local and state governments are using convict labor for data entry, record keeping, and call-center operations.[40]

Federal Prison Industries (FPI) produces *all* of the helmets used by the U.S. military, camouflage shirts and pants by the hundreds of thousands, various weapons components, and cable harnesses for TOW and Patriot missiles. In 2002, the company's total sales to the federal government amounted to $678.7 million, of which $400 million went to the Department of Defense.[41] And whatever FPI cannot supply, Woolrich, Inc., can: in 2005 it signed several contracts totaling

$100 million to use federal inmates to manufacture military pants and jackets.[42]

Sound like a good idea? Perhaps not to former Honda auto workers, who lost their jobs to prisoners paid one-tenth as much as they once were. Or to ex-employees of Linn County Mills in Oregon, who were replaced by a convict work crew that saves the company between $600,000 and $900,000 annually.[43] Or to inmates in California, where Governor Schwarzenegger has expanded for-profit work programs even as he cut educational funding by 20% and eliminated 300 prison teachers.[44]

Convicts do not even benefit by learning a trade they can use upon release,[45] because the most popular forms of correctional enterprise are garment manufacturing and telemarketing. Outside of prison, however, most U.S. clothing factories and call centers have been moved overseas. Thus Professor Gordon Lafer of the University of Oregon believes that using American inmates to perform this work is little more than a corporate public relations ploy to avoid the controversy over offshoring.[46]

In more enlightened times, the U.S. Congress passed a law—the Ashurst Summers Act, 18 U.S.C. §§1761-62—designed to make prison sweatshops financially unattractive. The statute prohibits the interstate transportation of inmate-manufactured goods unless the incarcerated workers are paid the prevailing wage or the minimum wage, whichever is higher. Unfortunately, the last prosecution under the Ashurst Summers Act was in 1929, and Congress repealed it altogether in 1979.[47]

EXPLOITING PRISONERS' FAMILIES

The ingenuity of correctional profit-mongers does not end there, however: in recent years they have discovered convicts' families as a major source of revenue. Because inmates typically earn only 22 to 45 cents per hour, cheating them out of their prison wages is hardly worth the effort. But some convicts, at least, have relatives and friends who want to relieve their incarcerated loved ones' misery—a potential gold mine for companies and their allies inside Departments of Correction (DOCs).

How do entrepreneurs and prison administrators siphon money from inmates' families into their own coffers? By privatizing all 240 canteens in Florida's correctional system, for example. As soon as Keefe Commissary Services took over in 2003, the corporation's willing helpers in the DOC allowed three 10% across-the-board price hikes and— to ensure that the higher prices did not result in a reduced sales volume—raised the weekly purchase limit twice, from $65 to $85 to $100. Convicts' paychecks typically amount to no more than $20 to $40 per month, so by themselves they could neither afford the increased prices nor take advantage of the higher purchase limits. To make this business model succeed, therefore, Keefe and the DOC were clearly counting on inmates to send begging letters to their relatives and friends.

And, of course, this ploy worked: the DOC's annual profits from canteen operations leaped from $15.6 to $23 million in one year, while its partner Keefe earned so much that it preferred not to disclose its income from the deal. Florida's auditor general issued a lengthy report, and it was scathing indeed. Virtually all of its criticisms, however, were directed at the DOC's failure to protect the state's financial stake in this moneymaking scheme.[48]

In fact, the commingling of government and corporate interests is the real problem here. In July 2006, after being ousted by Governor Jeb Bush, the former Director of the Florida Department of Corrections, James Crosby, and one of his division heads, Allen Clark, accepted plea agreements for "corruptly accepting" $130,000 in kickbacks from a Keefe subcontractor. No doubt the Sunshine State's auditor general would describe these men as two bad apples, not harbingers of a systemic or structural failure. According to the *New York Times*, however, ongoing investigations into Florida's prison system have yielded over twenty arrests.[49]

By far the most efficient way to financially exploit prisoners' loved ones is through correctional telephone services. Convicts are only allowed to make collect calls, with all sorts of fees and surcharges tacked on by corporations like AT&T, Verizon, and Sprint. As a result, the prison telephone business is worth $1 billion per year.[50]

In Virginia, each of the 32,000 inmates housed in state penitentiaries (as opposed to local jails) generates $225 annually for MCI WorldCom.[51] But that is nothing compared to the San Mateo County, California, jail: there, every prisoner runs up $1,375 a year in telephone charges.[52] Who pays these enormous bills? Convicts' relatives and friends, of course—almost always people with limited incomes who just want to hear their loved ones' voices.

For the privilege of gouging them, telephone companies pay DOCs commissions of 40 to 60%. Thus the New York prison system received $93 million per annum from MCI until 2007,[53] while a small state like Virginia gets a still-respectable $6 to $7 million a year. To maximize both the company's and the DOC's income, prison officials deliberately "rejected an earlier proposal that offered lower rates," according to court testimony.[54]

Thus a typical fifteen-minute long-distance call made from a Virginia correctional center until recently cost $9.20. In the federal Bureau of Prisons, by contrast, phone companies are not allowed to bilk convicts' relatives, so that same fifteen-minute long-distance call costs only $3.00 there. Price disparities like these led the Virginia State Corporation Commission (SCC) to order MCI to lower its rates in 2001.[55]

But, thanks to a special bill sponsored by Republican state Senator Thomas K. Norment, Virginia's general assembly retroactively removed the correctional telephone contract from the SCC's jurisdiction, thereby nullifying its ruling against MCI. Of course, Norment's quick and effective action had nothing at all to do with the fact that MCI had just given him the third-largest campaign contribution received by any legislator in the then-current political cycle.[56]

If the senator and his financial masters thought this ended the matter, however, they had not counted on Jean Auldridge of Virginia CURE (Citizens United for the Rehabilitation of Errants). She successfully lobbied the general assembly to create a debit card calling system that would cut the cost of prison phone calls by two-thirds. According to Republican state Delegate James H. Dillard II, the reform's sponsor,

"This has been an injustice for a long time.... Now is the time to do the right thing."[57]

All's well that ends well? Not in the world of the prison-industrial complex! The new phone system has meanwhile been implemented: MCI is still running the show, and that $9.20 call has been reduced by only 80 cents to $8.40. As Auldridge put it to the *Virginian Pilot*, "They're sticking it to us again."[58]

"SAVE SOUTHAMPTON CORRECTIONAL CENTER"

That was the slogan printed on T-shirts worn by three hundred guards and their family members as they demonstrated on the Richmond, Virginia, Capitol Square in 2002.[59] Immediately after his 2001 election, Democratic Governor Mark Warner proposed shutting down three of the state's forty-three penitentiaries: Southampton, Brunswick, and Staunton. Little did he realize just how difficult it is to trim back the prison-industrial complex.

Not only corporations like MCI, but also correctional officers' unions and associations will go to any lengths to keep prison dollars flowing. Guards have their Democratic henchmen in the legislatures, just as business has its Republican lackeys. In many cases, they work together.

Today more than 747,000 men and women are employed in corrections.[60] According to the Urban Institute, nearly one-third of U.S. counties have at least one jail or penitentiary; in Florida, 78% do.[61] A Virginia Department of Corrections fact sheet explains, "With layoffs in the coal industry [in the state's southwest], prisons are vital to the local and regional economy."[62] A similar brochure from the California DOC promises "600 to 1,000 new jobs and an annual payroll of $20 to $52 million" if towns agree to host a penitentiary.[63] To many politicians and voters in economically depressed areas, that sounds like a very good deal indeed.

Southside Virginia is one such poor region, and two of the three prisons that Governor Warner wanted to close in 2002 are located here. In response to growing local unrest, Public Safety Secretary John M. Marshall organized a hearing at which guards and local elected officials expressed their fear of mass unemployment in vivid terms: "This is tearing my life apart," testified correctional officer Mike Reynolds. Normally a proponent of criminal justice reform, Democratic state Senator L. Louise Lucas changed her tune when her constituents' jobs were at stake: "Hopefully your conscience will say to you, 'We can't do this to Southside.' "[64] Local residents collected 6,000 signatures on a petition opposing closure—quite an achievement, given the fact that the two towns hosting Southampton and Brunswick Correctional Centers have only 167 and 1,275 residents, respectively.[65]

In the end, all the petitions and protests were successful. Governor Warner came to realize that eliminating just 600 guards' jobs, out of 747,000, was simply too big a sacrifice. To save face, he shut down one prison: Staunton Correctional Center in northern Virginia, where there is plenty of other work. The two Southside penitentiaries would remain open, the governor explained, because the Department of Corrections had just handed him a new projection that called for *more* prisons, not fewer.[66] Nobody asked him why this should be so, at a time when the state's crime rate was falling to record lows.[67]

Is Virginia unique in this regard? Unfortunately not, as New York Governor Eliot Spitzer discovered in 2007. Because the Empire State's correctional population had fallen from 71,000 to 63,000 since 1999, he proposed forming a commission to study whether some prisons could be closed. But Lawrence Flanagan, president of the New York State Correctional Officers and Police Benevolent Association, immediately objected, "We're not open to any closures at this point."[68]

Having donated over $1.8 million to state lawmakers in recent years, the guards union could count on support from politicians like Republican state Senator Elizabeth O'Connor Little. "There are over 5,000 correctional officers living in my district," she told the *New York Times*. Prisons "have a tremendous economic impact"—both on her constituents and on her campaign fundraising efforts, no doubt.[69]

Smart pol that he is, Governor Spitzer soon recognized the futility of his plan to shut down unneeded correctional centers: "I don't want to suggest that it's happening soon," he told lawmakers in a budget address.[70]

Reentry for Guards

What the attempted closure of correctional centers in Virginia and New York shows is that America cannot conquer its addiction to prisons without a major retraining and job placement initiative for guards. Focusing only on the rehabilitation, education, and reentry of inmates is not enough. Unless correctional officers are given significant help in transitioning to a different line of work, they will fight to keep "their" penitentiaries open. Sadly and ironically, guards are locked into these hellish institutions as much as convicts are.

Fortunately, many correctional staff members have a keen insight into the insanity of this country's criminal justice policies and a strong desire to work somewhere, anywhere else. Lance Corcoran, a guard's union representative from California, says, "... after a lifetime, thirty-five years of working, you look back...and it's very difficult to take pride in what you've done."[71] This sense of hopelessness and frustration—sometimes taken out on convicts—could be very effectively redirected into a vocational education and employment program, if one were offered to them.

In addition to such direct assistance to guards, local politicians and residents of towns considering the hosting of a new prison must be educated about the economic and social impact they can expect. Researchers have found that, over a twenty-five-year period,

- richer and urban counties that had a penitentiary or jail showed no increase in their residents' income and the counties' total earnings, compared to similar counties without one
- poorer and rural counties with a correctional facility actually did *worse* economically than comparable counties that had none

These findings were confirmed by two other studies.[72]

According to the social scientists who conducted this research, the counterintuitive neutral-to-negative economic impact of prisons may be due to the fact that other industries consider them undesirable neighbors and move elsewhere. And there are other unexpected and unpleasant side effects to having a penitentiary move into town: divorce, domestic violence, and juvenile delinquency rates almost twice as high as before the prison's arrival.[73] Because guards cannot help but bring their work home with them, their families suffer even if their income is steady and secure.

Money—especially correctional money—is not the answer to all of life's problems, after all.

"Gross Abuses of Public Trust"

For a glimpse of what union-controlled penal policies can lead to, let us turn to the nation's cultural bellwether, California. The Golden State turns out to have the country's second-largest prison system, after the federal BOP. Thanks for that dubious distinction must go to the California Correctional Peace Officers Association (CCPOA), whose 31,000 members have essentially co-opted the entire political spectrum.

According to the *San Jose Mercury News*, the union doled out $12.6 million in campaign contributions to state legislators of both parties between 2000 and 2004.[74] That bought enough bipartisan fealty to push through a 37% pay increase for correctional officers in July 2004, over Governor Schwarzenegger's objections. The average guard's salary will now rise to $73,000—more than twice the average wage in the next-highest-paying state, and $20,000 higher than the average California teacher's salary.[75] (As everywhere else in the field of corrections, however, the full truth is even worse than these officially reported figures suggest: benefits and overtime raise the *actual* cost to taxpayers of one guard to over $100,000 per year).[76]

"In almost every way, the [CCPOA] seems to have the state administration outgunned," reports the *Washington Post*. Union representative Joe Bauman brags, "We sit down to the negotiating table, and we use our laptops. Meanwhile, [California government officials] are using a calculator that you get with a carton of cigarettes."[77]

But the CCPOA does not restrict its advocacy to standard union issues like pay and benefits. For instance, the organization considers private prisons a threat to its power, so it convinced then-Governor Gray Davis—recipient of $3.4 million in CCPOA contributions—to close four of them in a 2002 bill. After Schwarzenegger's election, the union showered leading Republican state Senator Jim Brulte with six-figure donations, whereupon he began lobbying Schwarzenegger to shut down the remaining five private correctional centers.[78]

Another CCPOA priority, according to the *Los Angeles Times*, is "terminating college and vocational education programs in prisons statewide."[79] Why? Because the correctional system needs a steady inflow of recidivists to keep penitentiaries at full capacity. If inmates were to reform and then fail to re-offend upon release, a few state prisons might actually have to close!

Fortunately for the guards' union, the CCPOA includes parole and probation officers as well, so there is no real danger of having "too few" recidivists.[80] Californian parole and probation officers send ex-convicts back to the penitentiary at *eight times* the rate of their Texan colleagues; even minor offenses, like being drunk in public or driving more than fifty miles from home, suffice to take a released inmate's freedom away again.[81] To the CCPOA, successfully reintegrated former prisoners are a threat to their members' job security—a threat that union parole and probation officers work hard to eliminate.

This kind of thinking also motivated the CCPOA's decision to spend $101,000 to lobby for passage of the state's "three strikes and you're out" bill in 1994.[82] In 2004, it invested another $1 million to defeat Proposition 66, which would have excluded nonviolent offenders from this draconian law.[83] To scare taxpayers into supporting its "keep the prisons full" agenda, the CCPOA's annual budget typically includes up to

$1 million for TV ads, a figure that rises to $10 million during election cycles.[84] Much less well-known is the fact that the union also donates six-figure sums to "Crime Victims United of California."[85] Could it be that crime victims are just another tool to help the CCPOA maintain access to correctional dollars?

According to a 2004 reform commission headed by former Republican Governor George Deukmejian, "there has been too much political interference, too much union control, and too little management courage" in the California Department of Corrections, leaving the agency "dysfunctional" and "in chaos."[86] Federal District Court Judge Thelton Henderson documented systematic "gross abuses of public trust [by] the CCPOA" in the interminable *Madrid v. Gomez / Madrid v. Woodford* case; his Special Master John Hagar found that "prison reform in the state has been undermined by high-level contacts between [the governor's] staff and the politically influential California Correctional Peace Officers Association."[87] Sad to say, Schwarzenegger immediately rejected the one reform that Deukmejian and the federal judge consider the essential prerequisite for all others: the establishment of an independent civilian oversight board, like those that regulate major metropolitan police departments.

Truly independent oversight would, of course, have limited the governor's ability to reward those members of the prison-industrial complex that support him: the Geo Group and other correctional capitalists. Schwarzenegger's "reform" plan of 2006 promised them two new penitentiaries at $500 million each and a program to house 4,500 female inmates in private prisons.[88] This cannot solve California's correctional crisis, of course—but corporate gratitude can make a decisive difference at election time.[89]

A HISTORICAL POSTSCRIPT

To students of history, the baneful influence of money in corrections should come as no surprise. In 1595 the Dutch city of Amsterdam established its first "house of correction," a workhouse for petty offenders, and soon this new, enlightened form of punishment spread throughout continental Europe. According to Christoph Hinckeldey of the Museum of Medieval Criminology in Rothenburg, Germany,

> the object of resocialization was thrust aside in favor of the idea of extracting the greatest possible benefit from the corrective institution. The houses of correction offered a large potential of extremely cheap labour, so what was more obvious than to utilize it in the interests of the state by setting up production shops [?] Things went so far that houses of correction were leased to private entrepreneurs who, however, had not the slightest interest in the crime-policy goal of these institutions, but only wanted to maximize their profits, even more so than the state. As a result of this misuse, these institutions declined into neglected confusion. Buildings and equipment fell into disrepair and low-grade supervisory personnel let discipline decline. All this and the crowding together of great numbers of criminals and non-criminals made the houses of correction "hot beds of crime."[90]

What part of that passage could not be used to describe America's prison-industrial complex?

*   *   *

To conclude our review of the role of money in penal policy, let us recall once more the two subjects never mentioned: justice and crime control. Neither the CCA nor the CCPOA—nor even those medieval "houses of correction"—care in the least whether their cash cows, the inmates, *deserve* to be incarcerated any longer, or whether they *need* to remain locked away to protect the public. To them, "tough on crime" rhetoric is simply a public relations ploy that helps keep the money flowing.

Before we capitulate to the power of the correctional profiteers, however, let us recall that America can do and has done better. Our next interview subject, Charlie Campbell, served as warden in the federal Bureau of Prisons and director of the Alaska Department of Corrections in the 1950s, '60s, and '70s—a time when rehabilitation, not money-making, was the purpose of incarceration. If we could all just stop bowing to the golden statue erected by the prison-industrial complex, we could see an alternative: Charlie Campbell.

INTERVIEW WITH CHARLES CAMPBELL

Q: Tell us a little about your background.

A: I was born in 1924 in Georgia, but I grew up in Virginia. My father was a Baptist preacher with vigorous churches and a good ministry, mainly by being a loving, enfolding kind of person rather than a great preacher or pulpit politician. My mother was very much a free spirit, but a wonderful partner for my father in his work. Right after high school, I was drafted into the Army and served in Europe as an airborne infantryman. I attended George Washington University under the GI Bill after the war and married my wonderful wife, Ellen, in 1948. We have four entirely satisfactory grown-up children and quite a few grandchildren.

Q: Tell us about your professional life.

A: After college, I took a job as a probation-parole officer in Virginia. I didn't know much of what the job was all about, but soon I became deeply interested in working with offenders. In 1955, I went to work for the U.S. Bureau of Prisons and had a twenty-year career with that agency, with assignments at seven different facilities as well as the BOP's central office in Washington.

Q: What did you do after you retired?

A: You could hardly say I retired. I did some writing, taught a course in corrections at Texas Christian University, and, in 1977, went to work for U.S. District Court Judge Sarah G. Hughes as special master in the Dallas County Jail case. This was a highly satisfying job because in those days the federal courts had not yet been restrained by higher court rulings and thus were able to do a good job of requiring prisons in the United States to be humane and decent.

Q: Did you do any further work in the field of corrections itself?

A: Yes: I did quite a lot of consulting with state correctional systems across the country. And in 1979, I agreed to take a job in Alaska as the Director of Corrections; they wanted someone to oversee implementation of the state's "correctional master plan." I left this job after three years, just as I had planned, but after about five years I went to work as Compliance Monitor for the court system in a class action lawsuit involving "conditions of confinement" issues. And along the way, I also wrote a couple of books, one of them in the field of penal history.[91]

Q: So you were able to witness firsthand what the field of corrections was like before the massive expansion of inmate populations over the last thirty years.

A: That's true. When I retired from the federal Bureau of Prisons in 1975, the total prison population in the U.S. was about 300,000. Today it is over two million.

Q: How were prisons then different from prisons now?

A: Well, the primitive side of incarceration—the old-time, Hollywood image of chain gangs and tough, brutal prisons—was certainly part of the picture back then, especially in the less progressive state systems. And yet, thirty or forty years ago, there was a much stronger counterbalance to the dismal side of corrections than there is today. Civility between inmates and staff was valued, not viewed with suspicion, as it often is today. Occasionally there was even something very close to affection between the old lifer, for example, and his boss-man in the plumbing shop.

Q: And that human touch is lacking nowadays?

A: Yes. Much of what we still call "corrections" in this country has spiraled down into a nationwide crisis-management operation over the last thirty years. The huge numbers of people being incarcerated nowadays simply overwhelm staff and resources. And that leaves human warehousing as the only recourse.

Q: Some might say that warehousing is all that convicted criminals deserve.

A: We hear that kind of thing a lot, but it truly misses the point. This is not a matter of kindness or compassion; it's about doing the right thing and having safe, orderly communities. Remember, 95% of all prison inmates are eventually released and come back to live among us. Because sentences these days are so excessive and nothing of value is done for incarcerated offenders, prisons in America have become a vast, brimming reservoir of anger and resentment. Hundreds of thousands of alienated young men are released into the community every year, without lawful skills or hope. This is a largely unrecognized national disaster.

Q: So, if I understand you correctly, you support better prison conditions because you believe that rehabilitated prisoners are less likely to commit new crimes when released.

A: Yes, but the term "rehabilitation" can sometimes be a problem because it raises too many questions and too much skepticism. Of course, I support rehabilitative efforts and good counseling programs, especially for people who have problems with drugs and alcohol. And, at the very least, inmates should be helped to learn the basic skills they need to function in the community: reading, writing, work habits, and social skills. But what I want most is for imprisonment to become less destructive to the human spirit, less wasteful and alienating.

Q: "First do no harm," the medical profession calls this principle.

A: That's right. Incarceration is an essentially destructive experience, and my belief is that the first responsibility for people in the corrections field is to make it less so. A lot of good people do take this approach. Even now, in these dark days of cynicism in our field, many strong correctional professionals—from line officers to state commissioners—know what I'm talking about here. Unfortunately, many others do not know, or they simply don't care, or they have another agenda.

Q: What do you mean by "another agenda"?

A: Well, private prison companies, for instance, profit financially from keeping offenders incarcerated as long as possible, and they have a vested interest in releasing inmates who are likely to commit further crimes. That's a basic flaw in the concept of prison privatization that somehow escapes people. And, quite apart from the privateers, we have to face the fact that imprisonment in America is now a multi-billion-dollar industry. Lots of big companies are flourishing beyond anything they ever would have dreamed of. What I call an unrecognized national disaster—the over two million people behind bars in the U.S.—is a financial bonanza for these companies.

Q: In spite of all that extra money being spent on prisons, though, there seems to be no increased expenditure for therapeutic and educational programs. Why is there so little rehabilitation going on nowadays?

A: It seems to me that in the 1950s and '60s, there was more imagination, more optimism, and a lot more dedication to the task of intervening in patterns of criminal behavior. Idealism had not gone out of fashion, as it seems to have done today. On the very first day I went to work for the Bureau of Prisons, it was made clear to me that the stated goal of the agency was "the correction of the offender." Maybe the same thing is still being said, but I don't see much evidence of it.

Q: I understand that you see this new, less rehabilitative approach to corrections being reflected in staff-inmate relations, as well.

A: Yes. Thirty years ago, even in tough, long-term penitentiaries, there was a lot of personal contact, a working relationship between line officers and inmates. You know, I've always considered line staff—especially "guards," as the general public calls them—to be the most important staff members, because they are the people most closely in contact with inmates. When basically decent men and women are recruited for these jobs, given adequate pay and good training, and motivated to have the right attitude, they can make a great difference for good. In the federal system and the more progressive state systems, this approach was common, and it made those prisons safer, more orderly and more worthy of being a part of a civilized society.

Q: Do you really believe that thirty or forty years ago prisons were safer and more orderly than today?

A: I can hardly say that. But the safety and security that prisons may have now comes at a high cost in the lost advantages of positive human contact. Prison design today relies on the management of inmates by way of TV monitors, electronic doors and PA systems, with officers isolated from prisoners in control booths. Another means of keeping prisons safe—if you want to call it that—is by use of the twenty-three hour lockdown. Sometimes whole prison populations are locked in single cells, except for the required one hour of exercise, in so-called supermax prisons. Some folks in the corrections field, as well as in the news media and politics, may call this progress. I call it brutalization.

Q: How did all of this happen? What were the factors that brought us to the overcrowding, the warehousing, and the abandonment of rehabilitative efforts?

A: As I mentioned earlier, various legal rulings by our conservative federal appellate courts have undercut the authority of the lower courts to oversee prison conditions. These higher-court rulings more or less legitimized terrible prison conditions and overcrowding across the country. And an equally important factor was the lure of "tough on crime" politics, which took over during the 1970s.

Q: Tell us more about the political developments that took place in that decade.

A: Well, politicians and their constituents began to nourish each other's ignorance about crime and the causes of crime. And then came the huge influence of money: it was learned that crime *does* pay, if not for the perpetrators, then at least for a variety of corporate interests. The worst of it got started in 1974, when a criminologist named Robert Martinson gained his fifteen minutes of fame by publishing what he considered to be a comprehensive survey of prisoner rehabilitation programs around the country.[92] This study proved to be seriously flawed, but before this conclusion was reached—and eventually conceded by Martinson himself—the study became something of a cause célèbre.

Q: So his study received wide attention on TV and in the newspapers?

A: Yes. Unfortunately, CBS's *60 Minutes* gave Martinson a national pulpit to declare that "nothing works." Throw-away-the-key advocates and hard-line politicians all over the country loved hearing that! President Richard Nixon's attorney general, William Saxbe, gleefully picked up on this and made something like a triumphal tour around the country, talking about the "myth of rehabilitation." Others joined in: respected social scholar James Q. Wilson, for instance, gained near-celebrity status by proclaiming that there are many "wicked people" in the world who simply need to be locked up.

Q: Surely there is some truth to that, isn't there?

A: What I really think is that Professor Wilson gained some PR points with that observation, but he also reflected a certain ivory-tower obtuseness about the matter. If we really could manage to lock up *all* the wicked people in our society, the ranks of the rich and the powerful would be seriously depleted! It troubles me that so often it is poor people—people with no real chance in life, especially minorities—who are sent to prison and written off as "wicked" or "sociopathic." Incidentally, I hate that term. Sociopathy is a greatly overused diagnosis, a throwaway label that serves as an excuse for not trying to help people.

Q: Most people would question whether criminals, whether from rich or poor backgrounds, deserve any help at all.

A: The conclusion I have reached, after more than five decades of association with the field of corrections, is that there is likely to be some measure of goodness and decency in almost everyone. Moreover, I've observed that there usually comes a point, even for long-term prisoners and recidivists, when they have had enough. They don't want to continue "doing life on the installment plan." If only they knew how, they would choose to join society's mainstream.

Q: Can you think of a particular example of an inmate who appeared to be hopeless, but learned to become a law-abiding citizen?

A: Oh, there are so many! An old-timer called Shakey Martin comes to mind—a fellow I knew when he was in prison, and also after he was released. In his youth he had been orphaned and neglected, and he ended up riding the rails. He was a confirmed loser by his mid-twenties, as well as a major abuser of alcohol. But he never spent more than a year or two at a time in state prisons in Indiana and Ohio—until he pulled a post-office burglary that put him in Leavenworth. From there, he was transferred to the Federal Correctional Institution Fort Worth, which I activated in 1970 and where I served as first warden until 1975.

Q: Tell us more about this facility. It had some pretty unique features, didn't it?

A: Well, yes. Primarily out of necessity, FCI Fort Worth became a coed prison—or co-correctional, as we preferred to call it. More importantly, Fort Worth was a place that took its helping and restorative roles very seriously. A few months there utterly destroyed Shakey Martin's convict value system.

Q: What did he do while at FCI Fort Worth?

A: He really "got with the program," so to speak: he signed up for high school classes and, at the age of sixty-five, actually earned his GED. He took an interest in all kinds of positive things—the kinds of things that all of his life had been foreign to him. The chaplaincy program, for instance, meant more to him than anything else. From the very first week he showed up at Fort Worth, he participated in my wife's Bible study group, and in time he became a "pillar of the church." This, as well as his participation in the institution's Alcoholics Anonymous program, put him in touch with volunteers from the outside, folks of the sort he'd had no experience with in his entire life.

Q: That all sounds very touching, but how long did he manage to stay out of prison after he left FCI Fort Worth?

A: When Shakey visited us for breakfast that last time before we moved to Alaska, he had been out of prison and living in Fort Worth for a year. He had settled into a good routine and was doing well.

Q: This man had breakfast with you?

A: Yes, and not just that one time. After I retired from the BOP, Ellen and I and two of our kids moved to a lovely house in the country near Fort Worth. Shakey Martin was not the only ex-offender to visit us there, but he was the one who always showed up early, in time for breakfast. So I'd have to yell down for him to come on in, pat the dogs, and have a seat in the kitchen. Ellen would give him a hug and get breakfast going for him. She always called him "Mr. Martin," never "Shakey."

Q: So what does a warden, the warden's wife, and one of his ex-prisoners talk about over a plate of scrambled eggs in the morning?

A: Shakey would tell us about his life in the free world, how strange it felt. He confessed that he was pretty lonely sometimes; some days, he would just ride the local buses around town, using his senior citizen's bus pass. At the senior citizens' center, he would play pool and sometimes have meals. The saving grace for Shakey was in the friendships he had among folks who had been FCI volunteers—all of them steady, churchgoing people. And, of course, there were the Alcoholics Anonymous meetings.

Q: Tell us more about those.

A: Shakey had consumed a lot of alcohol in his day, but I don't think he was a classic alcoholic. What mattered to him was the companionship, and he could find that at the AA meetings without the alcohol. Sometimes a nice sort of man whom he had gotten to know at the meetings would ask him to come to the brick plant office on Jacksboro Highway and earn a few dollars sweeping up and doing other chores. Shakey really appreciated that job; feeling useless was hard for him. Though it was hardly a full and meaningful life, I think my old friend made the most of it. And he knew that by going back to prison, he would be letting his friends down.

Q: Shakey had a long criminal record prior to his stay at FCI Fort Worth, and recidivists like him are not likely to get yet another "second chance" nowadays. Why do you believe that repeat offenders should be helped?

A: To begin with, it is important to understand that recidivists are not very often the kind of folks we suppose them to be. They are people who have learned how to "do time," but they have never had much success as criminals or anything else. In reality, *successful* criminals don't spend much time behind bars. There are many hundreds of thousands of imprisoned people in our country who have been released and gone back to prison a few times, but who nonetheless need and deserve help. Writing them off as hopeless losers is wrong.

Q: Is this where you see an opportunity for people of faith to intervene and bring new hope to repeat offenders and other criminals?

A: Yes, of course. I once had a pastor who insisted that it is the task of the committed Christian to reach out to "the least, the last, and the lost." Had it not been for committed, caring people reaching out to Shakey Martin, he surely would have remained among the least, the last and the lost. And he almost certainly would have resorted to alcohol, gone back to prison, and given up on life.

Q: Yet under the "three strikes and you're out" laws so popular today, Shakey would never even have been let out of prison in the first place, right?

A: Yes. Having committed three felonies—more than three, actually—he could have been sent to prison for life. What a waste and an injustice that would have been.

Q: Like recidivists, drug users and drug dealers have also been subjected to vastly longer prison sentences during the last thirty years.

But, again, you have a different perspective on this type of criminal, right?

A: I do indeed. The kind of drug offenders who are regularly sent to prison are often themselves the victims of drugs. Because law enforcement has little success in arresting upper-echelon dealers, street distributors—almost always users themselves—are given heavy sentences. This does nothing to impede drug traffic, because there are always plenty of users to recruit for street distribution, many of them hardly more than children. And the really cruel irony is that, while we're squandering tens of billions of dollars on keeping such people locked up, funds for drug intervention strategies have been cut.

Q: FCI Fort Worth, your final assignment with the Bureau of Prisons, had a strong drug treatment program, I understand.

A: Yes. Actually, Fort Worth had been a U.S. Public Health Service narcotics hospital before we reconfigured the facility as a Federal Correctional Institution for the BOP. The work we did with inmates who had drug dependency problems was an important feature of the effort we made there.

Q: Tell us more about how you and your staff addressed substance abuse issues at Fort Worth.

A: The facility was organized around five so-called functional units, each with its own unit manager and staff. Two of the units were for people with drug problems, ranging from hard-core heroin addiction to freebase cocaine dependency to long-term marijuana habits. We also had a separate unit for alcoholics and alcohol abusers. People tend to forget that alcoholism—or sometimes simple binge drinking—leads to more crime than any other kind of substance abuse. At FCI Fort Worth, we found that a routine based on the Twelve Step principle worked well with these guys, together with a close association with AA clubs in the community.

Q: Was Fort Worth the only BOP facility that provided this kind of program?

A: No. While it is true that some circumstances came together that gave us a very special opportunity at FCI Fort Worth, there were some terrific institutional programs at the FCIs Lexington and Pleasanton, as well as some great efforts in Illinois and

Massachusetts and North Carolina. Much of this has gone by the board now, because of what I call the decline of enlightenment that began in corrections during the mid-1970s. What we did then at Fort Worth could not be done anywhere today. But I think my colleagues and I demonstrated some valid penological principles.

Q: Explain that further, please.

A: In those days, one of the standard principles taught to people entering on duty in the more progressive correctional systems was that all people, including prisoners, tend to function according to expectations. So why not set positive expectations? We did that at FCI Fort Worth, and we decided to take seriously our responsibility to the inmates, since they were our fellow human beings. We were all children of God, though I'm not sure we ever used that term.

Q: How did these principles translate into practice?

A: Right off the bat, we decided to put together an array of positive choices and opportunities for the inmates. And we called them "residents," not inmates. We were helped by a rather distinguished criminologist, Dr. Esther Hefferman, who also happened to be a Roman Catholic nun. Sister Esther, as most of us called her, was with us at Fort Worth for about three years, off and on.

Q: How did she come to be so closely involved with the running of a federal prison?

A: She and a colleague had a contract to study the coed aspect of our program. From the very beginning, we had women inmates there, in one of our five functional units. A social scholar doing a study is not supposed to affect the subject that she (or he) is observing, but I think Sister Esther—Dr. Hefferman—probably did. She was and is such a fine and insightful woman; it's likely that just her presence helped us to get off to a good start in working with the female residents.

Q: How did you come to have a whole unit for female prisoners at an otherwise male prison?

A: Housing women inmates at FCI Fort Worth came about more by practical necessity than by a bold, innovative move by me or anyone else. It was a matter of the two federal prisons for women being dangerously overcrowded, and us having available bed space. As it turned out, the best way to work all of this out was to allow quite a bit of association between women and men residents, and to make all the programs accessible to both genders. Good staff supervision was essential, of course. And another huge help in our making this coed aspect work was the frequent presence of volunteers from the community, most of them good, solid church people who somehow knew how to connect with the residents.

Q: Surely the city's residents were a little suspicious and cautious when a BOP prison replaced the health service hospital.

A: Of course. So we more or less opened our doors to the citizens of Fort Worth, and soon we developed a terrific team of volunteers. At any one time, we had 200 active volunteers, for a prison population of just under 500. The townspeople quickly caught the spirit of what we were trying to do, and they worked very well with the staff. Bringing the inmates into that mix was especially important; this was the phenomenon that Sister Esther observed and described as "mutuality."

Q: This was one of the key components of the FCI Fort Worth program, so please tell us more about this.

A: The notion of doing all we could to reduce and maybe even eliminate the destructiveness of imprisonment was our guiding principle. In any situation, the best way to eliminate *what's bad* is to replace it with *what's good*. What's most bad about prisons are the subcultural influences among prisoners, characterized by scheming, lying, stealing, illicit drug use and trafficking, violence, and predatory sex—all of this, together with a lack of trust and regard between inmates and staff.

Q: So that is *what's bad*. What was the *what's good* that you and your staff tried to put in its place?

A: Our task was to fill the days of the inmates with positive activities and opportunities to improve themselves. Because of the unusual circumstance of our taking over a public health hospital and many of its staff, we had good resources and excellent people, including some very good clinically trained staff.

Q: Tell us more about these programs you offered the residents.

A: We had the staff and resources for a strong program of academic and vocational training, including study-release arrangements that enabled us to send inmates to schools and training centers in town. We had a particularly close relationship with Tarrant County Junior College, whose campus adjoined our facility. And

FCI Fort Worth itself eventually developed a whole array of therapeutic activities. I don't use the term "therapeutic" in a clinical sense here, although some of our programs were pretty sophisticated. But for the most part, we simply allowed lots of initiatives to develop, sort of spontaneously.

Q: Who came up with ideas for new programs?

A: Once we started, quite a few came from the residents themselves, and many others came from volunteers. Let me give an example: shortly after the women residents arrived at the facility, several women volunteers—some of them staff members' wives—began meeting with these gals to talk about such things as grooming, fixing their hair, beautifying the little cubicles where they lived, etiquette and manners, as well as the worries and concerns they had about their children back home. You can imagine how great these friendships were for the women residents.

Q: You spoke of "filling the days of the inmates with positive activities and opportunities to improve themselves." Tell us about some of these activities and opportunities.

A: Oh, there were so many small-group activities! Five or six of our staff did group counseling a couple of times a week. A professor from Texas Christian University, well qualified as a group therapist, worked as a volunteer with our residents for almost the whole time I was there. There were art groups and music groups and even a group that learned signing, to communicate with the deaf! Some of these small-group activities turned out to be not so small: the Alcoholics Anonymous meetings often had fifty or more residents and ten to fifteen outside volunteers, and the gospel choir had up to twenty-five members as I recall.

Q: You spoke of "good, solid church people" among the volunteers. In addition to the educational and therapeutic activities you just described, were the volunteers involved with the inmates in the religious programs at FCI Fort Worth, as well?

A: They were indeed. Bible study groups, prayer groups, the Sunday "rap sessions" after church services—all of these were heavily dependent on volunteers. You could really say we were bathed in prayer! And volunteers would frequently take those residents who qualified to their own churches in town, to make them a part of their own communities.

Q: Were most of your volunteers motivated by their religious convictions?

A: Yes. Many of them were evangelical Christians, but we also had a good relationship with a group of Catholic sisters, including the principal of a local Catholic school. She had her fifth graders write letters to our residents, and you wouldn't believe how meaningful this was. Some of our residents had never before gotten a letter from the outside!

Q: It occurs to me that much of what you have told me about would not have been possible if FCI Fort Worth had not been located on the edge of a good-sized city.

A: That's true. And, sad to say, many of the hundreds of prisons built in the U.S. during recent years have been tucked away in "out of sight, out of mind" locations. My view is that volunteers and access to other community resources are crucial to effective institutional corrections. Long years of isolation from society are not helpful in preparing people to reenter society. If given a chance, many God-fearing people with love in their hearts are inclined to reach out with friendship and support for the people locked up in their neighborhood prison. It should be the responsibility of policymakers to enable that kind of thing to happen, by locating correctional facilities close to urban areas.

Q: Since this is a book about faith in a criminal justice context, please tell us about the chapel services at FCI Fort Worth.

A: In a sense, the Sunday morning service was the central happening of the week at our facility. On any given Sunday, a hundred or more people would show up for the nine o'clock service—mostly residents, but quite a few townspeople, too. A few staff people would usually attend as well; we really were blessed with excellent staff there. And of course Ellen and our children always came to the service; this was *our* church as long as we stayed in Fort Worth.

Q: What was the highlight of the service?

A: The choir—it really brought the event to life! Twenty or more choir members, men and women, almost all of them African-American, would open the service by shuffling down the isle, singing "Walk in the Light." And Chaplain Summer never failed to give a good sermon; he was an excellent man, a Lutheran and therefore somewhat liturgical, but really appreciative of the spirit and energy of "the black church." Afterward, we always had a coffee hour with lots of mixing and mingling. Then came the "rap session," also led by the chaplain, and we had some wonderful discussions—always positive, "charged by the spirit." This mix of folks from inside and outside being there together added a very special dynamic—Sister Esther's "mutuality."

Q: Tell us a little about the chaplain's sermons.

A: Almost always, he called on us to celebrate the joy of life and the love of God that binds us together. He proclaimed hope but never forgot that there sometimes needs to be an acknowledgment of despair. FCI Fort Worth was a good place to serve time, thanks to the availability of friendship and help. But, given the individual circumstances of so many of our residents, all too often there was despair.

Q: And you saw it as your role, your Christian duty, to serve as a counterbalance to that despair?

A: It's probable that each of the good folks I worked with at Fort Worth, staff and volunteers alike, would put it differently. My feeling about it is that those of us who grew up in good circumstances—with the blessings of a happy childhood, loving parents, good friends, and good opportunities—simply don't have the right to an attitude of contempt toward others who had none of these advantages. Such things are utterly foreign to the overwhelming majority of the two million people who fill our prisons. To be sure, some of them are unredeemable in any human sense—but most of them are not. To write off so many of our fellow citizens is unworthy of a civilized society. And it is certainly not what I believe Christ wants us to do.

Questions for Reflection and Discussion

Scripture—Compare the defense speech of Mesach, Shadrach, and Abednego to those of Jesus before Pilate (Matthew 27:11–14), Peter before the High Priest (Acts 5:29 et seq.), Stephen before the Sanhedrin (Acts 7), and Paul before Felix and Agrippa (Acts 24–26). Contrast the portrayal of these speeches to the way defendants' court testimony is presented in the media today. Try writing a modern reporter's summary of Jesus', Peter's, Stephen's and Paul's defense speeches. Remember, they are all dangerous criminals, religious fanatics, and revolutionaries!

CRIMINOLOGY—The purpose of this chapter is to demonstrate that making money, not controlling crime, is the real goal of corrections. Carefully review the first five chapters of this book in light of what you have just learned. In the previous chapter, for instance, we noted that rehabilitative programs have been cut back in recent years. Do you now think that financial factors may be at work here—and how? Ask this type of question for each chapter.

SELF-EXAM—Study your own investment portfolio. How many of the companies whose stocks you own earn part of their profits in the corrections industry? Does any responsibility fall on you? Should you divest? See www.notwithourmoney.org.

INTERVIEW—Examine your reaction to Warden Campbell's description of FCI Fort Worth. Did you feel that any of the prison's programs "went too far"? When did you feel that way, and why? Relate your feelings to the subject of forgiveness.

INTERNET—Visit the Real Cost of Prisons Web site (realcostofprisons. org). Then go to www.prisonlegalnews.org and order a copy of Tara J. Herivel and Paul Wright, eds., *Prison Profiteers: Who Makes Money from Mass Incarceration* (New York: The New Press, 2008).

IMMERSION—Research the divestment and boycott campaigns directed against companies that invested in South Africa during the Apartheid era and in Israel today. Examine the possibility of organizing a boycott and divestment campaign against prison profiteers of *all* types. This could be a hugely powerful weapon against the prison-industrial complex. Once jails and penitentiaries no longer seem so profitable to corporations, alternatives to incarceration will suddenly become much more politically acceptable.

SPECIAL ASSIGNMENT—Some criminologists believe that the enormous expansion of this country's prison system over the last three decades was not a response to crime but to the oil price shock of 1973. As fuel costs rose, economic growth slowed and millions of low-skill jobs were eliminated through technology and outsourcing. Western European nations responded to this trend by creating an enormous underclass of more-or-less permanent welfare recipients; the U.S. responded by creating an enormous underclass of more-or-less permanent prisoners and guards.

If America incarcerated its own citizens at Western European rates, only about 400,000 men and women would be behind bars—not 2.3 million—and only 115,000 people would be working in corrections—not 747,000. A fair comparison between U.S. and Western European unemployment rates must therefore include these excess 1.9 million prisoners and 600,000 guards. (To further enhance accuracy, we must also count the estimated 1.4 million Americans who have become so discouraged that they stopped looking for work. The U.S. Department of Labor does not consider them unemployed, but European governments generally do.)

Go to the Department of Labor's Web site and find out the official number of unemployed Americans. Then add in this nation's excess convicts and correctional officers, as well as those who have given up the search for work. Now recalculate the actual U.S. unemployment rate and compare it to Western European rates.

If prison is actually little more than a system for absorbing unneeded workers, why not adopt the European model—free most inmates and put them on welfare? Why is it more acceptable in America to lock people up than to give them Social Security checks?

Chapter 7

Jesus and Prison Conditions

WHY BOTHER WITH improving prison conditions? One simple reason: Christ himself was a prisoner.

Stay with that thought for a little while: Christ was a prisoner. Not only that, but he died a prisoner, a "dead man walking." Incredible, really!

Most likely, your first reaction is to deny or mitigate or explain away this central fact of our faith. "But Jesus was innocent," you may say. Or, "Christ only allowed himself to be treated as if he were a prisoner; in reality he could have used his divine powers to get away any time." But both of these objections are entirely beside the point.

In Chapter 2 we learned about Joseph the Israelite, wrongly convicted of rape, and nevertheless very much a prisoner. If the U.S. legal system has an error rate as implausibly low as 1%—something no other institution would dare to claim—then there are 23,000 unjustly incarcerated men and women languishing behind bars at this time. Every one of them is very much a prisoner, no matter how innocent.

And, when Jesus was arrested in the Garden of Gethsemane, he explained to his disciples why his supernatural powers were of no avail: "Do you think that I cannot call upon my Father and he will not provide me at this moment with more than twelve legions of angels? But then how could the be fulfilled which say that it must come to pass in this way?" (Matthew 26:53, 54). To accomplish his mission, Christ had to "empt[y] himself" of his divine powers and "become like his brothers in every way" (Philippians 2:7; Hebrews 2:17).

This is the scandal of the cross, of course, "a stumbling block to Jews and foolishness to Gentiles," as Paul put it (1 Corinthians 1:23). If ours is an almighty God, then he really should have done better by his only begotten Son than to let him be crucified. That the "image of the invisible God" (Colossians 1:15) should be an executed convict simply sticks in our craw.

For that very reason, even good, sincere Christians nearly always leave out prisoners when discussing the Judgment of the Nations in Matthew 25. Jesus, you will recall, begins this parable by describing himself as "hungry and...thirsty,...a stranger,...naked,...ill and...in prison" (Matthew 25:35, 36.) When both the sheep and the goats object that they never saw him in these various predicaments, Christ explains that "whatever you did for one of these least brothers of mine, you did for me" (Matthew 25:40).

We rightly understand this teaching as the ethical foundation of our faith, the fundamental reason why we send food aid to Ethiopia, integrate Salvadorean refugees, operate shelters for the homeless, and support AIDS prevention and treatment programs in India. By the time we have lavished our charity on all these causes, however, we feel we have done our fair share. Let someone else worry about convicts and criminals!

I used to collect references to the Judgment of the Nations that neglect to mention prisoners. From popes to Puritans, from saints to *sola scriptura* reformers, nearly all of them somehow manage to miss the final group mentioned by Jesus: those behind penitentiary walls. My books are essentially one long, sustained attempt to correct this oversight.

Why do I consider prisoners so important? No doubt because I am a convict myself. But I also believe that we come closest to embodying God's selfless love ourselves when we reach out to those in prison.

What distinguishes divine love from the human variety is that the former is completely unmerited. While we can "earn" someone's friendship with repeated acts of kindness, there is absolutely nothing that sinful, limited man can do to earn the love of a perfect, infinite deity. "No one is just, not one," says Paul; "all have sinned and are deprived of the glory of God" (Romans 3:10, 23). Because we are endowed with a free will, our estrangement from God is in fact our free choice. Paul makes the point that this willful opposition to our Creator actually makes us his "enemies"—and yet he loves us anyway: "God proves his love for us in that while we were still sinners,...while we were enemies,...Christ died for us" (Romans 5:8, 10).

In the Sermon on the Mount, Jesus holds up God's unrequited love for a hostile, sinful humanity as the model all of us should follow in our love for others. Our "heavenly Father...makes his sun rise on the bad and the good"—or, as Paul put it, his "enemies" and his friends. So we too must "love [our] enemies and pray for those who persecute [us]" (Matthew 5:45, 44). And since "God is love" (1 John 4:8; cf. Ephesians 5:1), loving our enemies in particular actually turns out to be the highest form of the *imitatio dei*, the imitation of God.

Because it is so completely contrary to human nature to love those who hate or harm us, however, we do not make much of an effort to put this teaching into practice. The standard alibi is the word "persecute" in the passage above: supposedly, this means that our Savior only wants us to love religious opponents like the Pharisees. Since we are no longer being persecuted for our faith today, we can safely ignore this part of the Sermon on the Mount—thank goodness!

But the context of Jesus' remarks reveals the error in such thinking. In the lines preceding the command to "love your enemies," the Son of God speaks of criminals, not religious persecutors:

- The passage begins with the lex talionis, a piece of straightforward criminal justice legislation—"an eye for an eye" (Matthew 5:38)
- In the process of overturning this law, Christ gives the example of a simple assault, a "strike...on your right cheek" (Matthew 5:39)
- Then comes a lawsuit over a debt, something we would consider a civil dispute but in that culture could easily lead to "torture" or being "thrown in prison" (Matthew 5:40, 25; 18:34; cf. 30)
- Next we have a case of a Roman soldier pressing a Palestinian civilian "into service for one mile" (Matthew 5:41)—perfectly legal from the occupying military's point of view, but the equivalent of legalized kidnapping in the eyes of Israelites

- And finally Jesus mentions panhandling (Matthew 5:42), an offense that the city of Atlanta, for instance, criminalized in 2005 with a great deal of attendant controversy

These, then, are the "enemies" God's Son wants us to love: felons, not Pharisees. So we really have no excuse not to act upon his command today. And, thanks to the enormous expansion of the U.S. correctional system, there are plenty of crooks and convicts for every committed Christian to love.

What you will find if you do so is, of course, that every seemingly good-for-nothing prisoner is in fact a unique human being, created in and through Christ, with a past and a future and an eternal soul. God is no dummy: when he sent his Son to die for humanity, he knew that each and every one of us is worth trying to save. If we cannot see the infinite value of a caged felon, there is something wrong with our eyesight, not God's. And if we *can* see the child of God inside a mere convict, then we can truly say that "we have the mind of Christ" (1 Corinthians 2:16).

The great German theologian Karl Rahner even claims that it is easier to find Jesus in a prisoner's face than in any other. When we encounter someone like Mother Teresa, say, "we are so apt in such a case to stop short at the human greatness as such"—to love her for her kindness, her energy, her wonderful smile.[1] But when we meet convicts—"the mental and moral defectives; the unstable characters; the psychopaths; the vicious, the smooth, the cynical, the hypocrites and liars; the merely impulsive, the victims of circumstances, of addiction; the inevitable recidivists, the religiously impervious, the poor devils, the imbeciles"—then there is no human goodness to distract us.[2] All that is left to love now is "that which is most real and ultimate in this other person: God with his love and his mercy, who has conferred an eternal dignity upon this person and offers himself to him in the divine foolishness of love."[3]

But it is not only God or his Son whom we find in the prisoner, says Rahner: we also find ourselves, or rather, a profound truth about our own spiritual situation.

Every human being is continually running away from him-self... [from] the truth that we are all self-seekers,... always try-ing to serve God *and* ourselves.... [W]e are unfree, prisoners...in the prison of our own guilt,... our inability to perform any saving act.... [Thus the prison is] a true and real type, the making-visi-ble of a hidden reality....

But it might be objected [that] we ourselves are...redeemed,...no longer in servitude to sin.... But equally, so long as we are pursu-ing our pilgrimage in hope,... still marching and not yet at the goal, we are still as it were prisoners whose prison door is opening at this very moment....

So then we meet ourselves when we meet prisoners in prison. They present our own image to us, that image which we must face continually, day after day, if we hope to find the grace of God for ourselves; for that grace is only given to those who acknowledge themselves as sinners and build their lives on one thing only, the incomprehensible grace of God who takes pity on the lost.[4]

Now, the idea that "we meet ourselves when we meet prisoners" is probably unwelcome to most people. But, as uncomfortable as Rahner's assertion may make you feel now, I believe it is the *sine qua non* of successful prison reform and prison ministry. Inmates have abysmally low self-esteem, so the faintest hint of condescension by anyone imme-diately brings out all kinds of negative, even hostile reactions. If, by contrast, you appreciate them as equals before God, they often respond with intense gratitude for being taken seriously as human beings.

Not only will such an acknowledgment of your own state of spiri-tual imprisonment facilitate your relations with convicts, but it will also open the door for God's grace to flow into your life in a way that can only be called miraculous. That, in any case, has been my expe-rience over the last few years. Since this book's subject is Jesus and faith-based prison reform, allow me to give my own testimony of how Christ ministered to me behind bars.

For the first fourteen years of my sentence, my innocence was the one all-important, all-controlling truth of my life. The details of my case do not matter here, nor does it matter whether you believe me; the important point for understanding my spiritual journey is that I believed and believe that I am innocent of the crime of which I was convicted.

Just as you may perhaps look down a little on criminals and convicts, so too did I consider myself profoundly different from the men around me. (Almost) all of them were guilty, but I was not! In many areas of my day-to-day existence, I made decisions based solely on this factor. My eating habits (vegetables, not greasy stuff), reading material (classics, not westerns), TV viewing (PBS, not sports), choice of associates (hardly anyone)—all these and more were determined by my fervent belief that *I was not like "them."*

In late 1999, however, I came to a point where I could not go on. My lawyer was filing her last, increasingly hopeless appeals; I had recently been transferred to a horrific supermax penitentiary; and my prayer life had dried up completely. So, thanks to a wonderful United Church of Christ minister called Beverly Cosby, I tried something entirely new: Centering Prayer or, as it used to be called, contemplation.

Silent, wordless prayer has been practiced by the Church since the fourth century and, as I argue in my first book, quite possibly by Jesus himself. While there are many ways to explain or understand contemplation, my favorite definition comes from St. Catherine of Siena, who describes it as being "locked up in the cell of self-knowledge." Centering Prayer by this definition is a means of developing an incredibly clear and deep insight into our own sinfulness and consequent dependence on grace. In the silence within, with only you and God present, there is no place to hide: you have to face it *all.*

This is the kind of prayer I began to practice in early 2000, first twice and then three times a day. And what did I learn by locking myself in "the cell of self-knowledge"? That I am *not* completely different from the other prisoners with whom I am serving time.

I began to appreciate my own profound moral responsibility for the crime of which I was convicted. While I may not be guilty, I am far from innocent. My actions and especially my inactions hurt many people very badly—including even my codefendant.

And, when I compare myself to the men around me, I now see that many of them, though perhaps justly convicted in criminal court, are morally much less guilty than I. Many simply collided with the law while stumbling through life dazed by drugs, alcohol, mental disorders, or sheer hopelessness. If there is no light in someone's life, it is hard to blame only him when he knocks things over in the dark.

There was plenty of light in my life, however. I was just too cowardly and too selfish to do the right thing.

These truths about myself and my fellow prisoners were not easy to face. However, acknowledging that I truly belong with the two thieves crucified alongside Jesus had the effect of unshackling something within me that is larger than myself.

For the first fourteen years of my incarceration, I accomplished absolutely nothing; I was too busy being a victim of the legal system to do anything positive. But, in 2001, only one year after I entered the "cell of self-knowledge," my first book began to flow out of me...and then came a second...and a third...and now, even a fourth. And every one of them found a publisher.

Please note, however, that I do not claim credit for the above: I intentionally write that my books flowed out of me. I really do believe that something much greater than I has been using me for this work.

What work is that? To remind my readers of the two central truths discussed in this chapter: that Christ was a prisoner and that every one of us is a prisoner too. "Whatever you did for one of these least brothers of mine, you did for me"; "we meet ourselves when we meet prisoners." If my life has any purpose today, it is to ring these twin messages to as many readers as possible.

Now take a look at America's correctional system through these two lenses. As you learn more about prison conditions in this chapter, keep reminding yourself who is being subjected to this treatment: 2.3 million human beings who *are* Jesus and who *are* you! And notice who is doing this evil: *you* are. These are *your* tax dollars at work.

The Industrialization of Prison

In all fairness, it must be said that conditions in most U.S. penitentiaries are not overtly inhumane or cruel, and in some respects are actually improving. Thanks for this must go to the American Correctional Association (ACA), a prison-industry lobbying group that has played an enormous role in the overexpansion of the U.S. penal system. As part of its work of persuading lawmakers to build ever more correctional facilities, the ACA has developed a voluntary accreditation and standards system that, ironically enough, has made inmates' lives a little better.

Not all is sunshine and happiness, of course: there are still plenty of troglodytes like Arizona Sheriff Joe Arpaio, who has been noted for "holding people in tents in blistering desert heat and forcing them to wear pink underpants, eat green baloney sandwiches, and labor on 'equal opportunity' chain gangs for men, women and children."[5] On the Web site of the Commission on Safety and Abuse in America's Prisons, cochaired by former U.S. Attorney General Nicholas Katzenbach and federal Court of Appeals Chief Judge John Gibbons, one can find hearings transcripts that document further instances of this kind of treatment.[6] But such cases are increasingly the exception.

Why? Because negative publicity of the Arpaio kind is bad for business, and the prison-industrial-complex is a very big business indeed. The $63 billion spent annually on jails and penitentiaries constitutes 7% of state and local government budgets—an amount matched only by health care—and 747,000 men and women now earn their living as correctional officers.[7] To an enterprise of this magnitude, pink underwear and green baloney are an image problem that threatens the all-important bottom line.

But, while the industrialization of corrections is reducing some of the more glaring forms of barbarity behind bars, this trend has also vastly exacerbated the systematic dehumanization of inmates. The primary goal of prison administrators today is the minimization of cost factors, not the rehabilitation and welfare of the individual men and women in their charge. Although this businesslike approach does not lead to flagrant abuse, it does produce a uniform reduction of all services to a level just barely above the intolerable.

LET THEM EAT CAKE!

For instance, the state in which I am incarcerated spent over $3.00 per convict per day on food as recently as the mid-1990s.[8] Today, however, a typical penitentiary gets by with as little as $1.82, or 61 cents per meal.[9] Several Departments of Correction, including Virginia's, cut costs further by feeding inmates only two of those meals a day on weekends and holidays.[10]

Now take a moment to consider how much food 61 cents can actually buy. A meal at a Richmond, Virginia, homeless shelter costs $1.38, while the average American spends $2.71 per meal.[11] Of course, I am not suggesting that inmates should get more or better food than the homeless, but serving prisoners *less than half* of a soup-kitchen meal surely raises the issue of nutritional adequacy.

While I cannot provide hard data to support this, I and many other of my fellow long-term convicts have noted the dramatic rise in the number of diabetics in the correctional population over the last decade or so. We attribute this to the predominance of starches and refined carbohydrates in our new diets: at *every* meal, we get either bread and potatoes or bread and noodles. It would be interesting to see whether the savings from lower-quality meals are greater than the higher cost of treating so many more diabetics.

Does the new food regimen violate the Eighth Amendment's prohibition against cruel and unusual punishment? Correctional administrators would say no, because all convicts receive exactly the same diet: nothing *unusual* is done to anyone. Unfortunately, this kind of technical defense against claims of mistreatment succeeds regularly in court. To those who must survive on two or three 61-cent meals per day, however, each trip to the chow hall certainly *feels* like abuse.

"Not Clinical Problems, but Business Practices"

Most states' correctional systems also lower operating costs by contracting out medical care for inmates to private corporations like Prison Health Services (PHS), which has been blamed for two dozen deaths in New York alone. "What we were dealing with was not clinical problems but business practices," said James E. Lawrence, director of operations of the State Commission of Corrections, which investigated these fatalities.[12] Another private prison health care provider, Correctional Medical Services (CMS), has even developed "a long checklist of conditions, known as a 'protocol pathway,' [to] discourage treatment" of seriously ill convicts, according to *Harper's Magazine*. As Professor David Santacroce of the University of Michigan puts it, "The fewer patients they treat, the more money they make."[13]

What does privatized medicine behind bars look like in practice? Ask the family of Justin Farver, a twenty-three-year-old with cerebral palsy and a history of mental illness and suicide attempts. After he killed himself in an Illinois jail that contracted with Correctional Medical Services, it emerged that the nurse who had screened him upon intake had lacked any psychiatric training or experience whatsoever. Another nurse later testified that their supervisor had instructed them to refuse inmates mental health services "so that CMS would not get stuck with the medical bills."[14]

To keep costs down, state-operated correctional medical departments have adopted similar practices, as we learn from Elizabeth Dede of the Prison and Jail Project in Americus, Georgia. In October 2005, an inmate wrote her that the Autry State Prison in Pelham, Georgia was housing healthy inmates together with one who had active tuberculosis, a highly contagious and frequently fatal lung infection that requires the immediate isolation of those affected. She contacted Annette Anderson and Joseph Paris of the Georgia Department of Corrections (DOC) Health Services Division; Peggy Chapman, DOC Public Information; James E. Donald, DOC Commissioner; two reporters from the *Atlanta Journal-Constitution*; and Sarah Draper, DOC Ombudsman. Finally, Dede turned to Dr. Rose-Marie Sales, Chief Epidemiologist of the Centers for Disease Control and Prevention, and Elliott Minor, an Associated Press reporter.

These two discovered that 238 inmates and thirteen guards at Autry State Prison had developed latent tuberculosis. After Minor's Associated Press story about the outbreak appeared in state newspapers on December 22, 2005, Ms. Dede finally received a response from the DOC: Yolande Thompson, Director of Public Affairs, acknowledged that "a few" prisoners had had positive tuberculosis skin tests.[15] Two hundred and thirty-eight—"a few"?

Keeping medical expenditures to a minimum by systematically neglecting inmates' health care was developed into a high art in California, which operates the nation's largest prison system. Between 2002 and 2006, the Golden State failed to pay contracting physicians a total of $58 million for services already performed—in effect, an interest-free loan that the chronically cash-strapped correctional department granted itself at the unpaid doctors' expense. Meanwhile, medical staff employed directly by the prison system were paid salaries at least $24 million per year below fair market levels, producing yet more savings for the correctional budget.[16]

This large-scale nonpayment and underpayment of health care professionals had a direct impact on the quality of the services provided to patients, of course. According to Robert Sillen, appointed federal receiver for California's prison medical department under an inmate-filed civil rights suit in 2006,

I have run hospitals, clinics and public health facilities for the past forty years, and medical care in California prisons is unlike anything I've ever seen. Inhumane is the nice term for the conditions. From a clinical standpoint it is almost unrecognizable—an exam room without a sink, a fifty-three-bed medical unit with just one vital sign machine and an emergency room with broken defibrillators are just three glimpses at the bleak picture. The environment for patients, medical providers and custody staff is degrading, unsanitary and unsafe.[17]

More importantly, it is *cheap*—and that is the whole point. Fixing California's correctional health care system under federal Receivership may cost up to *$2 billion* per year in *additional* expenditures.[18]

How did California's prisoners survive before 2006, in a medical system that was underfunded by $2 billion annually? The simple answer is that many did not survive. In the court order appointing Robert Sillen, U.S. District Court Judge Thelton E. Henderson wrote, "it is an uncontested fact that, on average, an inmate in one of California's prisons needlessly dies every six or seven days due to constitutional deficiencies in the ... medical delivery system."[19]

"CAGED ANIMALS"

The modern, efficiency-oriented approach to prison management may have found its purest expression in the supermax penitentiaries that have become so widespread since the 1990s. Built to house the worst of the worst, these facilities keep inmates isolated in single cells for twenty-three hours a day. That may seem like an effective way to reduce violence behind bars, but a carefully designed study of three states' prison systems found that supermax units did little or nothing to lower the overall number of assaults. According to Oregon correctional Sergeant Gary Harkins, "The environment...actually increases the levels of hostility and anger among inmates and staff alike."[20]

What do supermax-style conditions do to the psyches of those housed in such facilities? A report by the New York Correctional

Association describes inmates as being in "states of extreme despera-tion: men weeping in their cells; men who had smeared feces on their bodies or lit their cells on fire; prisoners who cut their own flesh in a form of self-directed mutilation; inmates who rambled incoherently and paced about their cells like caged animals."[21] Fully 25% of prison-ers in that state's supermax S-Blocks have been diagnosed as mentally ill, and half of those surveyed attempted to commit suicide while con-fined there.[22] In Oregon and Indiana, as many as half of all supermax and long-term segregation inmates have been found to be psychologi-cally disabled.[23]

But supermaxes are cost-efficient, and ultimately that is the only thing that matters in the industrialized approach to prison manage-ment. Because supermaxes offer convicts no programs, for instance, New York saves $16,000 per inmate per year by housing a prisoner in an S-Block unit instead of a regular penitentiary.[24]

Thanks to this "bottom line" thinking, roughly 70,000 inmates are held in supermax-type units today, up from 48,000 ten years ago. The five largest state prison systems now house an average of 6.3% of their convict populations in isolation, sometimes for a decade or longer.[25] Since it is difficult to inflict that level of suffering on other human beings, many supermax guards experience their work as "degrading" and "humiliating," according to the New York Correctional Associa-tion: officers end up taking anti-depressants "to cope with the stressful and depressing nature of the job."[26] "When I see a human being who is reduced to throwing feces and urine, it wears me down," says one New Jersey supermax guard. "I am breathing the same canned air, sitting under the same fluorescent lights, listening to the same noises. I don't believe this is good for the officers or good for the prisoners."[27]

SHAKEDOWN

To help front-line staff members overcome their better natures, correc-tional administrators have developed training techniques that encour-age guards to treat all inmates as dangerous beasts. Former Oklahoma

Warden Jack Cowley explains that new guards are taught not to touch prisoners or use their names, but to call them by their numbers. In many correctional systems, officers are trained with a book called *Games Convicts Play*.[28]

Encouraging guards to view inmates as enemies inevitably leads to abuses, of course. In 2005, for instance, the *Atlanta Journal-Constitution* revealed that the warden of Rogers State Prison in Reidsville, Georgia, regularly supervised beatings of prisoners. His goon squad used special black padded gloves to prevent most visible injuries, and the medical department ensured that its records contained no reference to these incidents. As so often happens in such cases, the ensuing official investigation produced only modest results: seven misdemeanor convictions of guards and the retirement of the warden.[29] No one investigated the underlying problem of correctional management techniques that are based on dehumanizing inmates.

These management techniques need not always involve overt violence. What follows is an anonymous prisoner's account of an institutional shakedown at another Georgia prison. While reading this man's narrative, imagine what being required to participate in such an operation does, not only to the convict, but to the officers involved.

Although it was an unusually warm March morning, they were entirely overdressed, all in black: long sleeves, bloused pants, gloves, caps, and boots. They were images of the Third Reich's infamous storm troopers, but these were Georgia Department of Corrections Tactical Units. It was an unannounced assault on the state prison at Jackson, home to Death Row.

The agenda was to search-and-seize. The purpose was to isolate-and-intimidate. In the event there was any doubt, we were about to learn a lesson in dehumanization.

Three officers stood before this cell: two men, one woman. I was ordered to strip. The routine is standard. You open your mouth, you lift your genitals, you spread your cheeks, and you cough on demand. Attired in boxers, there was the directive to face the opposite wall. Over and again he barked, "Do you understand?"

I complied; but I did not speak. Nary a word.

Once my hands were cuffed behind my back, the female guard said, "I've got him." She wrapped her fingers around the chain that linked the handcuffs. Her other hand was placed on my shoulder. There were taunting questions, silly instructions, and inane comments. She then steered me out of the cell to a security fence. She pressed me against it. "Don't turn; don't talk."

She needed not worry. I looked through the steel and concrete maze until I located a section of sky. I prayed.

Twenty-five minutes later I was led back into the cell. More attempts to humiliate. More "Do you understand?" More silence.

As the door slammed, I became nauseated.

Personal property is limited: seven books, letters, photographs, underwear, towels, and shoes. The prison issues uniforms and linen. Everything I owned was scattered across the bunk, piled upon the floor, or dumped on the cabinet. No care, no consideration, no compassion, no concern—to the contrary. I believe they reduce us to a subhuman status to justify their subhuman behavior. Their actions were not designed to uncover contraband. They "tossed" the cell to degrade the occupant.

My Bible was beside the toilet. I struggled with tears as I bent to retrieve it. I turned to find them at the bars. I wiped my Bible with a rumpled shirt, kissed the cover, and informed the trio, "God will forgive you."

I had nothing illegal: so they took legal possessions. "You have to take something."

The one permitted coffee cup. A plastic bowl. A couple of sheets. They could not remove my dignity.

I have survived, a bit weaker by the experience. Everyone violated had his own story. Some had pictures soiled, others had papers wrinkled, others lost important papers or addresses of friends and family. The drug dogs pounced here, salivated there. At least the canines were not consciously cruel.

They did not discover weapons, escape materials, alcohol, drugs, or cash—only "nuisance contraband."

This fact tended to fuel their anger.

They condemn me.

I pity them.

Signed me,

A Human Being [30]

This account bears a remarkable resemblance to a well-documented and litigated incident at a medium-security Georgia prison nine years earlier.[31] My files contain nearly identical descriptions by inmates in correctional systems across the country; in fact, I chose this man's narrative precisely because it is so entirely typical of what virtually all of America's 2.3 million convicts experience regularly. This is average, normal, commonplace—standard operating procedure.

As the anonymous author above suggests, institutional shakedowns primarily serve a psychological purpose: creating and perpetuating an atmosphere of hostility between front-line officers and inmates. All day long, guards and prisoners must interact in the housing units and at work, so conversations about football or music are inevitable. Staff members cannot help but begin to see convicts as human beings, as Texas warden Jim Willett explains: "A simple example is a guy who's messed up on dope out there for a while and doin' all these crazy things, and he commits this horrible crime, and now he's down here for ten years, and he's dried out and his real personality comes out. Some of these guys got *great* personality."[32] That kind of thinking is terribly dangerous, of course, because it calls into question the whole prison-industrial complex.

If a man has spent ten years behind bars and is no longer addicted to drugs, why not release him? Every one of America's 747,000 correctional officers knows at least one convict who has "great personality" and should be sent home. But how many guards and administrators and Prison Health Service nurses would lose their jobs if 747,000 inmates were freed?

Institutional shakedowns are an effective way to avoid those questions. By requiring their officers to humiliate the prisoners they must deal with every day, correctional administrators effectively extinguish any friendly feelings or sense of a shared humanity that may have arisen between them. And habituating guards to treat inmates like naked, chained animals also makes it much easier to feed them 61-cent meals, deny them proper medical services, and isolate them for years in a supermax unit. None of this is cruel and unusual—just business as usual.

DISPLACED AGGRESSION

As necessary as dehumanization is to the efficient operation of today's correctional facilities, the sort of treatment described above does have some unwelcome side effects. The Commission on Safety and Abuse in America's Prisons reports, for example, that the number of inmate assaults on guards rose 27% between 1999 and 2000 alone.[33] And since convicts, like all human beings, often displace their aggression, we should not be surprised to find that the number of prisoner-on-prisoner assaults is also rising robustly—at a rate one and a half times that of overall penitentiary population growth.[34]

Because official statistics on violence behind bars are generally acknowledged to be very unreliable, I have chosen not to provide an estimate of the total number of assaults here.[35] The figures above on the rate of increase in reported incidents are useful, however, because they provide evidence of a powerful trend: the situation is getting worse. Much worse.

The contagion of violence cannot be contained behind penitentiary walls, of course. When those felons originally convicted of *nonviolent* drug, public order, or property offenses are released, respectively 18.4, 18.5, and 21.9% will be arrested for *violent* crimes.[36] Please read that sentence again and consider the implications: the experience of prison turns one in five or one in six nonviolent criminals into violent ones. Those are the bitter fruits of the modern approach to corrections: more victims in *your* neighborhood.

According to a new study by Professors M. Keith Chen of Yale University and Jesse M. Shapiro of the University of Chicago, "harsher prison conditions are associated with significantly more post-release crime." The study focused on a group of federal inmates with virtually identical criminal histories, but with slightly different Bureau of Prisons (BOP) security risk scores. Because some of these men's scores fell just below a BOP "cutoff," they were sent to less restrictive facilities; others, whose score fell barely above the "cutoff," were transferred to tougher prisons. The result? Those convicts who did time in maximum-security penitentiaries were *twice as likely* to re-offend within three years of release as their nearly identical counterparts who served sentences in medium-security correctional centers.[37] Think about that for a moment: tens of thousands of crimes could be prevented just by treating inmates a little less brutally!

"Entitled to Ordinary Respect"

Where can we turn to find an alternative to current American penal practices? To Europe, for instance, where the Committee for Prevention of Torture, a powerful independent commission established in 1987, has unlimited access to all places of detention: prisons, juvenile centers, psychiatric hospitals, and police holding facilities. By contrast, only three states in the U.S. have independent review boards to oversee conditions behind bars, and even they lack the authority to enforce change.[38] The Special Litigation Section of the Department of Justice once promoted reform in state and federal correctional systems; but between 1996 and 2004 the number of investigations declined from eleven to two, and the number of civil rights court actions fell from seven to zero.[39]

However, lack of oversight is only one example of the difference between European and American approaches to penology, as Professor James Q. Whitman of Yale Law School explains:

> Prisoners are supposed to be treated like ordinary human beings in continental Europe, entitled to ordinary respect.... Degradation

is regarded as so unacceptable in those countries that they have generally banned the use of prison uniforms—a far cry from stripping prisoners naked to humiliate them. … [I]nmates have privacy rights in Europe—which means, for example, that they are not housed behind barred doors. Certainly continental inmates are not obliged to use toilets in the open view of guards of the opposite sex, as they may be in America. In a country such as Germany, ordinary labor law applies to prison inmates, giving them the same kinds of protections accorded workers in the outside world. There are even rules requiring that prisoners be addressed respectfully, as Herr So-and-so.[40]

In Finland, incarcerated felons address guards by their first name and live in rooms resembling college dormitories. "We believe that the loss of freedom is the major punishment, so we try to make [prison] as nice as possible," a Finnish warden explains his country's approach to penology. [41]

In an article describing this "ridiculously lenient" treatment, an American journalist suggested that it was surprising Finland's crime rate had not exploded as a result.[42] Readers of this chapter should not be surprised, however, to learn that Finnish ex-convicts re-offend at much lower rates than their U.S. counterparts. More than likely, this is in large part *because* they were not subjected to the dehumanization of modern cost-effective correctional management techniques.

TACIT PREMISE

Some American prison administrators, such as former Kansas corrections secretary Patrick McManus, have come to see the advantages of the European approach to criminal justice: together with Dr. Andrew Coyle of London's International Centre for Prison Studies, he helped develop *A Human Rights Approach to Prison Management*.[43] Maryland's Department of Corrections is also "moving from a very restrictive philosophy of managing offenders to…a culture of safety, dignity, respect and accountability," according to Deputy Secretary for Operations Mary

Livers. "We're moving away from that feeling of being safe [only] when offenders are all locked up, to one where we're actually safer because we have inmates out of their cells, involved in something hopeful and productive."[44]

Although that last sentence certainly sounds encouraging, its implications are perilous. Please read it again, and consider: might the same principle be applicable to sentencing? Could it be true that "we're actually safer" if we have offenders out of prison, "involved in something hopeful and productive in society"—some form of community service and restitution, say?

In Chapter 2 we learned that other industrialized countries have answered those questions with a resounding "yes." The very same human rights considerations that persuaded Europeans to make their penitentiaries as humane as possible also compelled them to lock up their fellow human beings as rarely as possible. As a result, their incarceration rates are one-fifth (Great Britain) to one-tenth (Scandinavia) of America's.

And European crime rates? No worse than this country's. Prison turns out to have very little impact on levels of offending, as we saw in Chapter 2. From a practical viewpoint, it is difficult indeed to justify the caging of humans.

So *A Human Rights Approach to Prison Management* inevitably entails the closure of many, perhaps most, U.S. correctional facilities. But not even the Commission on Safety and Abuse in America's Prisons seems willing to recognize the long-term consequences of acknowledging the humanity of inmates. In its otherwise laudable report *Confronting Confinement*, the commission has much to say about prison conditions, but relatively little about oversentencing and excessive incarceration.

There is a reason for this reticence, of course: correctional officers' job security, a subject we examined in the preceding chapter. If the commission had openly declared that humanizing prisons means closing many of them, it would not have received as much cooperation from correctional employees. We, however, are not limited by such considerations and should guard ourselves against the unspoken assumptions of "experts."

To hear them tell it, the solution to the problem of mental illness in prison is better delivery of psychiatric services to inmates, for example. Incarcerated mothers need teleconferences with their children; elderly convicts should have wheelchair-accessible dorms and hospice programs; drug addicts ought to be housed in "therapeutic community" cellblocks. What is the tacit premise in each case? That better prisons are the answer.

But we can consider other alternatives. Perhaps the mentally ill should be in hospitals, mothers with their children, the elderly in retirement homes, and addicts in treatment centers. Perhaps a cage will always be a cage, no matter how humane it is made.

And perhaps we should bear in mind Winston Churchill's warning, delivered on July 20, 1910, in a speech to the House of Commons:

> The mood and temper of the public in regard to the treatment of crime and criminals is one of the most unfailing tests of any civilisation of any country[,... a] sign and proof of the living virtue in it....
>
> The first principle which should guide anyone trying to establish a good system of prisons should be to prevent as many people as possible getting there at all. There is an injury to the individual, there is a loss to the State whenever a person is committed to prison for the first time, and every care, consistent with the maintenance of law and order, must be taken constantly to minimise the number of persons who are committed to gaol.[45]

*   *   *

To conclude our examination of prison conditions, allow me to introduce to you one of the most extraordinary men I have ever met: Ras Talawa Tafari. How I wish that those politicians who favor a "tough on crime" approach to the judicial and correctional systems would meet him! But at least you will meet him, in our next interview.

Before we read his story, however, some background information is necessary. In 1999, the Virginia Department of Corrections changed its grooming policy, called DOP 864, to require all inmates to shave off their beards and cut their hair to no more than one inch in length.[446] Prison administrators claimed this was necessary to prevent convicts from hiding contraband in their hair, changing their appearance suddenly with a haircut, or identifying themselves as gang members by their hairstyles. As David Fahti of the ACLU points out, however, "some prison systems allow prisoners to have their hair any length so long as it's neatly groomed. So, the idea that you can't run a prison without having hair length restrictions is just not true."[47]

All this would be just a tempest in a correctional teapot, were it not for the fact that the Rastafarian faith and some Muslim sects require believers to leave their beards and/or hair uncut. While most inmate-members of these faiths complied with the grooming policy, several dozen refused—and were immediately moved to their respective prisons' segregation units. There they "remain in their cells twenty-four hours a day" and are allowed "three showers and three one-hour exercise periods per week," according to Larry Traylor, Virginia Department of Corrections spokesperson.[48]

Having spent six weeks in segregation myself, I can assure you that life in "the hole," as segregation is also known, can break many men. During my seg. time I personally witnessed, or met inmates who engaged in, aberrant behavior like drumming on their metal sinks all night; exposing themselves to the nurse on her morning rounds; becoming so paranoid that they refuse to leave their cells even for the three weekly showers; gouging chunks of flesh out of their forearms with sharpened pieces of plastic; or smearing the walls of their cells with feces. That is what prolonged isolation can do to the human mind. None of this is at all unusual in "the hole."

What *is* highly unusual is that the Virginia Department of Corrections has left those prisoners who refused to cut their hair in segregation *continually since 1999.* Only those who have had a taste of "the hole" can appreciate the monstrous cruelty of this punishment. Judging by my own six weeks in seg., all of these men *should* be stark raving mad.

But Ras Talawa Tafari was anything but insane when I spoke with him in the one-man "dog cages" in which seg. inmates are placed for their "exercise." In fact, he is one of the most pleasant individuals I have come to know in my entire penitentiary career. His amazing survival, both spiritually and psychologically, persuaded me that God is truly on his side.

In the summer of 2005, the U.S. Supreme Court's decision in *Cutter v. Wilkinson* gave Ras and his fellow believers some hope that their trial by fire might be coming to an end. The *Cutter* ruling upheld the Religious Land Use and Institutionalized Persons Act (RLUIPA), which forbids prison administrators to "impose a substantial burden" on religious practices in correctional facilities unless there is a "compelling" reason to do so.[49] Thanks to this decision, the ACLU suit on behalf of Rastafarian and Muslim inmates who refused to obey Virginia's prison grooming policy now will be allowed to proceed through the U.S. District Court in Richmond.[50]

Our next interview subject may become one of the first inmates to benefit from *Cutter* and RLUIPA. Let us proceed, then, to the talk with Ras Talawa Tafari.

INTERVIEW WITH RAS TALAWA TAFARI

Ras Talawa Tafari was sentenced to forty-seven years for armed robbery and abduction in 1990. [Interviewer's Note: In accordance with the interviewee's wishes, the text of this interview reflects his speech patterns and spelling preferences.]

Q: Tell us a little about your life before you were arrested for your current offense.

A: I was born in 1972 and reared in the metropolitan area of Washington, D.C., and Maryland, as well as in Jamaica. My father worked in construction, carpentry, automobile repair, food processing—whatever it took to support his family! My mother worked at a hospital and raised her children and, later, some of her grandchildren. My parents were not very religious, but they sent my brothers, sister, and I to Sunday School.

Q: Who introduced you to Rastafarian culture?

A: My older cousins. They always would tell me how Rasta should and should not live, and they quoted and read the Bible and the words of His Imperial Majesty, Emperor Haile Selassie I. They would take I along to Rastafarian services, called groundings, to give I a firm foundation, they said.

Q: What were you doing before your arrest?

A: I worked at a hospital, doing building maintenance and grounds work. But the wages were not enough to keep up with the ways of the world, so I was selling a little ganja [i.e., marijuana] on the side.

Q: Did that lead to your trouble with the law?

A: Not directly. One of my three victims beat one of my codefendants out of some money, so the six of us went to get the money back. We robbed him and his partner and some other people at the location, and they told, and we were arrested.

Q: How do you feel about your crime now?

A: First and foremost, I have come to see that my desire for vengeance and quick gain led to loss of freedom and the ability to share a life with the family who has always been there for I. I recognize that I am where I am at due to my own actions, and I am aware that I alone am responsible for my future behavior. The only way I can have any real enjoyment in life is to live crime-free; there is no quick road to success.

Q: Well, that sounds very good, but why did you not figure all this out before you committed your crime?

A: I was only eighteen when I came to prison, and I believe the most important thing I have done since 1990 is to make a major paradigm shift in terms of I thinking and, thus, I behavior. There is no doubt that the natural process of maturation has played a prominent role. Today [Interviewer's Note: The interview was conducted in 2005.] I am thirty-three, an age I feel is characterized by reassessing priorities, coming to terms with my past, and choosing how I want to live my life journey.

Q: What were your early years in prison like?

A: Basically, I tried to keep to myself and not get caught up in the folly that surrounded me. I knew I had already made one big mistake, and I was not going to do anything else senseless to keep myself in prison any longer than I had to be. I earned certificates for building maintenance and carpentry, and in 1994 I received my GED.

Q: Did you participate in any religious programs?

A: Yes, I went to Rastafari programs wherever they had them, but I have also attended other religious services so I could learn about them. True religion means to obey the laws of creation, and it leads to unconditional love for JAH—God—Allah—Grandfather Spirit, or whatever one may choose to call the Almighty. The goal is to lead you to spirituality and to build a personal relationship with JAH.

Q: What attracted you to the Rastafarian faith?

A: The love and peaceful vibe; the music, the food, and the [dread] locks; and the stories of martyrdom and heroism. But it was not until I became older that I started to understand the spiritual aspects of Rastafari, not just the physical parts. In prison, my faith in JAH has only become stronger; the prodigal son has returned home.

Q: Tell us more about Rastafarianism.

A: Well, the Bible is "JAH Word" and the foundation of Rastafari. Rastafari calls God the Father JAH, which is the praise form of Jehovah (Psalms 68:4). Rastafari knows that JAH the Son, Christ, was there in the beginning, and that the Holy Spirit is the breath of JAH Almighty, which gives life (John 1, Genesis 2, Job 33).

Q: How does Haile Selassie I, the first Emperor of Ethiopia, fit into all this?

A: King Solomon and the Queen of Sheba had a son, Menelik, who established the Solomonic Dynasty in Ethiopia, where the Ark of the Covenant rests today. Emperor Haile Selassie I, being of the line of Judah, root of David, and on David's throne, fulfills many prophecies of Scripture. Also, "Haile Selassie" means "the might and power of the Holy Trinity."

Q: How does Rastafarianism relate to Christianity?

A: In the Acts of the Apostles 8:26–39, Philip baptized the Ethiopian official, and from that day onward the Word of JAH has continued to grow in the hearts of Ethiopians—all Rastafarians.

Q: Please explain the role that marijuana plays in Rastafarian religion.

A: Ganja is an herbal plant divined by JAH for us to use. It heals the trinity of body, mind, and spirit; lifts you toward the higher levels of spiritual consciousness; and makes you aware of the importance of your personal identity to your functional wholeness, health, and growth. Ganja is used to lift depression, ease hypertension, and treat common diseases like glaucoma, asthma, bladder irritation, ulcers, and many more. When used in a gathering, it symbolizes the act of unification amongst those gathered together in the sight of the most I JAH—a sacramental act (Genesis 1:24; Revelation 22:2).

Q: Please explain the role that uncut hair, or the growing of dreadlocks, plays in Rastafarian religion.

A: Rasta believe strongly in the laws of nature, and growing our locks is the fullest expression of nature. Also, growing locks means abiding with HIM holy words of the Bible: "Ye shall not round the corners of your head, neither shall thou mar the corners of thy beard" (Leviticus 19:27). See also Leviticus 21:5; Ezekiel 8:3; Song of Solomon 5:11; Numbers 6:5; Deuteronomy 23:21–23. This is the vow of Rastafari! With all this in mind, one must come to understand that the growing of locks is our divine and human right.

Q: What other tenets of your religion do you observe in prison?

A: I am a vegan. In general, Rastafarians are very particular about what goes into the body. The human body is seen as a reflection of divinity, made in the image of JAH, and should be treated as such. I refuse to soil and desecrate my system by consuming dead flesh, or to make my stomach a cemetery by consuming meat, fish, eggs, or poultry.

Q: During the early years of your incarceration, were you able to practice your faith, and how?

A: Before 1999, the whole Rastafarian congregation held weekly scheduled services, one for worship and praise, the second for Bible study and life skills. We had festival celebrations on January 7 (Ethiopian Feast of the Nativity of Christ), July 23 (Birth of Emperor Haile Selassie I), and November 2 (Coronation of His Majesty, Emperor Haile Selassie I). At these gatherings, there would be video and audio documentaries, poetry, prose, display of artwork, and playing of instruments. It was a nice, peaceful experience to come together in JAH name to give thanks and praises, and to reason about positive subject matter.

Q: So what happened in 1999 to change things?

A: The Virginia Department of Corrections issued a new grooming policy, DOP 864, that requires all male inmates to wear their hair very short and to shave off their beards. The reasons given were safety, sanitation, identification, and the rubber-stamp catch-all: security. Sanctions for noncompliance are a mandatory three disciplinary charges for "disobeying an order," with five-, ten- and fifteen-day isolation increments as punishment; reduction in good-time allowance; loss of all programs and work assignments; increase in security level; placement in an isolation-style segregation unit; loss of visitation and phone calls, except with lawyers; commissary privileges restricted to hygiene and writing material; and no books or newspapers from the library.

Q: So you have been living in segregation under these conditions since 1999?

A: Yes.

Q: What were your feelings when you learned that you either had to cut off your dreadlocks or go to segregation?

A: My thoughts were, what does JAH want me to learn from this situation? I never had any thoughts of breaking my Nazirite vow, which is the consecration of JAH upon my head as an outward appearance of inward change. What I did was to continue to hold faith and trust in JAH to guide me through this plight.

Q: What practical steps did you take to try to help yourself?

A: I wrote complaints, grievances, and appeals—but to no avail. I also wrote letters to various organizations, seeking assistance. My goal was to get everyone together in the Rasta and reggae communities, and anyone else that would help.

Q: Many Rastafarians and Muslims [who initially refused to cut their beards] eventually decided to follow the grooming policy. What made you different?

A: I can only say that JAH never led me to feel that this situation was a burden enough to bow. I know that HIM would never forsake me! I fear not what man can do to me, but give thanks and praises unto the Almighty for what HIM has done and is doing to me.

Q: What do you think of those men who cut their dreadlocks off?

A: That is between them and JAH. I did have thoughts like, "If you won't stand up for a just cause, what will you stand for?" But I am personally aware of only five persons who bowed to the policy. A lot of people went home [because their sentences were over].

Q: What were the reasons those five men gave for cutting their dreadlocks off?

A: For example, one person's mandatory release date was 2002. He had already served eighteen years. [But, because of the disciplinary infractions for not complying with the policy, his release date] went up to 2008. Another person was trying to get a transfer to another prison to be with his brother, whom he had not seen in many years.

Q: Has your decision not to comply with the grooming policy affected your release date or your parole?

A: I am told by many people that the reason I am not granted parole is due to my stand against the grooming policy. My codefendants and I all had the same charges, and I do not have any institutional infractions that can be used against me, and I have a stable parole plan. But I am the only one left; my five codefendants all went home. What else could it be, other than the grooming policy?

Q: What did the Department of Corrections do with those of you who refused to cut off your locks?

A: After a year or so, they put us all in one segregation unit at Bland Correctional Center and then at Buckingham Correctional Center. There were thirty of us then. Being in one place gave us a chance to come together to worship JAH and plan a course of action. Every Sabbath, we would all stand at the cell doors and speak through the bars: chanting songs of praise, reading Bible Scriptures, and praying together. And we worked together to contact lawyers, DJs, and a publisher, to start knocking down the walls of Babylon. Overall, everyone knew the goal of the mission and was doing their part.

Q: How long did that last?

A: Until January 2004, when the Department of Corrections split us all up. I was sent here, to Brunswick Correctional Center, and for the first time since 1999, I was granted some limited library privileges. But other than that, things remain the same.

Q: How have the staff treated you?

A: For the most part, if you treat them with respect, they treat you with respect. You reap what you sow.

Q: No harassment at all?

A: Some of the guards would tell certain inmates that they should just cut their hair because they are causing the sincere practitioners of their faith to look bad. And they would apply psychological pressure, picking at them until they allowed their anger and emotions to cause them to do senseless things. But I personally did not have problems with the guards.

Q: Have you received any support from the staff?

A: Yes, I have received plenty of kind words and encouragement from guards and even administrators in every segregation unit I have been in so far. They would tell I to stay strong, keep faith, you are doing a good thing. Some of them would tell me that if they were in my shoes, they would not cut their hair either, and that they do not agree with the grooming policy. They have also told me that they do not see a [security] problem with a person growing his hair.

Q: How do other inmates, who pass through the segregation units for normal disciplinary charges, react to your decision not to cut your hair?

A: It be mixed vibes. Some of them are very supportive, but others think I am crazy. They speak of how they would miss their pacifiers: television, commissary, and cigarettes. But I have had some of the best experiences in my life while being in segregation, and I feel that some seg. time would do everyone some good—if they let it!

Q: I spent six weeks in a segregation cell across from yours, and I agree. But that was six weeks, and you have been in seg. for six years [at the time of the interview in 2005]! Surely you must miss some of the things available to inmates in general population?

A: Well, I feel—g.p. or seg., it is what you make it! When I was in general population, I did not eat the junk food from the commissary and I was not into TV—except for PBS, Discovery Channel, and the news. I do miss jogging on the recreation yard, but I can jog in place in the cell. If the DOC came into this cell and took everything and painted the windows black, I could still stand firm and not bow. King David said in Psalms 34:18, "JAH is near to those who are of a broken heart and saves such as have a contrite spirit."

Q: Do you miss contact with your family?

A: All inmates who refused to comply with the grooming policy were denied visits and phone calls from 1999 until August 2003. Since then, I can make two phone calls a month. I do not get visits because I do not want family and friends to travel a long way to see me behind glass. [Interviewer's Note: He means a "non-contact" visit, as opposed to the regular "contact" visits allowed for general population inmates.] I enjoy the solitude in seg.!

Q: How do you keep abreast of the news without TV and newspapers?

A: They let me keep my radio, so I can listen to NPR, BBC, and AM talk radio. Since I came here [to Brunswick Correctional Center, in 2004], I have been able to request books, and the library sometimes sends newspapers. I used to read a lot when I was in general population [i.e., before 1999], but in segregation I have more time to read and study the Bible.

Q: Do you miss talking to people?

A: In general population, I enjoyed going to the library to reason with people, and I miss that type of intellectual charge. I do not get much good conversation any more. Lately, all people want to talk about are perverted and senseless topics that I care nothing about. But when I do get a good conversation, I take advantage of it and learn and give what I can.

Q: How has your faith sustained you during your time in segregation?

A: I pray every day, and there have been many instances where the belief in the Almighty has sustained I in this plight. Since I have been in seg., my father has passed away, and at first my emotions were mixed up for a while. But I know that JAH is the creator, writer, and director of the script of life. JAH is before alpha and omega, and Rasta just treads through creation in a meditation on HIM vibration of truth. Babylon cannot stand up to JAH truth, for JAH light shine brighta, brighta! Give thanks and praises for life everlasting, for not having to taste death, which is the fate of this world.

Q: How do you think God feels about what you are doing?

A: I trust in JAH and HIM Word: "Blessed are they which are persecuted for righteousness' sake," Matthew 5:10! So I know JAH is elated with my actions, and I live to please JAH, not the DOC.

Q: Do you think of yourself as a martyr or hero, as in those stories your cousins told you as you were growing up?

A: When I think of martyrs and heroes, I think of persons who have endured so much more suffering than I. What I am doing does not seem so great. Many have done and are doing much greater.

Q: Have you and the others received support from the Rastafarian community?

A: Yes. They have written and called the DOC, the ACLU, and the Department of Justice. Also, they have run articles in the Rastafari and reggae magazines and newspapers, spoken about it on reggae radio shows and at festivals, and posted the situation on the Internet. The Rasta out in society has come together to help the Rasta within. Now it is in JAH's hands.

Q: How about the regular media?

A: Every media organization that I have written to did not respond. None of the mainstream media showed any interest until this year [i.e., 2005]. It is a blessing for us that the newspapers have decided to take an interest at last. I do not know why they have, but I give thanks.

Q: Does your family support you?

A: Yes. They are not the bowing type, and they are very vexed that the DOC would do such a wicked thing.

Q: What do you think will happen to you now that the U.S. Supreme Court affirmed the constitutionality of the Religious Land Use and Institutionalized Persons Act (RLUIPA) in *Cutter v. Wilkinson?*

A: Basically, we have won, and now the DOC will have to bow. Two of the lawyers had a meeting with [the Director of the Virginia DOC], and he said they may send us to another prison system outside of Virginia that does not have a grooming policy. HIM righteousness and justice will prevail.

Q: How would you summarize your sojourn in segregation?

A: Grace and faith! Maybe I am a madman, maybe I am a fool with a crazy notion, Selassie I know. Within the depths of I heart and soul, I feel that everything I am experiencing right now is given to I through the grace of the Most High to strengthen I and help I learn lessons that I could not learn but by going through such experiences. One day I will look back and reflect upon these experiences and see how they contributed to I life and making me the person I am destined to be. My faith has taught I that JAH has sent I here to show the power of HIM divine love, the love that reaches every living thing. This is what I try to do.

A Postscript

On September 19, 2006, inmates at Ras Talawa Tafari's prison were issued a memorandum entitled *Revision to Inmate Grooming Policy Enforcement*:

> Inmate grooming *standards*...have not been changed. The Department's procedure for *enforcement* of the standards has been modified as follows:
>
> - All inmates who refuse to comply with the Department's Grooming Policy will remain in segregation status....
> - Conviction of Offense Code 133 will carry a penalty of reprimand only....
> - Inmates who refuse to comply with grooming standards will not be restricted from earning good conduct time.

In other words, Ras Talawa Tafari must remain in "the hole," but the Department of Corrections can pretend that it is no longer punishing him! A 1995 U.S. Supreme Court decision called *Sandin v. Connor* established that segregation, by itself, is not punishment but one of the "ordinary incidents of prison life." By limiting punishment to a mere reprimand and allowing segregated inmates to earn good conduct credits, the Department of Corrections has cleverly finessed the new standards of *Cutter v. Wilkinson* to keep Ras Talawa Tafari on his cross. Pontius Pilate and the Sanhedrin would be proud.

QUESTIONS FOR REFLECTION AND DISCUSSION

SCRIPTURE—Before he was a prisoner, Christ was a suspect and a defendant. Go through the events of his Passion as recounted in the four Gospels and compare them point for point with police and trial procedures today. Begin with the use of a paid undercover informant and a nighttime arrest by a heavily armed SWAT team. Does Christ's coercive interrogation remind you of *NYPD Blue*? Continue all the way through to his execution.

CRIMINOLOGY—The author argues that correctional administrators use shakedowns not to find contraband, but to create an atmosphere of tension between front-line guards and inmates to prevent fraternization and maintain control. Is the government using similar ploys to create tension and maintain control in society at large? What law-enforcement actions appear to be motivated by security concerns, but produce no measurable results—other than sustaining a public atmosphere of fear and raising calls for yet more "law and order"? (Hint: Look for the use of the word "war," as in War on Drugs or War on Terror.)

SELF-EXAM—When the Abu Ghraib scandal came to light, Americans were particularly shocked by the sexual overtones of the abuse of Iraqi detainees. The author's description of a shakedown—and his description of his eleven-month stay in a supermax penitentiary in his previous book, *The Convict Christ*—indicate that mistreatment with sexual overtones also occurs in U.S. prisons. Try to imagine conducting shakedowns year after year: might you begin to enjoy this?

INTERVIEW—Do you believe the Department of Corrections' claim that the sole motivation for DOP 864 is security? Reflect on the military's ritual of shaving new recruits' heads to enforce conformity; in that context, compelling uniformity of appearance and behavior is considered acceptable. How does prison differ—if it does at all?

Internet—Visit the Web site of the Commission on Safety and Abuse (www.prisoncommission.org) and read the transcripts of testimony given by ex-inmates and former correctional officers.

Immersion—Find a prisoner advocacy group "near" you; this may require going out of state, unfortunately. Speak with a representative in person or by phone and learn more about the issues this group addresses. Begin donating to them regularly.

Chapter 8

Paul and Prison Ministry

In Chapter 6 we saw that Mesach, Shadrach, and Abednego were charged with violating King Nebuchadnezzar's new religious edict because the Chaldeans wanted to recoup their lucrative positions in the royal bureaucracy. Of course, there are many other scriptural incidents where financial motives lead to the arrest and execution of innocents: after Jesus chased the moneylenders out of the temple, for instance, the chief priests grew "indignant" and began plotting against him (Matthew 21:12, 15). So we should not be surprised to find economic factors at work when Paul was arrested in Philippi.

The apostle cured "a slave girl with an oracular spirit, who used to bring a large profit to her owners through her fortune-telling.... When her owners saw that their hope of profit was gone, they seized Paul and Silas and dragged them...before the local authorities," who "threw them into prison" (Acts 16:16, 19, 23). There, the slave girl's masters had Paul and Silas "beaten with rods" by the magistrates (16:22). They then "instructed the jailer to guard them securely," an order that he followed with apparent relish: "he put them in the innermost cell and secured their feet to a stake" (16:23, 24).

If that seems just a little excessive—Paul and Silas were charged with nothing more serious than advocating unusual religious customs, after all (16:21)—then we must remember that correctional departments throughout the ages have attracted people who enjoy punishing others. Of course, not every prison guard has this character defect—but many do. In the case of the Philippian jailer, we see the flip side of his punitive personality on display just a few lines later: he "drew his sword and was about to kill himself" when he suspected that all his prisoners had escaped (16:27). His mercilessness toward himself was simply another form of his mercilessness toward Paul and Silas.

However, the prison guard's cruelty did not deter our two heroes from launching an early faith-based in-house correctional program: they began "praying and singing hymns to God as the prisoners listened" (16:25). For those interested in helping inmates, this scene reflects a useful guiding principle for effectively changing lives behind bars: ministers and teachers cannot just swoop in, deliver their sermon or lesson, and then depart. To some extent, they have to join convicts in their lives and enter into their painful, lonely existence. Paul and Silas got the prisoners to listen because they related to them as equals, not from on high.

This approach proved to be very successful: "there was suddenly such a severe earthquake that the foundations of the jail shook; all the doors flew open, and the chains of all were pulled loose" (16:26). In those two sentences we find a wealth of correctional wisdom:

- Earthquakes were often a sign of divine action, as when Jesus "gave up his spirit" on the cross (Matthew 27:50, 51). But on this occasion there were no choirs of angels; God sometimes works miracles without revealing himself as their author.
- What brought about this particular miracle was the combination of Paul and Silas "praying and singing" *and* the prisoners "listening." If lives are to change, both sides must do their part.
- Reforming the Philippian inmates "shook...the foundations of the jail"; it undermined the very basis and purpose of the prison. *If criminals stop thinking and acting criminally, who needs penitentiaries?*
- Christ came to proclaim "freedom for the prisoners," as he explained in the synagogue at Nazareth at the start of his public ministry (Luke 4:18). When that passage is read nowadays, however, it is usually spiritualized out of all recognition: the "prisoners" are captives of sin, not ordinary convicts, and the "freedom" they gain is inner liberation, not release from literal chains. But in the Philippian jail we see that real inmates were literally freed from a real correctional center.

Could it be that this is what Jesus meant when he proclaimed "freedom for the prisoners"? I believe so—but only if inmates have really, truly reformed! The convicts in the jail at Philippi, for instance, demonstrated their changed character in the very next line of Acts 16: even though they were free to leave, they remained on the prison premises so their jailer would not commit suicide (16:27). Perhaps only someone who has been incarcerated himself can appreciate how much courage that took.

Note, however, that the Philippian prisoners were only able to prove themselves because they were given a genuine second chance—because they were extended real trust. In our interview with Kent I., he made this point as well: "you can never know unless you open the gate and meet" the person. What would happen if the same energy that is currently directed toward designing ever-improved security devices were instead directed toward inventing better ways for convicts to learn how to handle trust responsibly?

Perhaps something like this: the Philippian jailer converted to Christianity, took Paul and Silas in, "bathed their wounds," and "provided a meal" for them (cf. 16:30–34). As we saw above, this guard showed no mercy to prisoners or even to himself, so he must have been profoundly shocked by the mercy that inmates now showed him by not fleeing the jail. The scum of the earth had saved him from killing himself!

Remember, while our discussion above has treated Paul and Silas as in-house experts in prison ministry, the Philippian prison guard would have seen them as mere convicts. His job and quite probably his entire worldview were based on the premise that these two men were threats to society. For a jailer, of all people, to take them into his home and care for them personally—that is indeed a powerful testimony to the depth of his conversion (16:33).

Now imagine what might happen if prison systems across the country *paid* each one of America's 747,000 correctional employees to pick one convict, "[bring him] up into his house," and help that felon on a one-on-one basis! Why do we consider this crazy? Years later, after Paul's arrest in Jerusalem and extradition to Rome, he "was allowed to live by himself, with the soldier who was guarding him" (28:16). *Individual* correctional/reentry officers—ancient Rome was able to make that idea work, so why not America?

How did Luke, the author of Acts, manage to pack so many sound ideas about rehabilitating criminals into that short story about Paul and Silas's stay in the Philippian jail? Because the good doctor had in-depth, firsthand experience with one reformed offender: Paul. As we know from the "we" sections of Acts and from 2 Timothy 4:11, Luke accompanied Paul on some of his missionary journeys and stayed with him during his long final incarceration. But he never forgot that his good friend, the great apostle to the gentiles, was a killer.

Take a moment to read Acts 28:3–5, which describes what happened after the ship taking Paul to Rome sank off the coast of Malta and all the survivors spent the night camping outdoors. It was not by accident that a skilled and sophisticated writer like Luke placed this incident in such a prominent position, immediately before Paul's triumphant entry into Rome. What we have here is a classic case of dramatic irony: a character makes a statement that only the reader, but not the character, knows to be true.

"This man must certainly be a murderer," the natives of Malta exclaimed when the snake bit Paul's hand. And, of course, this was true: in any U.S. federal court, the apostle would have been convicted of felony murder for taking part in a hate crime, the stoning of Stephen on religious grounds (7:58–60). Similarly, a lookout outside a bank would be convicted of murder if his accomplices shot a teller inside.

Yet Paul not only survived the snakebite but even performed a miraculous healing immediately afterward (28:8). Why was he granted this deliverance from his own death, and the power to save others from death? Because God believes in second chances even for murderers, as Paul had written Timothy years earlier:

> I was a blasphemer and a persecutor and an arrogant man, but...Christ came into the world to save sinners. Of these I am

the foremost. But for that reason I was mercifully treated, so that in me, as the foremost, Christ Jesus might display all his patience, as an example for those who would come to believe in him for everlasting life. (1 Timothy 1:13, 15, 16)

The fact that "Christ came into the world to save sinners," not the righteous, is the very heart of the Gospel's good news (cf. Matthew 9:13; Mark 2:17; Luke 5:32). If only America could remember this simple truth, it might discover that modern-day Pauls—men like the five inmate interview subjects in this book—can shake off their pasts, like Paul shook off the snake, and do even greater things than he did.

Or, perhaps more accurately, men like Paul should be given the opportunity to live out the full consequences of their pasts. As noted theologian and author the Reverend Dr. John R. Stott of All Souls, London, has pointed out, Paul's bad conscience over his role in the murder of Stephen almost certainly contributed to his own conversion on the road to Damascus.[1] "It is hard for you to kick against the goads" (Acts 26:14), Christ told him—and one of those goads was surely the knowledge that he had helped shed innocent blood. Instead of punishing Paul the killer, however, Jesus converted him into Paul the "apostle in chains," the "prisoner of Christ." Reforming his fellow felons in the jail at Philippi was only one of many ways in which Paul's murder of Stephen bore beautiful fruit, thanks to God's intervening grace.

The remainder of this chapter will review three areas of prison ministry in which you can continue Paul's work: conventional religious volunteer work, faith-based prisons, and religious reentry programs.

CONVENTIONAL RELIGIOUS VOLUNTEER WORK

Prison ministers have been a central feature of the correctional landscape in America ever since 1829, when the first modern penitentiary was built under the guidance of the Quakers in Cherry Hill, Pennsylvania.[2] In most jails and prisons today, a (usually semi-official) chaplain coordinates the activities of religious volunteers who may participate in a one-off special event, like a Kairos retreat, or conduct regularly scheduled programs on a monthly or weekly basis.[3] Only one Department of Corrections in this country collects comprehensive data on the religious involvement of its inmates, so quantitative data on the extent and effect of prison ministry is virtually nonexistent.[4]

No matter how many or how few volunteers work at the particular facility that you are considering as your mission field, however, it is important to remember that prison ministers often are the only contact inmates have with the outside world. The majority of convicts receive no visits and very little personal mail. For many of these men, you will quickly become the primary emotional focus, your program the highlight of the month. This can be very rewarding for volunteers, of course, but the isolation and neediness of prisoners also have drawbacks.

On the bright side, there are incidents like the one that occurred one Christmas at my correctional center. Every December 25, Dennis and Loretta Beeman, whom you will meet in the interview following this chapter, add a special holiday service to their regularly scheduled monthly program. Here grown convicts can let themselves get a little teary-eyed while singing carols—an important event for all of us. After our 2005 service, a black inmate who has spent more than thirty years behind bars was speaking to Loretta, a middle-aged white lady—and inadvertently called her "mom." Neither one of them found this remarkable; they only smiled at each other to acknowledge the slip and then continued their conversation. In a very meaningful way, Dennis and Loretta have indeed become the center of a kind of family in here.

Perhaps less wholesome is the effect that female religious volunteers can have on men who have not seen a civilian woman in years. While many correctional centers now employ female staff—and plenty of convicts develop very unhealthy feelings for them—most prisoners find the guards' uniform to be a terminal turn-off, no matter how delightful the body inside that uniform may appear to be. The flowing robes worn by a visiting church choir, on the other hand, have no such deflationary effect on the inmate imagination: attendance at services for the largest denomination at my facility easily doubles whenever there is a special event featuring women singers.

Pointing out this simple fact is not meant to disparage the inmates, the civilian choir or the denomination. Even if prisoners come for "the show," they may still get hooked on Jesus, and my own denomination pioneered the use of liturgical pomp and circumstance. My only concern here is to point out that prison ministry takes place in prison, a place full of hazards less commonly found in the civilian world.

If female religious volunteers are forewarned of such matters, then they can in fact perform a tremendously important service to male inmates and their families. All these men ever see is women guards and the dancers on Black Entertainment Television (BET), so their perceptions of male-female relationships become severely distorted over time. By giving convicts the opportunity to interact with women on a totally different, spiritual level, female prison ministers call them back to something approaching reality and lay the foundation for them to develop healthier, less abusive relationships upon their release. This is *far* from a small matter!

Contact with female religious volunteers is not the only possible ulterior motive that prisoners may have for attending prayer groups or church services. Because life behind bars can be extremely dangerous, some men are simply seeking "a safe place, material comforts, . . . and a less stressful set of inmate-to-inmate relationships," says Dr. Thomas O'Connor of the Oregon Department of Corrections' Religious Services unit.[5] Of course, much the same can be said of civilians who attend church primarily for the social benefits and connections, or to placate their spouses!

In any case, providing a refuge from sexual predators and hostile guards should not be disparaged. Churches and monasteries have often become sanctuaries in times of war or persecution, and a prison chapel can serve the same purpose. A few years ago, for example, convicts and volunteers of my denomination made a point of reaching out to a young man of our faith who had been beaten up badly by his cellmate. He began attending services regularly again and then reconnected with his church in the civilian world, members of which later helped him find a job and an apartment.

"Tough guys," by contrast, rarely attend religious programs behind bars. For prospective prison ministers, it is helpful to keep this in mind: your clientele is, in a sense, the cream of the correctional crop, those who have already reached a point in their lives when they are ready for a change. My best guess, having spoken to the chaplain's inmate liaisons for all the faith groups at this facility, is that you will see only the most receptive 15 to 20% of the prison population.* Interestingly enough, the Oregon Department of Corrections estimates that 32% to 52% of their inmates attend religious programs. As the chaplain's inmate liaison for my faith group, I know how such attendance figures are collected and compiled. My belief is that the Oregon DOC's much higher *reported* religious program participation levels are due to double- and triple-counting within monthly data collection intervals.

Though religious volunteers deal with a fairly select group of convicts, they are still not spared the great scourge of the American criminal justice system: racism. There are a few religious programs that are integrated to some extent, but in most cases one race or the other predominates strongly. As in job placements, sports activities, and cell assignments, inmates tend to segregate themselves in church, too. Prison ministers may be tempted to challenge this despicable aspect of penitentiary life straight away; a wiser course would be to listen and learn, and then take a very oblique approach.

Just as in your world, interdenominational prejudices and conflicts can erupt unexpectedly behind bars, too. Unlike your world, however, the prison environment allows administrators and chaplains to enforce their views on members of minority faiths and outside volunteers. The Saluda jail in Middlesex County, Virginia, for instance, barred Catholic volunteers for several months in 2005 because they refused to sign an evangelical "statement of faith" required by the jail's private religious services contractor, Southeastern Correctional Ministry.[6] On most occasions, faith-based prejudices are not expressed quite so boldly

---

* See footnotes on pages 26 and 34.

but instead take the form of minor administrative hurdles and obstacles and "problems" that take their toll over time.

Finally, one more warning and one more mission field: convicts are not the only ones who must be handled with care. Some of the most successful prison ministers, like Reverend Emmett Solomon of the Restorative Justice Ministries Network, make a special effort to develop positive relations with correctional staff.[7] Even with such outreach to guards, however, religious activities behind bars are a magnet for snafus, scheduling conflicts and miscommunication of all types.

Volunteers should remember that in most cases such difficulties are not due to intentional obstruction or mean-spiritedness by correctional officers. Because they are trained to make security their utmost priority—and because so many convicts abuse every tiny little bit of leeway—guards are extremely cautious and inflexible about rules. This mindset can lead to decisions that may seem incomprehensible to outsiders, but to prisoners (and staff!) are just one more instance of the "same old same old." Best to consider such things a learning experience, your little taste of life in "the big house."

And, sooner or later, even hardnosed "super cops" will surprise you with unexpected helpfulness. Correctional officers who have direct contact with convicts, like Win Barber of the Nebraska State Penitentiary, realize that "a large number of inmates, rather hard customers if you look at their record, . . . have a sense of atonement for what they've done and are genuinely looking for some kind of forgiveness. . . . We try to give each faith group a reasonable equitable opportunity to practice their faith."[8]

I could give you numerous examples of extraordinary kindness shown by officers at my facility when it comes to religious programs. But if I were to provide details that divulge these staff members' identities, their superiors would inevitably call them in for a little talking-to. Even a well-meant compliment can become a danger on this side of the razor wire fence.

By the same token, however, prison ministers are in a unique position to offer discreet encouragement and thanks to those who otherwise do not receive a kind, quiet word from anyone. And that is an important ministry, too.

Faith-based Prisons, part 1

While "my" state does not have faith-based prisons, you may have the opportunity to work in this type of facility where you live, so we should spend some time on this subject here.

The concept of the faith-based prison was developed by Drs. Mario Ottoboni, Silvio Marques Neto, and Hugo Veronese in Brazil. In 1972/73, they and their team of lay volunteers began working in the government-operated Humaitá penitentiary in São José dos Campos. This facility was turned over to their group completely in 1984 and has been run on religious principles as a private correctional center ever since. Ecuador, Peru, Argentina, and New Zealand now also have faith-based prisons. In the U.S., Prison Fellowship Ministries (PFM) now operates such facilities in Texas, Iowa, Kansas, Florida, and Minnesota.[9]

Unlike normal penitentiaries, faith-based prisons have full-time, salaried employees who provide rehabilitative programs and classes with a strong religious component. The state benefits because an outside organization such as PFM pays the staff—though we should note that PFM, in turn, receives federal grants. And inmates benefit both immediately—because faith-based prisons offer better living conditions (including private toilets), enhanced visiting privileges, and special treats (like pizza parties)—and in the long-term—because the religious, educational, and therapeutic programs improve their chances of living crime-free after their release.

In the summer of 2006, faith-based prisons were dealt a serious setback in a widely reported federal court ruling. (This decision was affirmed by the U.S. Court of Appeals for the Eighth Circuit on December 3, 2007.) Chief District Court Judge Robert W. Pratt held that PFM's InnerChange facility in Iowa unconstitutionally used taxpayer money to indoctrinate inmates and required PFM to refund $1.5 million in federal funds it had received.[10] This decision drew a great deal of criticism from evangelicals, who were understandably offended by Judge Pratt's tendentious and inaccurate description of their beliefs.[11] In addition, many religious conservatives took the Iowa PFM ruling as an attack on religion in the public square generally. As a religious conservative myself, I might be expected to join the defense of PFM against meddling federal judges. However, my decades of penitentiary experience give me a different perspective—one that I ask my fellow religious conservatives to consider.

In my opinion, Prison Fellowship Ministries has correctly "identif[ied] sin as the root of [inmates'] problems." PFM is also correct in stating that only "God can heal them permanently, if they turn from their sinful pasts."[12] And finally, PFM has correctly recognized that one-on-one, individual ministry cannot accomplish this goal by itself; the entire institution of prison must be transformed as well.

As a writer and advocate, I have worked hard, and at some risk to myself, to promote the same twin missions of transforming prisoners and transforming prison. So it is as a concerned and somewhat troubled friend of PFM's that I ask: are faith-based prisons really the best way to achieve our objectives?

The fundamental, structural problem of the faith-based prison concept is that the religious staff members are ... *staff members*. In a regular penitentiary, religious volunteers are not employees of the facility; it is not part of their job to keep inmates locked up. In a faith-based prison, by contrast, religious staff are part of a workforce whose task is to confine, to control and ultimately to punish inmates. Jesus gave Peter the "keys to the kingdom of heaven"; should Christians really hold the keys of jail cells containing fellow Christians?

Of course, one Christian can write another Christian a traffic ticket if one is a Christian highway patrolman and the other is a Christian speeder. But in a faith-based prison, staff members exercise their confining, controlling and punishing authority *based on religious criteria*. Should one Christian judge another Christian's spiritual maturity, for the purpose of writing an official evaluation for the prison administration?

Consider the following three components of the PFM InnerChange program in Iowa:

- Almost without exception, PFM employees are dedicated, even fervent evangelical Protestants. So far, so good! But an important part of their work is to assess the spiritual progress of inmates who belong to other denominations and faiths.
- Prisoners in InnerChange facilities are *required* to attend PFM worship services, even if those services are contrary to their own religious beliefs.
- If inmates fail to attend, PFM employees must write disciplinary reports. These disciplinary reports are entered into inmates' institutional files, can lead to transfers to higher security level prisons, and become part of the set of records submitted to parole boards (where parole still exists).

Now put yourself in the shoes of say, a PFM staff member: could you write a positive spiritual progress report on a Catholic prisoner who refuses to accept Jesus as his personal Savior and instead insists on worshipping "the Whore of Babylon"? How about a Nation of Islam inmate who is ethically impeccable but also sincerely believes that you are a "white devil"?

Now put yourself in the shoes of, say, an Episcopalian prisoner. You strongly believe that your church was right to ordain a practicing homosexual as bishop—but your PFM caseworker regards homosexuality as a grave sin and the Episcopal Church as apostate. Would you feel comfortable about your caseworker's ability to evaluate your religious maturity?

Consider the experience of prison psychologists. In the idealistic 1960s and '70s, many psychology majors went to work in penitentiaries with the desire to help and to heal—to cure criminals of their offending behavior and thought patterns. Inmates, however, soon came to see mental health staff as nothing more than a different type of guard, because psychologists ultimately report to the prison administration. Their purpose is to snoop on our thoughts and feelings so that we can be controlled even more efficiently. For that very reason, I myself never consulted a prison psychologist and never will.

And if I thought that our priest were writing spiritual progress reports on me, I would immediately stop going to Mass. My faith is the *only* part of my life where the prison has no power; I will not permit the prison to sully this, too.

Faith-based Prisons, part 2

Unfortunately, the faith-based prison concept has another fundamental, structural problem: staff motivation. In any other operation, a highly motivated staff would be an asset. In a faith-based prison, by contrast, the more highly motivated the staff, the greater the risk that the staff will subtly or overtly pressure inmates to convert! And the fact that religious prison employees have great worldly power means that the pressure on inmates to change their faith can be overwhelming.

Faith-based staff are really caught in a terrible trap: on the one hand, they truly believe that prisoners can only be saved if they give their lives to Christ. On the other hand, can an inmate's conversion really be genuine in the context of spiritual progress reports and disciplinary charges for failing to attend worship services? There is a great danger here that faith-based prison employees may be doing harm to the souls of inmates—and thus to their own souls, too (Luke 17:1, 2).

The track record of PFM staff members in this regard is not confidence-inspiring, precisely because they are so dedicated, so fervent, so enthusiastic:

- Both PFM employees and PFM-supervised volunteers in the Iowa InnerChange facility repeatedly criticized the religious beliefs of non-evangelical Protestant inmates. According to PFM President Mark L. Earley, such comments do not reflect the philosophy of Prison Fellowship Ministries.[13] But is it actually reasonable and realistic to expect PFM employees to remain silent about their faith?

- In the Kansas InnerChange prison, PFM staff tried to circumvent this problem by training inmate "disciples" to pressure newly arrived non-evangelical Protestants into changing their beliefs.[14] This is especially insidious because it injects religion into the inevitable power struggles of penitentiary life. To maintain his privileged position, a cellhouse missionary will use "any means necessary" (a favorite expression among convicts).

- Florida's Lawtey Correctional Institution is operated by local Southern Baptists, not PFM, but here too there is overt denominational discrimination. While most convicts attend the "Evangelism Explosion" in the gym—featuring pizzas, cookies, and conversion stories—the prison's three Muslims meet in a mop closet. Pastor J. Stephen McCoy's comment: "This is the Bible Belt, you know."[15]

What we have here is a perfect illustration of the law of unintended consequence. I have my doubts about the crowd in the gym, but those three fellows in the mop closet—they interest me! Would it not be fair to say that their courage and faith make them *more* worthy of early release than the men who conveniently find Jesus while Pastor McCoy is watching?

I think the best advice in this regard comes from our third interview subject, Carlton L.:

We are a vast culture of many faiths, and so I have to be ready to help regardless of whether I have the same faith as that person or not. Jesus summed that up in one word: love. If you give these men love and forgiveness, you have already brought Christ to them, even though you might not have used the word "Jesus" in your conversation.

FAITH-BASED PRISONS, PART 3

Finally, faith-based prisons raise significant constitutional, public policy and criminological questions that cannot simply be dismissed as sour grapes from federal judges and liberals.

The Establishment Clause of the First Amendment was intended to prevent the federal government from forcing free citizens to join a state-sponsored church—a threat that exists nowhere in the U.S. today, *except in prison*. Most Americans, accustomed to their free choice, find it hard to imagine that there are these little corners of the country—the jails and penitentiaries—where genuine choice is impossible. Prisoners must do *everything* they are told to do: attend a drug counseling course, report to the kitchen for work, or—if they are housed in an Inner-Change facility—meet with their faith-based caseworker for a quarterly spiritual progress evaluation. Refusing to meet with caseworkers at my current prison can result in a disciplinary offense report, and no doubt the same holds true in a PFM penitentiary. If that does not violate the Establishment Clause, what does?

Even some supporters of faith-based prisons recognize that the fundamentally coercive nature of penitentiary life creates genuine constitutional hazards. "[I]f the only way to get preparation for release is to go into a 'single-faith' program, that seems to be a coercion of religion," says Douglas Laycock of the University of Texas School of Law.[16] Prisoners, unlike civilians, do not have the option to go elsewhere to obtain needed services, so non-religious inmates or those of other faiths would be compelled to fake their faith in order to get drug rehabilitation, say.

When it comes to the public policy aspect of faith-based prisons, I strongly suspect politicians of exploiting the good will of religious folk to avoid paying for regular rehabilitative programs that the state should be providing to all inmates. The term "faith-based initiative" originally designated existing church charities that would henceforth receive government funds despite the First Amendment's Establishment Clause. With faith-based prisons, by contrast, the funding stream is reversed: religious organizations pump money into an institution, the penitentiary, that was hitherto financed by the state. The federal government then partially subsidizes this dubious arrangement with grants to faith-based groups. No one benefits from this murky business—except state governments.

In Florida, for instance, the Department of Corrections has entirely eliminated substance abuse programs, even though 80% of that state's inmates have addiction problems.[17] Now the faith-based Lawtey facility is the only one offering this kind of essential service. And the cost is borne by the congregations of participating nearby churches, not taxpayers in ritzy Miami Beach and elsewhere.

The same principle is at work in Kansas, where the state's prison system cut in half high school equivalency classes and eliminated substance abuse programs in 2003. But in the 140-man faith-based wing of its medium-security correctional center in Ellsworth, PFM pays for such programs and provides the staff to operate them. Roger Werholtz, the secretary of the Department of Corrections, admits that PFM "follows the form, if not the content, of a therapeutic program. [But] I'm interested in any kind of resources we can employ that will be effective on a low-cost or no-cost basis."[18]

Whether faith-based prisons are indeed "effective" is very much in dispute. In a study paid for and frequently cited by PFM, only 8% of the graduates of its Texas InnerChange facility re-offended, compared to a statewide recidivism rate of 35%. But that study did not count inmates who dropped out, were kicked out, or failed to hold a job for six months after graduation. If those are included, the InnerChange recidivism rate is actually 36.2%.[19]

Dr. O'Connor has noted that all of the research on the impact of in-prison religious activity on recidivism is beset with severe methodological problems: research design, measurement, statistical analysis, and controls are all inadequate. In a meta-analysis of the twelve least-flawed studies, he found that "they provide some evidence of a significant relationship between religious involvement and rehabilitation but are accompanied by contradictory findings and weaknesses.... [W]e cannot equate their findings or make definite conclusions."[20] According to the American Correctional Association journal *Corrections Today*, "there simply is no credible evidence that such programs reduce recidivism or improve other post-release outcomes. Of course, future research might prove otherwise, but such research will need to rest on considerably stronger research design."[21]

RELIGIOUS REENTRY PROGRAMS

In Chapter 6, we examined rehabilitation and reentry programs in detail. Here I only want to note that prison ministers are uniquely situated to make reentry programs succeed. Because religious volunteers can and should befriend members of their incarcerated congregations, they can become living bridges that connect soon-to-be-released convicts with churches in the civilian world. Personal relationships and trust are essential for this to work, and these are precisely the areas in which prison ministers excel.

As I pointed out in my second book, religious reentry programs could in fact dismantle America's vastly oversized correctional systems. Only a little effort, two or three years, and some national coordination would be needed. While even some of my friends and supporters tell me, "It will never happen," I can only say, "Why on earth *not?*"

What I propose is incredibly simple: it comes down to practicing what we all say we believe, which is to love our neighbor as ourselves. Or, to be precise, loving two neighbors a year, for two or three years. The key is universal implementation of the astonishingly successful Transition of Prisoners (TOP) program, developed by Joseph Williams in Detroit.

After spending thirteen years in the illegal narcotics trade, Williams recommitted his life to Christ at age twenty-eight and earned several college degrees. Then he joined with Prison Fellowship Ministries to create TOP, which has local churches "adopt" high-risk ex-convicts. By giving a released inmate a caring support network, perhaps for the first time in his life, TOP-participating churches achieve the near-miraculous recidivism rate of 1%.[22]

What works for the worst of the worst in Detroit could work everywhere. In 2001, America's 134 mainline Christian denominations had 317,580 houses of worship.[23] If each congregation "adopted" just *two* of the 672,000 convicts released from prison each year, there might only be 6,720 recidivists (at TOP's rate of 1%) instead of 453,000 (at the current national rate of 67.5%).

This would, of course, throw America's correctional departments into a profound crisis. If 453,000 former inmates failed to get themselves sent back to the pokey, the way they are "supposed" to, hundreds of penitentiaries would suddenly stand empty! Tens of thousands of guards would find themselves unemployed, and several hundred million dollars would not be deposited into the accounts of prison profiteers like Correctional Corporation of America.

All forms of early release for convicts would immediately be stopped to end the national "disaster" of unneeded, unused penitentiaries. But, thanks to "no parole" policies, virtually all inmates serve their entire sentences anyhow. The following year's batch of 672,000 prisoners thus would *have* to be released, because their court-ordered terms of incarceration would be over.

Then each of those 317,580 churches would simply "adopt" another two convicts, for a total of four per congregation—a burden, yes, but not an impossible one. And by the end of the second year, another 453,000 ex-inmates would fail to re-offend, leaving *nearly half* of the penitentiaries in the country empty. And the beast would die.

Impossible? Dennis and Loretta Beeman, our next two interview subjects, do not think so. Having begun as prison ministers at my facility, they have come to see that effective reentry programs really are the key to *all* the problems discussed in this book. Meeting real "live" convicts—and bringing them the body and blood of our Lord in their monthly Communion Services—not only turned out to be, according to Dennis, "the most rewarding thing I've ever done," but has given them a vision of how to transform America, one reintegrated prisoner at a time.

Interview with Dennis and Loretta Beeman

Q: Tell us a little about your lives and jobs.

Dennis: I was born in 1946, Loretta in 1949. We are the parents of four daughters, all in their twenties. I am the director of Christian Formation at the Catholic Diocese of Richmond, and Loretta is the assistant principal—as well as math and religion teacher, and religion coordinator—at Our Lady of Lourdes Elementary School, which covers grades pre-K through 8.

Q: Tell us a little about your work with your local church.

Loretta: Both of us have been very active in our parish for many years. I have worked with the First Sacrament Program and the Liturgy, Art and Environment, and Christian Formation Committees. Dennis has served on the Liturgy and Christian Formation Committees, taught Confirmation class to fifteen- and sixteen-year-olds, and often leads adult education. As religion coordinator at Our Lady of Lourdes, I also work with Caritas to help the homeless in Richmond, and with Catholic Relief Services to help people in Haiti.

Q: But neither one of you had been involved with prison ministry, is that right?

Dennis: That's correct. That only started in 2003, when we came to Brunswick Correctional Center with then-Bishop Walter F. Sullivan. We were part of a group that attended a Mass led by Bishop Sullivan.

Q: What did you see during this Mass that sparked your interest in prison ministry?

Dennis: I saw men who were very attentive, extremely thankful just for the opportunity to have Eucharist, and eager to talk about serious things. These men were hungry and receptive. I said to myself, "Holy cow, they are like starving people!" And I can very easily provide some nourishment for them. So I said, I've got to do something about this. This shouldn't be, and I can do something about this.

Q: So what practical steps did you take?

Dennis: I went back to Richmond and contacted Kathleen Kenney, at that time the Assistant Director of the Office of Peace and Justice for the diocese and the prison liaison. She got me in touch with the volunteer coordinator at the prison. I went down and had an interview with the volunteer coordinator and got fingerprinted, for the security check. The interview was very brief, really just an explanation of dos and don'ts. I remember her saying, If by any chance you are taken hostage, we will not negotiate. That made me think, but it didn't stop me. Getting the security clearance took two or three months, but I was able to come once before that as a special visit.

Q: What kind of service do you offer the men at Brunswick Correctional Center?

Dennis: I can't preside at Eucharist because I'm not a priest, so I do a Communion Service. It begins with a Liturgy of the Word, just like at Mass—those are readings from the Old Testament, the Epistles and the Gospels. Then, in place of a homily—a sermon—we have a shared reflection on the Bible readings, for twenty or thirty minutes. Finally, we say the creed, offer prayers and petitions, say the Lord's Prayer, and exchange a sign of peace. Then Loretta and I distribute consecrated host we've brought with us from our home parish. Oh, and, of course, we sing hymns!

Q: What was it like to enter the prison for the first time to perform a Communion Service by yourself?

Dennis: I walked in the front door of the administration building, met with the guards, signed the logbook, and had the staff check through the things I'd brought with me: prayer books, the communion bread, and all of that. Next, they patted me down and gave me a visitor's badge. I felt anxious the first time, but it all went easily, really. Then I entered the visiting room through a sliding door. When that door clangs shut behind you, you definitely get a prison feel!

Q: What happened next?

Dennis: The setup crew arrived—five or six inmates who arranged the chairs, and so forth. I knew a couple of them from the visit with the Bishop. About twenty minutes later, the congregation arrived: we have between twelve and twenty men show up for our services. The first time, I tried to make them all feel welcome, introduced myself to each one by name, and tried to remember their names. Before we started, I explained the kind of service we were going to have, since it's different from a Mass.

Q: Did you feel scared?

Dennis: No, more like worried that the guys would accept or benefit from the kind of service I was offering. I wasn't worried about my safety.

Q: So how did you first service go?

Dennis: Fine. I felt good at the end, like something good had happened. The men were so grateful that I'd come, and I received four or five letters from different men afterward.

Q: And what was your first service like, Loretta?

Loretta: The first time I came was with Dennis at Easter, just after he'd started. We were going away to North Carolina for a little vacation. I really wasn't looking forward to going, but Brunswick is on the way from Richmond to North Carolina, so I said I'd do it—just one time, as a special visitor.

Q: What do you remember most about coming into the prison?

Loretta: I was in awe about the fact that a door closes behind you, and no other door opens. You have no control at all. It's a very weird feeling.

Q: So what did you do when you met the men?

Loretta: I'm basically a shy person; I wasn't sure what to do. I said hello to people and tried to talk a little before the service. What really moved me and what brought me back was the faith sharing the men did during the whole service—and how everyone conducted themselves, so respectful. The whole spirit—they were there for the right reason, to worship and form a community. I remember sitting there as Dennis was leading the reflection on the Bible readings, feeling surprised.

Q: Why surprised?

Loretta: I had expected things to be a lot more negative, for people to be down on God because of their situation, being in prison. But it was just the opposite—much more positive and uplifting.

Dennis: I remember the theme of that Easter service: light overcoming darkness. People were giving amazing examples from their own lives of how they keep faith and hope going.

Q: Did that service persuade you to join Dennis in becoming a prison minister, Loretta?

Loretta: Yes. On the way to North Carolina, we were talking and sharing. I was so in awe of what had happened, how much it had affected me in a way I hadn't expected. I felt I was in one of Jesus' parables and had to rethink my whole perspective of prison and prison life and the faith of prisoners.

Dennis: We were expecting to have a hard sell, convincing people that God loves them and that life is worth living, and that you have to stay hopeful.

Q: Apart from your message, did you feel that the men accepted you personally?

Loretta: Yes. And them accepting us made it easy for us to accept them. The whole thing about people thanking us afterward—I felt very ashamed, because I hadn't wanted to come in. I feel I got more from them than they got from me, in a way.

Dennis: When you give of yourself, you receive so much more back.

Q: As a woman in a man's prison, were you worried about your personal safety, Loretta?

Loretta: Before I came in, I did. That was a real concern. And I wondered whether I, as a woman, could say or do anything that could help those men. But once I came in, I never worried about my safety—I felt very safe. I worried: what can I contribute?

Q: And, what can you contribute?

Loretta: I'm not sure. I hope the men feel I accept them for who they are, and that my acceptance in turn means that God has accepted them and forgiven them. I look at the prisoners as people who deserve dignity and respect, regardless of their pasts.

Q: Do you know what crimes they committed?

Loretta: No, and I don't think it matters. People don't discuss their crimes with us—that's not the point of the visit. As Christians, we are called to love the person, no matter what he's done.

Q: Does the issue of forgiveness ever arise during your visits to the prison?

Dennis: We haven't had a service that focused directly on the question, Do you feel forgiven for what you've done? But Loretta and I both feel that the most powerful service we had was about the Prodigal Son, or the Forgiving Father. I had a whole lesson that I'd brought with me, to start off our reflection period after the Scripture reading. But after just two or three paragraphs of that lesson, I asked, has anyone here experienced anything like the story in this parable? And four or five people shared really deep, personal experiences of either being the Prodigal Son or the Forgiving Father, of either being hurt or being forgiven for causing hurt.

Q: Tell us more about those personal testimonies.

Dennis: One man shared that he had almost literally lived this story. His son had managed to take all his possessions, his bank accounts, everything—and he had been a well-to-do person before coming to prison. So now he was in there, with absolutely nothing. I remember he said out loud to the group, I don't know if I can forgive my son! And then another man spoke up and talked about his relationship with his family. He felt that they, too, had abandoned him and hurt him while he was in prison. But finally he realized that he needed their forgiveness even more, because originally he had abandoned them by getting himself locked up. So he prayed to be forgiven, and out of the blue, his wife contacted him, and he was able to ask her forgiveness. That service was one of the most moving services I've ever been in, inside or outside of prison.

Loretta: It was very evident that God was there at that gathering. And then there was also our service last week, which was Ash Wednesday. That same man spoke up again and commented on the cross we all had on our foreheads. [Interviewer's Note: On Ash Wednesday, Catholics put a cross of ashes on their foreheads as a sign of sorrow for their sins.] He said that there was no black or white or brown—we have some Hispanic inmates attending, too—because we all wore the same cross. We're all sinners, even Dennis and I, and God still welcomes all of us to his banquet.

Dennis: That cross is also a sign of repentance, of course. The words that the celebrant says when he anoints each congregation member with the ashes is, "Turn away from sin and believe in the good news." It's about being restored into God's love and into his community.

Q: Do you ever discuss your prison ministry with your students, Loretta?

Loretta: Yes. All students at our school are required to do two hours of community service, so I tell them about the kind of community service that I do.

Q: How do they react?

Loretta: They are surprised, a few of them look at me like I'm crazy. Some of them ask me questions like whether I'm scared, or what crimes the prisoners committed. I tell them, those men are just like you. I tell them that we shouldn't push those prisoners out of our lives just because they have broken the law. I tell the students, if you do something wrong, that doesn't mean that I push you out of my life, either. It all goes back to Jesus: he loved the person. He always treated the person with dignity and respect.

Q: Do you tell your adult friends about your prison ministry?

Loretta: Yes, and they have the same sorts of questions as the students. I was telling our Spanish teacher about it, and now she is going to get Hispanic inmates some material in their own language. Maybe, in time, she'll start to come with us. Talking about this raises people's consciousness.

Dennis: When I tell people what I do, almost everyone reacts with surprise: "Really?" They also wonder where we go. They don't realize that all of these prisons have been built out in the middle of nowhere, where people can't see them. It's like we've hidden it all away, the inmates and the prisons—like we don't want to look at them.

Q: Is there a prison ministry at your parish?

Dennis: No, and that's a good example of what I'm talking about here. The Henrico County Jail is only two miles from our church, but in the twenty-five years we've been there, there's never been an outreach to the jail. It's easier to pretend it doesn't exist. But this prison ministry at Brunswick, it's the most rewarding thing I've ever done in my life!

Loretta: I'm hoping that others will become interested and involved by our sharing our experiences with them. I don't tell people, Look at me, how wonderful I am. But I try to draw them in. And I hope that the eighth-grade students I teach will grow up with a better perspective on prisoners and prison ministry.

Q: How about your diocese? Is there an organized program for prisoner reentry there?

Dennis: No. We have a diocesan refugee resettlement office that tries to get the parishes to help resettle immigrants and so forth. But there's nothing to help reintegrate released inmates into the community. For us, that became very evident when one of the men at our services who is about to leave prison asked us for help. As far as we can tell, there is no Catholic group in the entire Tidewater area that could help him, and we couldn't find a single Catholic halfway house in the entire state.

Q: Do you feel called to a new kind of ministry in this area, maybe?

Dennis: Well, our new bishop has brought in a new director of the Office of Peace and Justice, and they are trying to get some deacons together to get a halfway house going. For me personally, though, the next step is to try to change the whole system. I plan to join Virginia CURE and start lobbying politicians, attending General Assembly sessions, that sort of thing. What Loretta and

I do is fine and totally worthwhile, but to really make a difference, we need to make larger changes. The same problems keep happening over and over again, and building more and more prisons just isn't solving those problems.

Loretta: I want to do more to open children's minds about prisoners. It's important for them to see that Jesus is calling us to love all people, not just those that are considered good by society. That's why the Gospel of Luke is my favorite Gospel. Throughout Luke, Jesus reaches out to those people in society that society doesn't accept: the sinful woman, the dishonest tax collector, lepers, Samaritans. That Gospel makes you think about how you treat other people, and how you accept them into your own life. Jesus didn't exclude anyone, he loved them all.

QUESTIONS FOR REFLECTION AND DISCUSSION

SCRIPTURE—Reflect on the fact that God grants forgiveness *before* repentance is expressed: see Luke 15:20, Romans 5:8–10, and 1 John 4:10. Compare to Luke 17:3. Does repentance *have* to be expressed before forgiveness is granted—among humans, at least? How does the answer to that question impact your approach to prison ministry?

CRIMINOLOGY—Discuss the problem of faith-based initiatives and funding: local churches end up carrying the financial burden for essential substance abuse programs, while citizens who do not participate in prison ministry contribute nothing. Is the good will of Christians being exploited here? By whom, and why?

SELF-EXAM—Reflect on the problem of implicit compulsion in faith-based initiatives, taking into account your own spiritual life. If immediate, earthly rewards are attached to conversion, how can anyone determine if faith is sincere? On the other hand, why should spiritual transformation not be rewarded with this-worldly benefits?

Interview—Dennis Beeman mentioned that his parish church has no outreach program to the nearby county jail. Does your church have a prison ministry program? Why or why not? Does your pastor ever discuss or preach about prison outreach?

Internet—Visit the Web site of Transition of Prisoners (TOP), the phenomenally successful reentry program developed by Joseph Williams in Detroit (www.topinc.net).

Immersion—Meet with a prison minister or volunteer at your church or another one. Learn about this work.

Chapter 9

ONESIMUS AND DEATH BY INCARCERATION

O F THE NINE biblical criminals and convicts in this volume, Onesimus is the only one who was not a prominent figure. He was just a runaway slave—a nothing, a nobody. If he had not "serve[d Paul]…in his imprisonment" (v. 13) and then returned to his master, we would never even have heard about him.

But, as we shall see below, Onesimus was in fact just as courageous and heroic as the more famous crooks and prisoners in this book, and the early Church clearly recognized this by including the letter about him in the New Testament. Before we can see what made Onesimus so special, however, we will have to rid ourselves of our twenty-first-century blinders.

From our perspective, the most important thing about Onesimus is that he was a slave and therefore the victim of a great social evil. But that is not at all how the free citizens of the first century would have viewed him. In their eyes, he was an inferior, even "bad" person who deserved to be held in servitude.

We can begin to get some sense of how Onesimus's contemporaries saw him by reflecting on what kinds of people became slaves, and what their modern counterparts might be:

- Some slaves were captured during war, like the Taliban or Al Qaeda today
- Others were enslaved because they had fallen into debt—saddling honest folk with the consequences of their financial irresponsibility, like Jeffrey Skilling and Kenneth Lay of Enron fame
- Finally, many slaves were the children of slaves, considered defective by virtue of their breeding, much as pit bulls are considered inherently vicious

Now imagine living in the same house with someone from one of these groups; imagine having to rely upon this person to cook breakfast for your children! If you can picture that, you will have a much better idea of how free people felt about slaves two millennia ago.

But Onesimus was much worse than an ordinary slave: he was a criminal, a thief twice over!

- As verses 18 and 19 of the letter make clear, he had taken some item of value from his master: Paul tells Philemon, "Charge it to me.... I will pay"
- Onesimus was the legal property of Philemon and thus, by running away, stole both the cost of his own purchase *and* the value of the work he would have done, had he remained

Because our own emotions are so caught up in the terrible injustice of slavery, we modern-day readers of Scripture completely overlook the evident criminality of Onesimus' actions. My favorite Bible scholar, Professor Raymond Brown of Union Theological Seminary, devotes an entire subsection of his *Introduction to the New Testament* to the "Social Import of Paul's View of Slavery"—but only a one-sentence footnote to the fact that "Onesimus stole something when he fled."[1] At the time Paul wrote the Letter to Philemon, however, the fact that Onesimus was an egregious felon would have been foremost in all three of their minds.

Of course, the fact that Paul asked Philemon to treat a slave as an equal is central to understanding the importance of this epistle. But in their age and culture, it was not that uncommon for a master to manumit a favorite slave, or to allow him to purchase his own freedom; there was some dim recognition that slaves were indeed human. What makes Paul's plea to Philemon so remarkable is that Onesimus was a particularly bad slave, a thief—one who definitely had not earned his freedom.

For today's Christians, this insight into Onesimus's status as a slave *and* a criminal is especially important because the standard reading of this letter allows us to dismiss it as irrelevant. We no longer practice slavery, so we can safely feel superior to Philemon, right? Wrong! Once we understand that, even two thousand years ago, Onesimus would have been considered a thief, we can begin to see that the Letter to Philemon still has much to teach us about how we treat thieves today.

So let us examine in some detail what precisely Paul was asking Philemon to do with the felon Onesimus:

- First of all, Paul wanted the thief to escape punishment and to be released—not exactly "tough on crime!"
- The apostle to the gentiles also made a point of expressing his affection for a crook—"my child," "my own heart"—and explicitly suggested that Philemon too should love him—"a brother, beloved…to you" (v. 10, 12, 16)
- And, perhaps most radically, Paul wanted the master and crime victim Philemon to accept the slave and criminal Onesimus as an equal in Christ: "Welcome him as you would me" (v. 17)

History buffs may note that Paul's three requests of Philemon are also the slogan of the French Revolution, with the last two items in reverse order: *liberté, fraternité, égalité*. And indeed, what is more revolutionary than loving your enemy, a social inferior who stole from you?

Those who would apply the Letter to Philemon's teaching to the 2.3 million Onesimuses in America's prisons should think twice, however. Far from putting all the burden on Philemon, Paul himself offers to pay for any damages the thief has caused. But Onesimus does not escape the consequences of his actions, either: as the apostle makes clear, he expects the runaway to make himself "useful to" Philemon (v. 11). It seems the victim/master and criminal/slave are to live, if not together, then at least in the same neighborhood.

So far we have treated Onesimus in the standard way, as a fairly passive person sent back to his former master by Paul (v. 12). As with the issue of Onesimus's criminality, I have yet to find any scholarly writings that challenge this approach. But the truth is that Onesimus was far from passive, and Paul had no authority to send him anywhere.

Onesimus *chose* to return to Philemon, and that is what makes him a hero.

As a slave of the Virginia Department of Corrections, I can assure you that it is very, very difficult for slaves even to imagine escape. We are so accustomed to following orders and routines that most of us would not walk through a hole in the perimeter fence even if one miraculously opened up right in front of us. Having run away in the first place marks Onesimus as a slave of exceptional independence and initiative.

He was also a man of considerable spiritual sensitivity, since he befriended Paul in the latter's imprisonment (v. 10). Over the course of what must have been many jailhouse visits, Onesimus grew to trust the apostle enough to tell him his dangerous secret: that he was not the free citizen he appeared to be, but a runaway slave. Onesimus must have been very sure indeed that Paul would not turn him in to the authorities.

Of course, Onesimus's *past* enslavement did not give Paul any legal power over him *now*. Only a slave's master had the authority to give him a command. Since Paul was neither Onesimus's owner nor a magistrate, he could not order the runaway slave to return to Philemon.

Therefore the apostle's statement that he was sending Onesimus back to Philemon must be understood metaphorically. Philemon was meant to understand that Onesimus had chosen to accept Paul's spiritual authority—and that he should do the same.

It is also hard to imagine that the apostle would even attempt to *command* his friend to return to his former master. As everyone in antiquity knew, slave owners had complete power over their property, and we have records of truly stomach-churning punishments meted out to disobedient slaves. Paul would have had to be a complete monster to have tried to *order* Onesimus to expose himself to that sort of danger.

I believe it is far more likely that Onesimus himself had the idea of returning to Philemon. All his life, remember, he had chafed under the yoke of his servitude: he knew, he *knew* that he was no less of a man than his masters! By running away, he thought he had proved his equality—but he remained a second-class citizen, an outlaw, a hunted man. How he longed to be truly free, to have his humanity fully acknowledged.

And then he met Paul and was captivated by the power of the Gospel. As he learned more and more about Jesus at the apostle's feet, he would have come to understand the spiritual judo that Christ had performed and that his new friend and teacher was even now repeating. What they did was so beautifully counterintuitive. Jesus had conquered death by voluntarily accepting his own execution on the cross, and Paul was transcending his chains by embracing the role of "prisoner of Christ" (Ephesians 3:1, 4:1; Philemon 9). By willingly taking on what men fear most, by letting themselves become completely weak and vulnerable, these two became "more than conquerors" (Romans 8:37). So could he, Onesimus, also overcome his enslavement...by somehow embracing it?

I believe Onesimus said yes to that question: he voluntarily returned to Philemon, his former master, in order to become truly free.

If Jesus was who Paul said he was, then it would not even matter whether Philemon forgave or punished him:

- Being reconciled with his master would prove that Christian love was stronger than the institution of slavery
- Being sold to the salt mines would make him a martyr who gave his life for the proposition that "there is neither slave nor free...in Christ" (Galatians 3:28)

As his friend Paul had put it, "to me life is Christ and death is gain" (Philippians 1:21); Onesimus too could not lose.

Those of us who want to reform and transform the prison system have much to learn from Onesimus's example. For starters, both convicts and citizens need to develop his kind of courage—the courage to allow ourselves to become completely vulnerable, to embrace what we fear most. If Onesimus could bet his life on the power of love, how can prisoners today refuse to reach out toward civilians? And if Philemon could take back Onesimus as "more than a slave, a brother, beloved...as a man and in the Lord," how can law-abiding Americans today refuse to take back their 2.3 million "beloved" brothers and sisters (v. 16)? Are we less courageous, less Christian than they?

It would appear so. While ex-convicts do not get anything close to a genuine second chance, I think it is incomprehensible and basically inexcusable that 67.5% fail to make good on the second-rate second chance that they do get upon being discharged from prison. Released inmates need to do much, much better.

And, of course, society needs to give them the opportunity to do better! Instead, this country keeps beating prisoners with bigger and bigger sticks: "three strikes" laws, parole abolition, mandatory minimum sentences, and life sentences with or without parole. What these correctional policies amount to is death by incarceration—there is no other way to put it. If Onesimus had been told that one of these punishments would be meted out to him upon returning to Philemon, he would have never left Paul's side.

Bigger Sticks

In Chapter 4 we learned that since the 1990s, the primary cause of prison growth has been longer sentences. Lengthier terms of incarceration were the justice system's response to two near-simultaneous phenomena: the sudden sharp rise in the crime rate known as the crack "spike," which we noted in Chapter 3, and a series of shocking, high-profile cases such as the abduction-murder of Polly Klaas, which largely inspired the rise of the victims' rights movement discussed in Chapter 4.

As we saw in Chapter 3, sensationalistic reporting by the media distorted the nature and extent of these problems. Beneath the hype, however, there really was a rise in narcotics-related offending, and a few parolees really did commit unspeakable acts.

To most Americans, the only conceivable way to deal with these twin criminological trends was to punish offenders more harshly. What else do you do with crooks but beat them with bigger sticks? Well, at least theoretically, there might have been other responses to crack addicts and homicidal parolees. How about a national crash-program to treat as many drug users as possible, thereby removing some of the financial impetus behind the narcotics trade's turf battles—and a national crash-program to make U.S. penitentiaries fit for human habitation, so prisons would produce fewer angry, embittered, and traumatized recidivists?

My point here is not that these alternative policies would have been more effective—though I think it would be easy to make that argument—but instead to note that the two options above were never even attempted. The *only* response to the crack "spike" and paroled maniacs was bigger sticks, lengthier terms of incarceration. And that raises a very interesting question: Why?

Criminologists have proposed a variety of answers, chief among which are these:

- Thanks to this country's Puritan heritage, the justice system continues to be inspired by a Calvinist love of "fire and brimstone" retribution. But if this is the case, our courts must be among the last upholders of an influence that seems to have faded long ago from all other areas of public life.

- Because this is a nation that valorizes rugged individualism, Americans focus less on the social causes of crime and more on personal responsibility. The primary difficulty with this hypothesis is that in Australia, where the tough, straight-talkin', son-of-a-convict mentality is a national stereotype, the prison system is as rehabilitation-oriented as any European country's.

Undoubtedly history and culture contributed to the punitive streak in America's national character. But I believe there is a much simpler reason why the U.S. responded to crack dealers and psychopathic parolees *only* with longer prison sentences—a reason we glimpsed briefly in the discussion of California's "three strikes" law in Chapter 6.

"Three Strikes and You're Out"

Of all the various manifestations of the bigger-sticks response to crime, California's version of the "three strikes" legislation is perhaps the worst. The Golden State imposes a mandatory life sentence on all three-time offenders, including nonviolent ones. Even worse, under the "petty with a prior" provision, a misdemeanor theft can qualify as the third felony that triggers life.

The U.S. Supreme Court reviewed California's statute in 2003, in a case involving a repeat offender's attempt to walk out of a store with $68.64 worth of videotapes shoved down his pants. According to America's wisest jurists, giving this man a life sentence for that crime did not constitute cruel and unusual punishment.[2] Thus California prisons now hold hundreds of lifers whose third strike is nothing more than a misdemeanor, and thousands more whose felonies are nonviolent.[3]

In a study by the RAND Corporation, parent training and early childhood intervention programs were found to be four or five times as effective as the "three strikes" law in reducing violent crime.[4] So why did the Golden State's legislators pass the latter but fail to fund the former? At least in part because of the financial largesse of the California Correctional Peace Officers Association (CCPOA), as we saw in Chapter 6. Neither America's Puritan heritage, nor even its individualistic frontier spirit, but cold, hard union cash are behind this particular bigger stick.

Parole Abolition and ALEC

As wasteful and ineffective as "three strikes" legislation is, it impacts only a few tens of thousands of prisoners across the U.S. By contrast, parole abolition—also called "truth in sentencing" or the "85% law"—affects virtually every one of this country's inmates either directly or indirectly. Perhaps not surprisingly, this policy too was born of love of money.

When private industry wants to manipulate government, it has an option not available to organized labor: the American Legislative Exchange Council (ALEC). This group drafts model laws friendly to business and then lobbies state legislatures to pass them. To help companies avoid the cost of cleaning up their own pollution, for instance, ALEC created a bill called "Environmental Audit Privilege," versions of which were passed in three states.[5]

The "truth in sentencing" statutes that were enacted by forty states during the early 1990s were also drafted by ALEC, making parole abolition its most successful legislative product ever. Under these laws, all inmates newly entering the system have to serve at least 85% of their sentences. Thus Virginia's Department of Criminal Justice Services reports that "a large number of violent offenders are serving two, three, or four times longer under truth-in-sentencing than criminals who committed similar offenses under the parole system."[6] Whereas first-degree murderers once spent an average of fifteen years behind bars in Virginia, they can now expect to serve forty-six.[7]

Who profits when convicts stay in "the big house" for much longer periods of time? The prison-industrial complex, of course: all those inmates have to be housed, fed, medicated, Tasered, telephoned, and Keefed. So who do you suppose sat on the ALEC committee that created the model 85% legislation? The Correctional Corporation of America (CCA)!

What is especially disturbing is that state lawmakers were not told who was behind the parole abolition bills they voted for so enthusiastically. Said a dismayed Walter Dickey, former director of Wisconsin's Department of Corrections, "...there was never any mention that ALEC or anybody else had any involvement in [that state's 'truth in sentencing' statute]."[8]

Subterfuge and deception played a role not only in the passage of 85% laws but also in their subsequent implementation, as we will learn in greater detail below. For now, let us note that even the legislation's name is misleading, since prisoners actually serve 91%, not 85%.[9] That extra 6% can make a big difference, year after year after year; remember, time literally is money for CCA, Aramark, PHS, and MCI.

Finally, we should also note that not only corporate cash but also government funds fueled the parole abolition craze. The federal Violent Crime Control and Law Enforcement Act (VCCLEA) of 1994 offered prison construction grants and other financial incentives to states that passed "truth in sentencing" bills—a very enticing bit of bait indeed.[10] In our discussion of mandatory minimum sentences, below, we will see that many observers believe that particular bigger stick to have been motivated by the legislative branch's desire to restrict the judicial branch's freedom. Is it possible that a similar power play was behind the VCCLEA? Could it be that this statute and its attached federal dollars were part of Washington's long-running campaign to bring those unruly state legislatures under centralized control?

And, if so, what does any of this have to do with justice or crime control?

Parole Abolition and Crime

As we saw in Chapters 2 and 4, raising incarceration rates has a marginal to nonexistent effect on levels of offending. More prisons do *not* make communities safer. If we take a look at the way the 85% legislation actually operates, we can see why.

"Most serious crimes are committed by people between the ages of eighteen and thirty-two," says Virginia's Republican Attorney General Robert F. McDonnell.[11] On the graph on the following page, we can see that murder, rape, armed robbery, aggravated assault, property and drug offenses occur only very rarely in the forty-and-over population.[12] Dr. Richard Kern, Director of the Virginia Sentencing Commission, points out that "felons in their twenties [are] much more likely to commit another crime than those twice their age."[13] Therefore, pulling convicted criminals out of circulation until they have reached their late thirties is not such a bad idea.

The Expected Timing of Different Types of Offenses
LogNormal Probability Density Distributions for Six Types of Felony Crime
(set so that area under each curve = 100%)

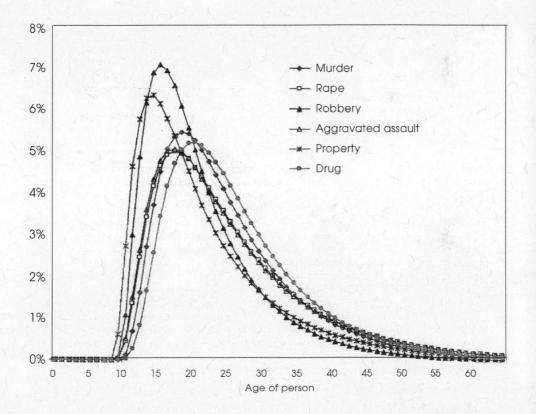

Source: Washington State Institute for Public Policy

According to McDonnell, Virginia's parole abolition law was intended to achieve this precise purpose: "If you make the penalties so harsh for a first offense,…by the time they get out they are older and less likely to commit a new crime."[14] The problem is that the prison terms imposed under the 85% scheme are not calculated to release offenders when they have aged out of their crime-prone years. Instead, sentence lengths appear to reflect emotional reactions to the nature of the offenses.

Below, for instance, we will read a letter by a thirty-one-year-old bank robber who received a sixty-year term of incarceration. Since he will have to serve no less than fifty-four years of that term under "truth in sentencing," he will be eighty-five before he sees freedom again. Will society be any safer by keeping this man locked up throughout his sixties, seventies and half of his eighties?

Under the old parole system, by contrast, he would have become eligible for release after fifteen of those sixty years, at age forty-six. A repeat offender like him would have been denied parole many times before being discharged—in his mid-to-late fifties, say. At that point, he would no longer have been a threat, and the prison cell he freed up by leaving could have been occupied by a real danger—a robber in his twenties, perhaps.

PAROLE ABOLITION AND CRIMINALS

What does it feel like to be sentenced under the 85% law—to be told that there is absolutely no hope of earning a second chance? Read the following letter, sent by the bank robber mentioned above, to a nontraditional prison ministry organization called the Human Kindness Foundation.

I'm pretty much losing my f*cking mind—what's left of it, anyway. I'm thirty-one years old and doing time is nothing new to me. I have been in one institute or another for the past nineteen years. What's new to me is never getting out again. I have over fifty years to serve on my sentence. Basically, I'm f*cked. I don't know what to do. I never really have, I guess. I didn't belong on the street, and I don't belong in here. I just don't fit in anywhere. I have accomplished nothing in life except hurting those who love me. I have no friends—never have—never had any girlfriends, never worked a job longer than a month in my life, never had a license for a car, never had an apartment or a bank account, nothing. I've either been locked up or on the run. I've sold my body for food, killed people for pocket change, all the while looking for "something." Always that "something." Well, I've never found it, and I'm sick of the anger, pain, loneliness and misery. I want to die, plain and simple. Bo [Lozoff, founder of the Human Kindness Foundation,] I'm not crazy—desperate, yes, but not crazy. I just don't know what to do anymore. Reality is slipping away, and my mind is getting sticky. Please help me, if that's even possible, I wonder.[15]

No need to wonder—there is absolutely nothing that can be done to help this man. Because he will never be released, the Department of Corrections will not waste its limited rehabilitative resources on him. And why should he try to better himself on his own? No amount of self-improvement or repentance can change his mandatory release date. His life is reduced to waiting for death.

It is interesting, though, that he is "looking for 'something'"; clearly, he *is* reachable. Clearly, even in his miserable state and condition, he still has a heart human enough to yearn.

PAROLE AND "OLD LAW" PRISONERS

Because criminal statutes cannot be applied retroactively in most cases, those offenders convicted before the 85% legislation was enacted are still eligible for parole. Virginia's Department of Corrections still holds roughly 6,000 such "old law" inmates, or approximately one-sixth of the penitentiary population of 32,000 (plus 3,000 DOC-sentenced prisoners in jails).[16] If Virginia can be assumed to be fairly representative of those states that also adopted "truth in sentencing," we can estimate that there are at least 200,000 such convicts in state facilities nationwide.[17]

These men may still be technically eligible for early release, but in practice parole has been abolished for them, too. Parole boards long ago read the signs of the times and dramatically cut back the number of discharges granted. According to Jane Alford, a former Virginia parole officer, "it's really the political agenda, and if you want to keep your job [as a member of the parole board], you need to follow the political agenda."[18] In New York, Albany Supreme Court Justice Edward Sheridan noted "an undeniable inference that the [Parole] Board has 'gotten the message' and is implementing executive policy" by reducing parole grant rates dramatically.[19]

The change in parole grant rates in Virginia illustrates what is happening to a greater or lesser extent nationwide. In 1994, the last year before "truth in sentencing" was adopted, 40% of eligible inmates were released by the board.[20] Today the Virginia Parole Board's Web site proudly announces that, in the first half of 2006, only 2.9% of parole eligible male convicts were granted release.[21] (Women prisoners have higher parole grant rates.)

Even the 2.9% figure does not reflect reality, however, nor does the 8% number that is sometimes cited by the parole board itself.[22]

- Those 8% include so-called mandatory paroles—inmates who have served their entire sentences up to their mandatory release dates and then have to spend six months under mandatory parole supervision. Because the term "mandatory parole" includes the word "parole," laypeople conclude that some form of early release is involved, whereas the opposite is true.

- The 2.9% figure gives no indication that almost all of these "early" discharges take place within eighteen months or so before the mandatory release date. This stratagem is a staple of parole boards across the nation: in Colorado, for instance, 96% of those prisoners granted parole were so close to their release dates that they were not in fact discharged until they reached their mandatories.[23] To jaundiced eyes, there can be only one reason for making convicts serve almost their entire sentences and then granting them parole just before the very end: to create the appearance that the parole board is actually doing its job and determining which inmates ought to be freed.

Over the five years prior to this writing, I have been personally aware of only *two* discharged "old law" prisoners who were neither "mandatory paroles" nor within a few months of "mandatory parole"—and I have a rather wide circle of acquaintances and contacts. One of these men appears to have been paroled as part of his plea agreement many years ago, and the other is D. V. "Delicious Vanilla" Jackson.[24]

"Delicious" is a real *convict*—a loudmouth, a showoff, a bully to the weak, and a bootlicker to the strong, a con man and deal maker, and, inevitably, an "undercover" homosexual. To hear him tell it, he was convicted of second-degree murder as a juvenile in the 1970s and served twelve years of a forty-eight-year sentence before being paroled. Of course, he then abused his freedom by burglarizing a relative's apartment. For that offense he spent another fifteen years behind bars, during which time I had the dubious pleasure of meeting him.

"Delicious" is not a bad fellow, I suppose, but just about the last person who should ever have been paroled a second time. As *everyone* in the criminal justice field knows, prisoners who have failed under previous parole supervision, as he did, have an 80% recidivism rate when freed again.[25] Yet the parole board discharged "Delicious," of all people, although he had more than a decade left until his mandatory release date.

Why not one of the interview subjects in this book? Why not any of the literally dozens of inmates at this facility alone who are first-time offenders, have unblemished prison records, and have served more than twenty years? Their recidivism rate, as we will see below, is roughly 20%. Why "Delicious"?

Could it be that the parole board intentionally chose someone who is statistically almost guaranteed to re-offend? Is it possible that, if the board were to release hundreds of convicts who behave themselves, the whole notion of being "tough on crime" would be exposed as a sham? Could it be that, like the guards' unions, parole board members, too, need to keep a sizeable contingent of parole-eligible prisoners behind bars to justify their $120,000-a-year jobs?

Those who would dismiss these questions as convict paranoia on my part may wish to consider the case of Bobby K. Whitworth, former chairman of Georgia's parole board. In December 2003, he was convicted of taking a $75,000 payoff from his friend Lansome Newsome in exchange for initiating and pushing through a piece of legislation called SB 474. This statute effectively transferred supervision of about 25,000 misdemeanor offenders from the state's probation and parole department to Detention Management Services, Inc.—a company that just happened to be owned by Newsome.[26]

Of course, the point here is not that parole boards generally are corrupt. But for every Whitworth who crossed the line, we can be sure there are many others who legally manipulate the system to their own advantage. An annual salary of $120,000 is a very powerful motive—certainly a more powerful motive than the $75,000 that bought Whitworth.

In the case of "Delicious" Jackson, the Virginia Parole Board got what it wanted: he violated the conditions of his release by fleeing the scene of an accident, according to the prison grapevine. And who was the very next long-termer at our facility who received parole? Another man who had violated parole on a previous sentence! Another near-certain recidivist; another small piece of job security for the parole board.

Parole Abolition and the Future

If "truth in sentencing" were reversed, parole could be made into an effective crime-fighting and budget-saving tool. Here are a few commonsense principles to guide possible reforms.

Create a politically and institutionally independent parole board. This is the key to any reform in the field of corrections, as California governor Arnold Schwarzenegger's prison reform commission and federal District Court Judge Thelton Henderson noted in Chapter 6.

As long ago as 1967, the President's Crime Commission urged that parole boards be staffed by professionals, not political appointees.[27]

This recommendation was never adopted, with the result that parole grant rates fluctuate wildly as administrations come and go. In Pennsylvania, for instance, grant rates went from 77.4% in 1992 to 38.8% in 1996, and finally to 50.9% in 2002.[28] If anything like objective criteria had been used in the decision-making process, those rates should have stayed at roughly the same level over the years.

Protecting parole boards from being influenced by the mentality and financial interest of Departments of Correction is just as important. In Virginia, the offices of the board are located in the DOC's headquarters building, correctional personnel supply the board's staff, and the chairperson is a former prosecutor. How about a staff supplied by the Department of Social Services—people trained in solving problems, not hiding them away in prisons? And how about board members from the insurance industry—people trained in assessing risks objectively, using cost-benefit analysis?

Use risk-assessment tools. Over the last few years, criminologists have made great strides in determining the likelihood that a particular offender will recidivate. Virginia happens to be a national leader in this area: in both the *Washington Post* and the *New York Times*, this state's 71-point Probation Violator Risk Assessment (PVRA) was celebrated as the wave of the future.[29] "They've been able to, with near scientific certainty, distinguish who is going to be a future risk," says Delegate David R. Albo (R-Fairfax), chairman of the State Crime Commission.[30]

For some peculiar reason, however, the PVRA is used only at sentencing, to determine whether a newly convicted felon is sent to prison or placed on probation. Why is a risk-assessment tool like the PVRA not used for parole decisions? Because the same hard, scientific data that work so well for the PVRA indicate that most of the 6,000 parole-eligible, "old law" convicts in Virginia no longer pose a threat to public safety.

Develop realistic expectations of success. A common objection to parole is that nobody and nothing—not even the PVRA—can guarantee that a particular parolee will not re-offend. While this is true, however, perfection is not a realistic measure of success in any human enterprise. The prison system as a whole currently achieves a recidivism rate of 67.5%, so any figure below that should be applauded as an improvement over the status quo.

As we saw in Chapters 4 and 7, drug and property offenders have violent recidivism rates three to four times as high as released lifers. That is cold comfort if you happen to be harmed by a paroled murderer as opposed to a paroled burglar. But who would you rather have living next door? As so often in the field of criminal justice, the *intuitive* answer is the wrong one—and then everyone is surprised and outraged when disaster strikes again.

Develop a realistic sense of time and sentence length. To the best of my knowledge, few if any psychologists in the U.S. are conducting research on how much time a human being can spend behind bars before breaking down mentally. However, long-term convicts like me have observed that the twenty-year mark appears to be some sort of deep-rooted, inherent limit, beyond which lies madness for most inmates. This raises a significant public policy question: is it really wise governance to destroy hundreds of thousands of prisoners' minds?

These men and women are in effect being turned into permanent burdens on taxpayers' wallets; even if they are released eventually, they will have to be housed in mental hospitals or, more likely, local prisons. According to the Criminal Justice Institute, 27.5% of the adult U.S. correctional population, or roughly 525,000 convicts, are serving sentences of twenty years or more.[31] That means there could be as much as $12 billion at stake here, given the annual per capita incarceration cost of $22,650.

Even if American criminologists appear to be uninterested in the mental health consequences of long-term incarceration, other industrialized countries' court and correctional systems do take such factors into account. European attitudes to sentencing are different, anyway: prison terms over five years are considered long, terms of ten to twelve years are deemed very long, and twenty years is the outside limit.[32] "No one stays twenty years in prison," said an Italian judge while pardoning Mehmet Ali Agca, the man who attempted to assassinate Pope

John Paul II.[33] And in 2005 a German court paroled Mohammed Ali Hamadi, a Lebanese terrorist convicted of murdering a U.S. Navy diver during an airliner hijacking in 1985.[34]

Apply Christian thinking to parole decisions. Republican Mark L. Earley served as Attorney General of Virginia from 1997 to 2001 and then become President of Prison Fellowship Ministries (PFM). After meeting many convicts at religious events in penitentiaries across America, he had this to say about parole:

> Through my law and politics career I would have said I thought most prisoners were incapable of rehabilitation.... [But] I've seen an awful lot of prisoners [since joining PFM] that committed crimes in their late teens, early twenties, and now they're in their forties or fifties and they shouldn't be in prison anymore. What happened was a terrible act of misguided youth.... After a significant period of the sentence is served, should we provide some opportunity for look-back?[35]

Mandatory Minimums

Mandatory minimums are the third of the four bigger sticks that this nation used to beat back the wave of lawlessness of the early 1990s. Under these laws, judges are required to impose a specific number of years for specific quantities of narcotics, say—no exceptions! Supporters claim that firm, harsh punishments effectively deter drug dealers, while opponents argue that too many lives are needlessly ruined by removing judges' discretion to consider mitigating circumstances.

Many observers have come to conclude that, in the federal system at least, man-mins are less about fighting crime than about the legislative branch's desire to control the judicial branch. As with the CCPOA and "three strikes," and ALEC and "truth in sentencing," so too do mandatory minimums come with their own hidden agenda. However, the greatest power shift is not between the legislative and judicial branches, but between judges and prosecutors.

As the American Bar Association notes, man-mins do not remove district attorneys' discretion to charge defendants with all, some or none of the drugs found in their possession. That initial charging decision determines the level of punishment, and it is not reviewable by trial or in most cases even appellate judges.[36] For defendants, the only way to obtain mercy is to provide "substantial assistance" to prosecutors.

This provision has the ironic effect of helping primarily kingpins, however. Because they have the most information to trade, top-level dealers constitute only 6% of those offenders sentenced under federal mandatory minimums.[37] It is overwhelmingly "mules" and minor players who are slammed with the full force of these statutes.

Thanks to another quirk of federal mandatory minimums, they tend to affect African-Americans disproportionately compared to Caucasians. Just five grams of crack suffice to trigger a five-year sentence, whereas it takes five hundred grams of powder cocaine. Since the former is used mostly by blacks and the latter mostly by whites, guess who goes to prison more often and for longer periods?

The American Bar Association, former federal drug "czar" General Barry McCaffrey and most Christian denominations have explicitly called for the abolition of mandatory minimums.[38] Even one of the earliest proponents of these laws, former Michigan Governor William G. Milliken, joined the chorus of critics in a 2002 op-ed piece for the *Detroit News*: "I have since come to realize that the provisions of the law have led to terrible injustices and that signing it was a mistake— an overly punishing and cruel response that gave no discretion to a sentencing judge, even for extenuating circumstances."[39] Three months later the then-current governor of Michigan, Republican John Engler, signed legislation eliminating most of the state's man-mins, thereby saving Michigan $41 million in correctional expenditures each year.[40]

Life Sentences

When it comes to the fourth of our bigger sticks, life sentences, it is difficult to garner public sympathy or support for reform. More than

90% of lifers were convicted of violent crimes; 68.9% are murderers.[41] If ever the maximum penalty under law is appropriate, then surely it is for these men, women and juveniles.

No one—not even I and the many lifers I know—would argue that the crimes of which we were convicted do not merit lengthy terms of incarceration. In some cases a lesser penalty might have been more just: roughly 24,000 lifers are mentally ill, 9,700 were juveniles at the time of their offenses, more than 10,000 are nonviolent drug and property criminals (often "three strikers"), and an indeterminate number were convicted under "felony murder" statutes that impose a life term on a lookout outside the bank if an accomplice inside kills a teller.[42] Most of us, though, deserve our punishment.

What really needs to be asked when it comes to lifers is what taxpaying citizens deserve. Because convicted murderers and rapists are considered unworthy of attention, very few people have noticed the financial and public safety implications of life sentences. But these implications are truly enormous, and ignoring them is a disservice to the community.

According to the Sentencing Project, there were 127,677 prisoners serving life terms in the U.S. in 2003, or 9.4% of the total penitentiary population.[43] The number of lifers has risen 83% since 1992, far outpacing the growth of the rest of the correctional population.[44] And every year, another 5,000 or so new inmates with life sentences enter the system.[45]

The most conservative estimate of the annual cost of incarcerating these men and women is $3 billion.[46] As we will see below, however, elderly convicts require more medical services, which makes them on average three times as expensive to house as other inmates. Lifers are by definition older than the rest of the prison population, so a more realistic, but still conservative estimate of their total incarceration cost might be $6 billion per year.

Is this money well spent? Certainly not if public safety is the criterion: in Chapter 4 we saw that only 20.6% of paroled lifers re-offend, compared to 67.5% of ex-convicts generally. Moreover, at 3.7%, lifers have the lowest *violent* recidivism rate of any category of released inmates. If *all* of America's life-sentenced prisoners were freed today, they would collectively commit fewer than one hundred new violent crimes in each of the fifty states—too few to register in criminologists' statistics.

Why do lifers pose such a low risk upon discharge? One reason is their age at release: even before "truth in sentencing," virtually no lifer was paroled before he reached his late thirties at the earliest. Another, perhaps more important reason has to do with the offenders' character and the character of their crimes: according to Warden Burl Cain of Angola State Penitentiary, "Many of the lifers are not habitual felons. They committed a murder that was a crime of passion," and they tend to be "docile, mature and helpful."[47]

Life versus LWOP

As we learned in our discussion of "truth in sentencing," above, parole boards have virtually stopped discharging those convicts who are technically still eligible for parole. Inmates who have fixed sentences—that is, a determinate number of years—eventually reach their mandatory release dates and leave. Since lifers have no "mandatories," however, they can never finish their sentences.

This is why it is pointless to distinguish between "regular" life terms and "life without parole," or LWOP. It is certainly true that the number of LWOPers has increased even more dramatically than "regular" lifers—by 170% between 1992 and 2003.[48] But in reality lifers with parole are no better off in having hearings that never result in release.

A federal district court in California made a finding of fact in 2005 that the Golden State's parole board "operated under a *sub rosa* policy that all murderers be found unsuitable for parole."[49] Significantly, the board did not challenge this finding but merely argued that for each case there was "some evidence" to deny release.[50] "What we have is a [system] that holds out the illusion of redemption but in fact denies people any fair chance of living in a free society," says attorney Keith Wattley of California's nonprofit Prison Law Office.[51]

What is happening in the Golden State is representative of what is happening around the country:

- Fourteen states reported that they freed fewer than ten life-sentenced prisoners in 2001, the last year for which data is available; another eight states reported that they paroled fewer than twenty-four.[52]

- Michigan's politically popular slogan for parole-eligible lifers is "life means life." During the entire decade of the 1990s, only thirty-one were discharged.[53]

- Georgia's parole board boasted in a 1998 news release, "There's a popular misconception that life in prison doesn't mean all of one's natural life. In just the last year, there are twenty-one lifers who are no longer around to tell you otherwise"—because they died behind bars.[54]

- Angola State Penitentiary, which houses over 5,000 convicts, is being converted to hold only life-sentenced inmates.[55] Of New York's 64,000 prisoners, 19.4%, or roughly 12,400, are lifers.[56] These numbers will continue to swell because there is no way out but death.

- In California 27,375 prisoners, or 18.1% of the state's correctional population, were serving life terms in 2004.[57] About 4,000 of these men and women have board hearings each year,[58] of whom fewer than 1% are recommended for release. Generally, 80% of that 1% are then turned down by the governor.[59]

  During Democratic Governor Gray Davis's five years in office, he paroled only eight lifers. Republican governor Arnold Schwarzenegger, by contrast, freed just over 100 in his first two years in office—only a handful, but still too many for the CCPOA.[60] On April 22, 2005, the guards' union and the crime victims' group it funds staged a rally at the state capitol to protest the "action governor's" parole releases—whereupon he bravely cut his grant rate in half.[61]

What does all of this mean? It means that 130,000 prisoners have no other way of leaving state custody than in a body bag.

LIFE SENTENCES AND THE VICTIMS' PERSPECTIVE

Even some death penalty advocates express doubts about the policy of confining prisoners until they die. "Life without parole is a very strange sentence," says Professor Robert Blecker of the New York Law School. "The punishment seems either too much or too little. If a sadistic or extraordinarily cold, callous killer deserves to die, then why not kill him? But if we are going to keep the killer alive…why strip him of all hope?"[62]

Former warden Ron McAndrew, who supervised three executions during his tenure at the Florida State Prison at Starke, now publicly advocates the abolition of capital punishment with the argument that life without parole is "worse than the death penalty." He observes, "the most severe punishment you could ever give anyone would be to lock them in a little cage made our of concrete and steel… with a steel cot, a mattress that is two inches thick, a stainless steel toilet that does not have a lid, and you leave them there for the rest of their natural life. There can't be a more severe punishment than that."[63]

Some victims' relatives prefer life without parole over capital punishment precisely because they see it as a harsher penalty. In an op-ed piece for USA Today, the daughter of a victim of the 9/11 attacks wrote this about Zacarias Moussaoui:

> I want Moussaoui to die a slow, painful death. I do not want to give him the dignity of a planned execution, time to say his goodbyes, eat his last meal. His comrades did not give that to my mother. Let him sit in a cold, dirty cell alone for the rest of his long days, unable to direct his rants at anyone. [64]

Michelle Cottle of the New Republic also came out against capital punishment for Moussaoui "because it would be too easy…. Better to throw the failed jihadist into a cell with a large, surly redneck with a scorching case of xenophobia and let him spend the rest of his miserable life learning about pain and terror firsthand."[65]

Such feelings must be respected. But there is another way to deal with terrorists sentenced to life in prison, as the British journal *The Tablet* tells us.[66]

During the 1960s and '70s, the Red Brigades came close to over-throwing the Italian government with a campaign of assassinations of high government officials. Al Qaeda can only dream of being as "successful" as this homegrown terrorist organization was. In 1980, one of its female members scored what may have been the Red Brigades' greatest "victory": the murder of Vittorio Bachelet, a man so eminent that he has been described as the de facto vice-president of the Italian Republic.

Millions of viewers watched his state funeral on national TV. Speaking from the lectern over the flag-draped coffin, Vittorio Bachelet's son Giovanni stunned the congregation during the Prayer of the Faithful: he forgave the killer personally and on behalf of his family. Instead of giving the customary response, "Lord, hear our prayer," the assembled worshippers broke into applause.

The young woman who fired the fatal shots and several other Red Brigade members watched this event on the TVs in their penitentiary. Three years and countless discussions later, eighteen of the terrorists collectively sent a letter to Father Adolpho Bachelet, SJ, Vittorio's brother and Giovanni's uncle:

> We want you to come to the prison so that we can listen to whatever you want to say. We remember very well what your nephew said at his father's funeral. Those words of his keep taking our minds back to that ceremony where life triumphed over death, and we too were overcome. In the aftermath we were deeply touched and kept asking questions, trying to find within ourselves what were the roots of our transformation. The reason why we tried to change was the example you, the family, gave us: it made us realize that it was possible to live life another way.

Another four years later, Father Adolpho had built up a network of 150 to 200 Red Brigade members in prisons across Italy. He and others helped them transition back into civilian life, get jobs, and integrate into parish life. On one occasion, he celebrated a Mass of Reconciliation for the leader of an assassination team and the family of his victim.

"It all goes to show," says Father Adolpho, "that every age, in spite of everything, is the Messianic Age." In Italy today, the Red Brigades are no longer a significant public safety problem. Superior police work and forgiveness defeated terrorism—not bunker-busting bombs or hellholes like the federal supermax in Colorado, where Moussaoui has been sent.

Can America learn what the Red Brigades learned: that it is possible to live life another way?

LIFE SENTENCES AND THE LIFERS' PERSPECTIVE

Paul Wright, editor of *Prison Legal News* and an ex-convict himself, calls a term of life imprisonment "a death sentence by incarceration. You're trading a slow form of death for a faster one."[67] Of course, one can quibble that "death by incarceration" is not *really* a form of capital punishment; there is no point at which a needle is inserted into a vein or a noose is placed around a neck, after all. But, having learned about the realities of penitentiary life in the pages of this book, are you willing to argue that suffering through those horrors is better than death?

As readers of my first and third books will know, I myself traded death by electric chair for death by incarceration, so I am able to offer an informed opinion on which form of capital punishment, fast or slow, is worse.

I spent the first three and a half years of my incarceration under threat of execution; my own lawyers assured me that I had no hope of avoiding the electric chair. Then, in a surprising and indeed precedent-setting decision, the European Court of Human Rights refused to extradite me to the U.S. until death penalty charges were dropped. But just one year later, in 1990, I was sentenced to two terms of life imprisonment, to be served consecutively.

The fact that the judge specified consecutive instead of concurrent sentences is significant. If the two terms had been imposed concurrently,

I would have reached parole eligibility after fifteen years; but since they were consecutive, I had to wait seventeen years until my first hearing. The only reason to stipulate the latter instead of the former is that the judge expected me to be released (and deported to my home country of Germany) fairly soon after reaching parole eligibility. Had "life means life" applied in 1990, he could have sentenced me to just one life term to ensure my perpetual incarceration.

So I began my long trip "up the river" in the full expectation that I would eventually be freed. But then the rules changed, and the death sentence I thought I had escaped in 1989 caught up with me after all. Capital punishment on the installment plan!

When I allow myself to think about what my future holds, I primarily experience a powerful sense of guilt. My life—or, rather, my two lifes—are so much richer than virtually any other convict's:

- I am able to practice Centering Prayer three times a day
- I have interesting and meaningful work, in the form of my literary activity
- I have many friends and supporters in the "real world" who write and visit me

How dare I complain? I look at the lifers and long-termers in my circle of acquaintances, and I wonder how they manage to bear their existence.

- Most of them have no experience of joy or transcendence—except the brief, twisted glimpses provided by drugs, home-brewed alcohol and homosexual activity
- Most have nothing meaningful to do—which may explain why so many develop odd compulsions, like keeping the floor of the dayroom polished to a supernaturally sparkling brightness
- And most of them have little or no connection to the outside world; months pass without a letter, years or even decades without a visit

To me, it is a miracle that my fellow convicts can go on under these circumstances, and I am awed by their strength.

Yet even I, with all my blessings, feel the vise of time squeezing the life breath out of me. Behind me is the ever-increasing weight of all those wasted years; ahead is the ever-decreasing number of at least theoretically still possible "good years" and that list of "things to do before I die." Time is a rock on your chest that crushes you slowly, slowly.

A few years ago, in a moment of complete idiocy and weakness, I kissed a beautiful young woman in the visiting room; the guards allow this at the beginning and the end of each visit. My first kiss—after, at that time, eighteen years of incarceration! All I can remember is how incredibly, unbelievably, almost frighteningly soft her mouth was....

After the visit I returned to the mayhem of the housing unit: BET blaring on the dayroom TV, inmates arguing over a card game, the female floor officer flirting with her favorite convict. My cellmate was using the toilet, so my usual place of refuge, the cell, was not available. Resourceful fellow that I am, I stepped into the mop and broom closet, pulled the door shut behind me—and cried.

I have a good cry every two or three years, just to let off some of the pressure. Was this cry any different? I don't know.

But I do know this: for the few seconds of that kiss, I was a real human being—a creature made by divine Love to love and be loved (cf. 1 John 4:7, 8, 12). Eighteen years had nearly wiped away the memory of what it is to be human, and experiencing that feeling again after so long truly pierced me. If that kiss had not been so wonderful, I would say that it was one of the most painful events in my life.

The only thing worse than this reminder of my lost humanity is the knowledge that I will probably never experience another kiss. I will most likely never be allowed to be human again.

So, America, congratulate yourself: you have managed to invent a punishment worse than death.

Life Sentences and the International Perspective

As we saw earlier with Mehmet Ali Agca and Mohammed Ali Hamadi, not even the worst of the worst are considered beyond redemption in the de-Christianized and decadent nations of "old Europe." Only 3.1% of inmates in my home country of Germany are lifers, and both Germany's highest court and the European Court of Human Rights have held that life sentences must include the possibility of release. In England just 23 out of 4,206 lifers have no parole eligibility dates.[68]

America's closest cultural cousin, Canada, has granted parole to one-third of its life-sentenced inmates. Beginning in 1990, the Correctional Services of Canada (CSC) have operated an innovative program called LifeLine, wherein paroled lifers return to prison to counsel those still incarcerated how best to prepare for their eventual discharge. Newly released lifers go to a special residential facility, St. Edward's House, where they can slowly ease back into civilian society. In August 1998, the American Correctional Association (ACA) certified LifeLine as a model "best practice."[69]

Only one U.S. jurisdiction has adopted it: Colorado, in an exceptionally small pilot program.

Bigger Sticks and Elderly Prisoners

In Chapter 2 we saw that "three strikes," parole abolition, mandatory minimums, and more life sentences produced a 51.6% expansion of the U.S. correctional population during the 1990s. What effect did this have on crime rates? A reduction of just 4.4 to 7.9%, once factors like a booming economy and demographic changes are taken into account.

Instead of being merely inefficient, however, the four bigger sticks discussed in this chapter produced a brand new problem of their own: a rapidly expanding population of elderly inmates. The number of convicts aged fifty and over jumped from 41,586 in 1992 to 120,933 in 2002, an increase of about 170%.[70] While older prisoners constitute only 8.6% of all inmates today, that figure is expected to rise to about 25% by 2025.[71]

There is no consistent definition of what "elderly" means in corrections, but a lifetime of drug abuse and poor health care typically makes an inmate's physical age fifteen years greater than his or her chronological age.[72] Thanks largely to their greater need for medical services, aging convicts typically cost $69,000 per year to incarcerate.[73] Thus elderly prisoners are considered one of the primary factors contributing to the explosion in correctional health care expenditures—42% just between 2004 and 2005, for instance.[74]

By 2023, California expects to pay $4 billion per year just for the state's projected 50,000 elderly convicts.[75] But that estimate does not take into account the federal court's fall 2005 take-over of the California correctional department's entire medical services system.[76] To bring its prison health care up to something closer to civilized standards, the Golden State's annual correctional expenditure is expected to rise from $8.2 to $10.2 billion.[77] And that estimate does not even include the two new $500 million–apiece penitentiaries discussed at the end of Chapter 6; they are supposed to be special medical facilities, where aging convicts can get their heart bypass surgeries and Alzheimer's treatment.[78]

Whether this is a wise investment of crime-fighting dollars may be doubted. According to a Department of Justice study, "some of the most dangerous and/or persistent criminals sentenced to life in prison without parole thirty years ago are now old, debilitated, frail, chronically ill, depressed and no longer considered a threat to society or the institution."[79] Offenders paroled after age fifty-five recidivate at a rate under 2%.[80]

Elderly Prisoners and Life behind Bars

For older inmates, coping with prison life can be difficult, a study by the National Institute of Corrections found. They "feel unsafe and vulnerable around younger people," leading to "abrasive relations" and "explosiveness" or "anxiety" and "withdraw[al]."[81] Among elderly first-time offenders, "suicide,...mental disorder[s and] victimization by others" are especially common.[82]

Thirty-five states have attempted to address the special needs of aging convicts by constructing so-called geriatric prisons.[83] But these institutions can only hold a small percentage of all older inmates, and they vary greatly in quality. While Ohio's Hocking Correctional Facility is considered a model nationwide, for instance, an internal report by Florida's Correctional Medical Authority determined that its own prison "staff's lack of training in recognizing the medical and mental health conditions of elderly inmates often exacerbate [their] problems."[84]

Virginia's geriatric facility prides itself on keeping its per-convict cost far below the national average. How does it achieve this distinction? Instead of paying professional staff, it hires younger prisoners at $42 a month to push aging inmates' wheelchairs and help them with activities like eating and dressing.[85] Not surprisingly, the many older men at my current prison live in absolute terror of being transferred there.

The housing unit that I call home—this facility's "honor building"— holds mostly elderly convicts. Because everyone is so well behaved (or just plain sleepy), it is a comparatively pleasant place to do time. But we are all acutely aware that more of us leave by dying than by making parole. Every few months, it seems, another of our number is wheeled out to the medical department, never to return. Then Carlton L., our third interview subject, comes around again with a condolence card to sign; this has almost become a ritual around here. Lately Carlton has even begun to hold special memorial services for beloved old-timers.

Because so many convicts are dying behind bars, twenty-nine states have set up hospices or "end-of-life units" in selected correctional centers.[86] Louisiana pioneered this concept because 90% of Angola's 5,018 inmates are expected to die in state custody.[87] Thanks to staff member Tanya Tillman, RN, prisoners now receive thirty hours of professional training to prepare them for the difficult work of helping their fellow convicts die with dignity. One inmate volunteer described an unexpected benefit of the program in an interview for *The Angolite*:

Before I got in the program,…I didn't really care about anyone else's problems because I had a lot of my own. But after doing hospice care my whole attitude changed. I have a willingness to help others, especially those who are dying and have no hope. And I find I'm more tolerant with everyone.[88]

Elderly Prisoners and Those 63 Billion Reasons

If the passage above touches your heart, you have once again forgotten what prisons in America are really all about. The National Institute of Corrections points out that "hospice may save money because inmates are not dying in the hospital where care and services would be more costly.…Because staffing is minimal at the end-of-life program…the program operates at a low cost."[89]

Dollars and cents also control so-called compassionate release programs for terminally ill convicts. "We'll release somebody to the outside if so doing will save the state a significant amount of money and it is safe to do so," says Mark Stern, director of medical services for the Washington State Department of Corrections. Only about one hundred inmates nationwide are discharged each year under some form of "compassionate release";[90] in the state of Virginia, not a single one has been freed.[91]

As the New York Times put it, "the United States has created something never before seen in its history and unheard of around the globe: a booming population of prisoners whose only way out of prison is likely to be inside a coffin."[92] Those who have truly understood this book will read that sentence and ask, "I wonder which company got the convict coffin contract?"

*　　*　　*

Before we turn to our last interview subject, Bud T., let us spend a little time on the topic of incarcerated veterans. Bud T. flew a Huey in Nam, making him one of roughly 225,000 military men who are now serving time instead of their country. As late as 1998, an estimated 56,500 of these were Vietnam veterans—nearly as many as died in the war itself.[93]

In 1998 there were also about 18,500 Persian Gulf War veterans in this nation's jails and penitentiaries.[94] And as I write these lines, the first few veterans of the Afghan and Iraqi wars have trickled into the system. They will eventually become an entire army behind bars, so you may as well learn about this important part of the future of American corrections.

More than one-third of U.S. soldiers and Marines returning from Iraq sought mental health treatment,[95] and one-fifth are expected to develop post-traumatic stress disorder (PTSD).[96] While many veterans with PTSD never run afoul of the law, post-traumatic stress disorder and PTSD-related substance abuse are two of the four primary causes of criminality among former members of the military.[97] Defending their country has in effect handicapped veterans in a way that sets them up to fail when they return home from the front.

According to military psychiatrists, the four classic symptoms of PTSD are nightmares, severe and persistent memories, feeling numb, and being constantly on guard or easily startled. One soldier who is clearly at risk for PTSD described his dreams after fighting in Fallujah: "The truly terrifying ones are when someone I love gets shot because of a war that follows me home.... Or the people I care about are dying because of my sin.... I kind of worry about coming back [to America] from here."[98] Another soldier found himself unable to sleep more than three or four hours at a time after his return stateside. "Any little noise, and I'd jump up out of bed and run around the house with a gun.... I'd wake up at nights with cold sweats."[99]

To Bud T., these soldiers' accounts are sadly familiar; they describe his own life more than thirty years ago. He holds out little hope that traumatized veterans of the Afghan and Iraqi wars will be treated any more compassionately by the criminal justice system than he and his fellow Vietnam veterans were. In America, old soldiers never die, they just get sent to prison.

Interview with "Bud T."

Bud T. was sentenced to one hundred and twenty-seven years for first-degree murder, malicious wounding, use of a firearm, and numerous counts of aggravated sexual assault and sodomy in 1983.

Q: Tell us a little about your life before you were arrested for your current offense.

A: I was born in 1946. My father was an aeronautical engineer and my mother a nurse. We attended our local Baptist church almost every weekend; my father was a deacon and trustee there. In my late teens, though, I joined the Lutheran Church. I graduated from high school and then went to a junior college in New York to prepare for my entry into a Lutheran seminary. My plan was to become an institutional chaplain.

Q: What happened to change your plans?

A: The Vietnam conflict. In 1967, I volunteered to join the U.S. Army and went to Warrant Officer Flight School, to become a helicopter pilot. I arrived in Vietnam in 1968 and flew combat operations in the Mekong Delta. While I was there, my brother, who also flew helicopters, was shot down and killed. I was shot down myself on three occasions.

Q: When did you return to the U.S.?

A: In 1973, after a long rehab in Japan for my injuries. After about a week with my family, I took a cross-country trip to personally visit the families of all fourteen members of my flight school class of fifty-two students that I knew had been killed; there were probably more KIA and MIA-PD that I didn't know about.

Q: What was that like?

A: It was the hardest thing I've done in my life. I stayed drunk almost the entire time—binge drinking and passing out for days at a time—and I took lots of Valium and Demerol.

Q: What did you do with your life after this trip?

A: I served as a flight standards pilot in North Carolina and left active service with an honorable discharge in 1975. Between 1975 and 1983, I worked in, oh, about three dozen different jobs: retail manager, real estate agent, insurance broker, maintenance crew foreman in a Virginia prison, operator of an aluminum recycling business, gun dealer, produce manager. On and on, you name it, I've done it.

Q: Did your problems with alcohol continue during this period?

A: Of course, and they got worse. In the final year before my arrest in 1983, I was drinking a fifth of whiskey per day, or a case to a case and a half of beer—every day.

Q: Was your faith of any help during this period? You had once planned to become a Lutheran minister, after all.

A: I was too self-absorbed to think about any kind of salvation. I occasionally attended church services. And sometimes I would just sit outside the church, listening to the music inside, and drink. I was always drinking, more and more and more.

Q: What happened in 1983 to bring all this to a climax?

A: It actually started in 1982, when I checked myself into a Veterans Administration alcoholism clinic. While I was there, I was arrested on aggravated sexual assault and sodomy charges. Actually, I drove myself from the VA alcoholism clinic to the police station, made bond, and immediately returned to the clinic. But the rules were that you couldn't leave the premises for any reason, so I wasn't allowed back in. I became upset, and I ended up being involuntarily committed to a psychiatric facility on the same compound. I was released from there a few weeks later, toward the end of 1982, and then things really exploded in 1983.

Q: Before we get to that, please describe the aggravated sexual assault and sodomy charges.

A: I was charged with numerous counts of aggravated sexual assault and sodomy, involving the thirteen- and eleven-year-old sons of an occasional girlfriend of mine. The older boy was living in a group home; his mother had lost custody of him. He was caught in bed with another resident, and things unraveled from there.

Q: Have you developed any insight into how you ended up in this predicament? Had you been sexually abused yourself?

A: I wasn't abused! To say that is to continue part of the denial system, and I don't deny anything. As a nine-year-old, I had had a homosexual experience with a twelve-year-old boy; actually, we had a relationship that lasted six years. When I met this boy—the one I was charged with sexually assaulting—I felt I saw a mirror image of myself at his age. He was in desperate trouble: his mother wasn't able to provide for him and his brothers, they were living in this horrible tenement....I remember there was a dead dog lying out in front of the door for days and days. Well, anyway, I believed or thought that I was providing for him. Of course, I was completely drunk all the time in those days. But I'm not trying to make excuses.

Q: So, after you were charged with the sexual assaults, and you returned to the VA hospital and eventually left there toward the end of 1982, what happened next?

A: I got some private treatment with a psychiatrist. And then I got an income tax refund check, which I spent on an aquarium for a friend and some liquor for myself. That's when I decided to kill myself.

Q: How were you planning on doing that?

A: In those days, I always traveled with my two favorite guns in my car: a .30 fully automatic M2 carbine, and a .44 revolver with a 71/2-inch barrel. I always had those with me—always. But those are not the sort of guns you can kill yourself with, because of the barrel length, so I drove to a friend who owned a gun store and bought a .357 revolver. I was going to shoot myself at Yorktown battlefield, where Cornwallis surrendered to Washington and America won its independence in battle. It seemed like the appropriate place.

Q: But that didn't work out as intended.

A: No. On the way to my friend with the gun store, a recapped tire on my car started to disintegrate. After I bought the gun, I drove to another friend who owned a tire store, because I believed he had sold me the bad recapped tire. He hadn't sold it to me, but I thought he had; I was completely drunk, of course. Anyway, I shot and killed him, and I shot his brother-in-law three times, severely injuring him. When I went back into the store, I picked up the phone, which was off the hook because my friend had been using it when I shot him. The person on the other line must have heard the shots and gotten an operator on that line. I heard her voice and picked up the phone, and she asked me, "Sir, are you hit?" That set me off again, I can tell you! I thought I was back in Vietnam and started shooting at everything—the TV, the phone, everything.

Then the SWAT team arrived, and I started shooting at them, too; thank God I didn't hit any of them! After about six hours of firing my weapons constantly, I ran out of ammunition. That's when I decided to take six Valiums and drink half a bottle of pre-mixed Tequila Sunrise—on top of everything else I had drunk that day. But that didn't kill me, either.

Q: Did the police arrest you at that point?

A: Yes. I was taken to jail and put on extremely high doses of Thorazine, a strong psychotropic drug, for about ten months. During this time, I was taken to Central State Psychiatric Hospital several times to be examined by court-appointed psychiatrists for my competency to stand trial. The doctors said I was insane, but having seen the inside of Central State before my trial, I decided I didn't want to spend a decade or two in that place; they have some really crazy people there. So I pleaded guilty to first-degree murder, in order to be sent to a regular prison. Even the judge said that he wouldn't have found me guilty of first-degree murder if I had not pleaded guilty.

Q: Did you also plead guilty to the aggravated sexual assault and sodomy charges?

A: Yes, but that wasn't to avoid going to a mental hospital.

Q: So what was the reason?

A: In the jail, I didn't have access to alcohol, so for the first time in I don't know how long, I was sober. I mean, *really* sober! And I was so ashamed of what I'd done, so ashamed. I was also concerned for the welfare of the boys. The thing is, my lawyer told me that I had winnable cases. And in the end, the judge only gave me a year on each count.

Q: At the plea and sentencing hearing for the murder of your friend and the malicious wounding of his brother-in-law, did you have an opportunity to express your feelings to the victims' families?

A: You have to understand, the two men I shot were friends of mine. I had known the owner of the tire store since 1960. And I had known his brother-in-law for many years, as well. There's not a day that ever goes by when I don't wonder why I didn't just finish the job I had started that day—why I didn't continue on to Yorktown battlefield and shoot myself. I could have spared all these people so much heartache! In court, I apologized to the tire store owner's daughter, who was in her late teens at that time. She said, "Yes, but that won't bring my daddy back." Those were the exact words another child had used in 1973, when I told him that his father had been killed in Vietnam. It just struck me: this is like *Groundhog Day*, I'm going through it all over again.

Q: And at the plea and sentencing hearings for the aggravated sexual assault and sodomy charges, did you have an opportunity to express your feelings to those victims?

A: No, at that time I did not. During my subsequent therapy sessions, I was told that I could write a letter to my victim, to apologize for what I'd done, and I did that. The letter was given to the victim's psychiatrist, who shared parts of it with the victim during his therapy. After he turned seventeen, he got the entire letter.

Q: Did he ever write you back?

A: Not that I am aware of.

Q: Tell us about your prison career, after you left the Department of Corrections reception center.

A: In 1984, I was sent to Mecklenburg Correctional Center, at that time the state's supermax. I arrived right before the big death row escape in May of 1984, I was there during the riot in August, and then in the fall I was transferred to Buckingham Correctional Center.

Q: Having begun the process of sobering up in the jail, before your trials, were you able to get any help with your problems while at Mecklenburg Correctional Center?

A: Yes. I was extremely lucky. Some old coworkers of mine, from the time when I had been a maintenance crew foreman at another Virginia prison, made sure that I got one-on-one counseling there, once a week. The psychiatrist was pretty good; after the escape and riot at Mecklenburg, the whole prison stayed locked down for months, and she got me transferred to Buckingham so I could continue my therapy there.

Q: So what was Buckingham Correctional Center like, after Mecklenburg?

A: The night I arrived, I sat on the edge of my bunk and cried like a baby. For the first time in months and months, I had people I could talk to and see. I had a cellmate.

Q: Did you get counseling there?

A: Yes, from a psychologist—one-on-one, once a week. Very, very unusual back then, and completely impossible nowadays.

Q: What kind of job did you get?

A: I worked as a teacher's aide for the HVAC sheet metal course, teaching inmates how to make heating and air conditioning ducts. But I've had all kinds of prison jobs over the years.

Q: And did you join the Alcoholics Anonymous group at Buckingham?

A: Yes, it was...well, very shallow. The program was only about two years old when I got there, and the inmates in it still had the convict mentality: not disclosing the truth about who you are, what you've done. But our two outside sponsors—civilians who volunteered their time to come in once a week for our meetings—they were willing to try something new with me.

Q: And what was that?

A: Basically, a program of fearless and thorough honesty! We got some outside speakers to come in, and I did three one-hour programs in which I told my own story—every gruesome detail, every last one. When we started, we had about seventeen guys; by the end, there were about seventy.

Q: Did telling your story encourage others to be more open?

A: Yes. Look, it took some balls to come into a prison as a convict and tell a bunch of inmates, I used to work for the Department of Corrections, and I'm in here for murder and pedophilia! To prisoners, a maintenance crew foreman is the same thing as a guard—a marked man. And a sex offender whose victims were underage boys is likely to get attacked, too.

Q: How did the prisoners at the AA meetings respond to you?

A: They started telling their own stories. They couldn't use the excuse any more that they weren't being treated as full human beings, so they didn't have to act like full human beings. I *did* treat them as full human beings, so they could behave that way, too! All of a sudden, something was offered to them that gave meaning and purpose to their doing time. And that freed all of us; we could cry together and even had group hugs!

Q: You're crying now.

A: I'm just remembering. At those meetings, I received such an outpouring of forgiveness, at no cost, from my God. And that enabled others to do the same.

Q: What other activities did you engage in, aside from the AA group?

A: In 1985, a counselor at Buckingham who sponsored the AA group began to see that a lot of us were psychologically damaged combat veterans. He managed to put together a program for us through the Veterans Administration, with a psychologist who came in from Richmond once a week. After sixteen weeks, the funding stopped, so the program stopped. But the twelve of us who had participated continued to meet informally, as a support group. We were each other's family in there.

Q: And you also reconnected with an old friend of your literal family, your parents, at this time, isn't that right?

A: Yes, Bill Twine. He was and still is a member of Norview Baptist Church, to which my father also belonged. When Billy was growing up, my father drove him and the other kids to Little League games. Bill's father and mine had served together in World War II.

Q: During this time, the early to mid-1980s, he was building up Onesimus House, too.

A: That's correct. Some of the inmate groups I was involved with began to collect donations, which we sent to Billy. And he would sometimes seek my advice on a particular man he was considering for Onesimus House. Bill would ask me if this individual was participating in therapeutic programs such as AA and if he was serious.

Q: Over the last twenty years or so, how many men have you recommended to Onesimus House?

A: Oh, about two dozen. More than half of them still write me, years and years later.

Q: Like Rusty J., whom our readers met in the Reverend Bill Twine's interview.

A: Yes. He was the first violent offender, the first sex offender, that Billy ever accepted at Onesimus House. I had gotten to know Rusty and his background very well because we lived in the same housing unit. He was a good kid who'd just made some terrible mistakes because of alcohol.

Q: And he wrote you after he went to Onesimus House?

A: Yes. I still have three of his letters from when he first got there, in the fall of 1992. And he just wrote me again, from Arkansas.

That's where he came from originally. [Interviewer's Note: One of Rusty's 1992 letters and his 2005 letter to Bud T. follow this interview.]

Q: You met Rusty through the AA program, but you were also involved with several other groups. Tell us about those.

A: Well, there was the Jaycees—the Junior Chamber of Commerce. At that time, the Jaycees were allowed to operate programs within Virginia prisons that dealt with anger control, stress management, developing managerial skills and leadership qualities—the kinds of things inmates need both inside prison and after they leave. These programs were self-financing: inmates sold greeting cards, collected soda cans, took photographs, that sort of thing. The profits were put in accounts and financed all kinds of things. One summer, we actually sent a local Boy Scout troop to a summer camp for two weeks. None of that exists any more, of course.

Q: Why is that?

A: After the 1993 gubernatorial election in Virginia, the new governor, George Allen, brought in a new director of the Department of Corrections, Ronald Angelone. Mr. Angelone believed that prisons should be as tough as possible. Within a few years, he managed to shut down all these outside groups that were coming into prisons to work with inmates—not just the Jaycees, others too.

Q: Well, even back in the mid-1980s, I wouldn't have expected the Jaycees to be in Buckingham Correctional Center. Why were they there?

A: They believed that community service was the best thing you could possibly do, so they encouraged their members to work with us. We were still considered members of the community back then—we prisoners, I mean. One of the lines of the Jaycee creed has stayed with me, even all these years later: we believe that faith in God gives meaning and purpose to human life. I remember that one line, because I believe that any spirituality needs to encompass everything, one's whole life. You can't restrict your spirituality to one hour at church on Sundays! It's similar to what we teach at AA: the return to honesty has to be cared for and lived twenty-four hours a day.

Q: In 1987, you requested a transfer to Brunswick Correctional Center, to be closer to your parents. What did you do there?

A: Pretty much the same thing I had done at Buckingham. The AA group had lapsed completely. I restarted it with three staff sponsors, one of whom was a very courageous lieutenant. We started with six inmates at the first meeting, and within two years we had a core group of twenty-two, with up to sixty-five people coming each week. For our big quarterly meetings in the visiting room, with family members and outside AA members, we sometimes had over one hundred. But by 1997 Mr. Angelone had managed to shut us down.

Q: How did he do that?

A: We couldn't get outside sponsors. Most alcoholics have arrest records, and under Mr. Angelone's new security rules that meant they couldn't come in to sponsor AA meetings. We're still continuing, though, with about eight to ten people showing up each week. It's hard to get men interested in coming because they can't get any kind of credit for attending AA.

Q: I hear this might be changing.

A: Maybe. Mr. Angelone left in 2003, but a lot of his cronies are still in office in the Virginia Department of Corrections.

Q: You also started a Veterans Insight Group at Brunswick, right?

A: No, that was already in existence when I got there. But it was basically just a weekly bull session, with a counselor there to supervise. After I got here, though, twelve of us decided to become better organized. We wrote up a constitution, developed programs and activities, and eventually had forty to forty-five men involved.

Q: What sorts of things did you do?

A: We and some other groups got approval for a family day—at that time, a twice-yearly function where inmates could visit with their children outside, in a picnic-type atmosphere. We purchased self-help books specifically for veterans, and we had a peer partnership group for young inmates coming into the system who needed guidance. Most importantly, we had weekly support group meetings for veterans. Outside speakers came in twice a year, on Memorial Day and Veterans Day: two Virginia state senators, a Medal of Honor winner, and the past president of the Vietnam Veterans of America, among others. We were hoping to get the Department of Corrections to give us veterans some relief.

Q: Did Ron Angelone shut the Veterans Insight Group down, too?

A: Yes. The last meeting was in 1997. Another new security rule he came up with was that every group also had to have a staff sponsor. Of course, all Department of Corrections staff knew that their boss, Mr. Angelone, did not like rehabilitative programs for prisoners; it was supposed to be all punishment, all the time. So it was almost impossible to find staff sponsors. [Interviewer's Note: Under the new anti-fraternization rule discussed at the end of the Kent I. interview in Chapter 5, staff involvement in inmate programs is now also forbidden, so inmate groups must now obtain an outside sponsor with no criminal record.]

Q: How about the Community Involvement Group—that still exists, doesn't it?

A: Only in name. It used to be a very active group, but at that time—before the Angelone era—I wasn't a part of it. I only joined in 1997, after everything else was terminated. By then, the CIG was actually sponsored by the Brunswick Literacy Council.

Q: And what do they do?

A: They provide us with four outside volunteers—two retired teachers, a retired U.S. Navy captain, and a businessman—as well as classroom supplies and training. All the inmate tutors have to take a two-day training course in the Laubach system, which has now merged with the Literacy Volunteers of America system. We meet once a week after work, for two hours, to help non-readers develop basic literacy in preparation for the prison's LIP (Literacy Incentive Program). I'm the senior tutor and staff liaison.

Q: CIG works one-on-one, I understand, so tell us about your student.

A: He is an African-American man, born in 1953, who was developmentally handicapped due to environmental and nutritional factors and did not go to school at all after age twelve. His family had no electricity in their home until he turned nine. When he began with CIG in 1993, he could not read at all or even write his own name in cursive. One of the outside sponsors taught him the basics, the shapes of letters and pronunciation of sounds. Then I took him over in 1997, because we knew each other from our prison jobs.

Q: And how has he responded to your teaching?

A: Well, he understands concrete things, but not abstract concepts. For example, he can understand that the word "tend" can mean "to care"—for sheep, say—but he can't grasp the alternate meaning of "to incline." If I don't practice with him constantly, he'll lose what he's learned. And he's learned a phenomenal amount, considering his background. He loves to have me read to him; stories about wild life and old people are his favorites. His biggest accomplishment now is to write his former tutor, the outside sponsor, a simple letter once a week. He has no other connection to the outside world—none. In the more than thirty years that he has spent behind bars, he has received only a handful of visits, and none at all since 1980.

Q: In all the different activities and programs we've discussed, you never once mentioned attending religious services. Why is that?

A: Our AA meetings always began and concluded with a prayer, and we used to have a Serenity Group. That's a small AA group that deals with the spiritual side of our program. The prison's chaplain served as our sponsor for many years, but then he left. The chaplains that came after him—well, let's just say that they weren't very supportive. Once a month, though, a Lutheran minister comes here to bring me Communion.

Q: Earlier, you mentioned that you experienced a sense of being forgiven by God at your AA meetings. Tell us more about that.

A: It was extremely hard for me to accept that I could receive forgiveness. I am used to being a giver. In my family, as a little boy, I was always the peacemaker. I didn't want anybody to be as alone as I was, so I always put my own needs in last place. But I had a spiritual change in the first few days in jail, after my arrest in 1983.

Q: Describe that change.

A: The jail guards had put me in an isolation cell, with nothing but my drawers and socks—and plenty of Thorazine, of course. But then, on the night shift, a black guard brought me a telephone; I'll never know how he got the extension cord to stretch all the way back to the isolation cell! I told him I wanted to call my mother, and he dialed the number for me.

Q: And what did she say?

A: She said, Oh, Bud, thank God! I've probably received a hundred phone calls in the last few days, and everyone wants you to know how much they care about you. And she said, "You know, Bud, God still loves you." Then she asked me to say the Twenty-third Psalm with her. She knew I'd said it every day in Vietnam, in spite of all the insanity and all the alcohol. And I stood there, and I couldn't remember the words. So she said the words for me, the words to the Twenty-third Psalm. And I stood there, completely dismantled.

Q: Dismantled?

A: Yes. A bucket of mush. Here was my Lord and my Savior, in the voice of my mother, and he was telling me that I needed to live and to fight for what I knew my true purpose was: to meet and greet all who suffer from the same sickness of soul that I have. Let no man come among you and not feel welcome. No matter what our past or future, our Lord loves us all. That's what my life has been about, as best as I can maintain it, since 1983.

Q: Do you ever think about freedom, about rejoining your family?

A: Any man with an imagination leans toward hope, and hope carries with it the perception of freedom. My wife would dearly love for me to come live with her. My daughter kept putting off her wedding in hopes that her dad would be there to give her away, but she's going ahead this fall [i.e., 2005]. Still, it has been my experience that, if I am to live well this day, I have to concentrate on the here and now and not worry about tomorrow. I can be of service to my fellow man, be it in or out of prison. There's freedom enough for that.

Questions for Reflection and Discussion

Scripture—In Chapter 1 we saw that divine justice does not consist of measuring out enough punishment to balance the scales of Themis, but of restoring covenant or relationship. Analyze the different ways in which Paul wants to restore and indeed transform the relationship between Philemon and Onesimus.

Criminology—Why do you think Americans have such a radically different attitude toward time, in the context of sentence lengths, compared to Europeans? What do you think of the twenty-year mark that the author—and, apparently, European nations—posit as the outside limit?

SELF-EXAM—Reflect on Italy's experience with Red Brigade terrorists in the context of Al Qaeda and 9/11. Is restoration possible? Why or why not? How do you know without trying?

INTERVIEW—Do you think Bud should be granted parole? Why or why not? Compare the summary of his criminal record at the beginning of the interview with all you learned later. How do you relate the two?

INTERNET—Visit the Correctional Services of Canada Web site (www.csc-scc.gc.ca) and learn not only about LifeLine, but about an entirely different approach to criminal justice. Could and should the U.S. adopt the Canadian model?

IMMERSION—Through the connections you have established in the previous Immersion experiences, contact a life-sentenced prisoner; get to know him or her through letters and visits; then advocate for the lifer's release. This is, in essence, what Paul did with Onesimus.

LETTER FROM "RUSTY J." TO "BUD T.," OCTOBER 10, 1992

Dear Bud,

Greetings to you, all the fellows at AA, all the fellows at the Vet[erans] Group, and the gang. Be sure you are all a part of my heart and memory and shall be for the rest of my life.

I have a job working for a landscaping company. It pays $5.00 an hour, and I enjoy it. It's outdoor work. I'll let you know if I still enjoy it in the dead of winter and the dog days of summer!!!

As you probably know, Bill [Twine]'s program is something of a work-release program with plenty of stress management thrown in. I try to hold down my bitching by constantly reminding myself that where I am now beats where I've been by far! I hope you can all say that sometime soon.

I went to a church picnic on October 4th. It rained. We played football in the rain. I cussed in front of the Christians and had to apologize profusely! Old habits are hard to break indeed.

I am attending AA meetings twice a week, and I am pursuing and sometimes truly recognizing and appreciating my serenity. God is truly kind and forgiving. Tell everyone in AA to follow the steps. *Work the steps!*

One of my weekly meetings is a step study. We read a chapter of the twelve steps and discuss its content and how it applies to each of us. It is an enlightening experience. I'd like to do a step study program. But, of course, you are pursuing your own sobriety for yourselves, not for me, just as I pursue my sobriety for myself and nobody else.

Well, I'll close for now. This letter will have to suffice in lieu of the many I owe. [Onesimus] House is keeping me very busy. My day starts at 4:30 A.M. and ends at 11 P.M. (later on Mondays!). So, take care, my friend, and remember me to all.

Your grateful friend, Rusty

LETTER FROM "RUSTY J." TO "BUD T.," FEBRUARY 22, 2005

Dear Bud,

I hope this letter finds you as well as can be expected under the circumstances. I hope you enjoy hearing from me. I'm aware that my correspondence is many years overdue and may be unwelcome for that very reason. For what it is worth, I have thought of you often with gratitude. I do not believe I would have ever adjusted to freedom without the help of Onesimus [House], and given the size of the ministry, I have no doubt that I would not have received their help without your recommendation. So, I write to thank you.

Life has been pretty rough back home. People remember and love to gossip, and I am still capable of awful poor judgment. I was able to attend college on a JTPA program administered under Bill Clinton's Presidency. However, I was attending with the children of people who had heard where I had been and thought they knew why. I have several malicious cousins and neighbors who spread the rumor that my crime was child molestation, as if the truth were not bad enough. Add to that my own poor choices in alcohol consumption and skirt chasing, and it wasn't long before they cut my funding and ostracized me.

So I went to Georgia to lick my wounds. I do not know if you remember Frank P. He was a "Mopar" nut and a mechanic working for Lonnie M. in the bus barn. We've stayed in touch over the years, and he and his father—a Korean War Marine—welcomed me with open arms, dusted me off, and restored my ego.

I'm back in Arkansas now. I have a very good boss. He is tolerant of my behavioral disorder and content with my labors. He says he will always have a job for me. I hope so. I live in an apartment over his shop, and my rent is about half of what I could expect to pay anywhere else.

I have not been squeaky clean. I spent ten days in jail for two DWIs in a one-month stretch. I've had a couple of failed relationships. I spent a weekend in jail for misdemeanor marijuana possession. I gave up marijuana. Not for fear of prosecution, but because I swear the last time I smoked it, I could feel blood oozing down the right side of my brain. It was a frightening enough sensation to make me quit for good.

I hope you will forgive me for my failings. I do not wish to betray the faith you put in me fifteen years ago. I'm a weak man in many ways. I avoid as much human contact as possible. People are superficial for the most part. They are proud of their cruelty. Not so much because they truly believe other people deserve cruelty, but more because they take strength and courage and a sense of self-actualization from their acts.

I'm fortunate. I have to run across idiots like that sometimes, but most people I meet are civil if not compassionate in nature. At least I am still out here plugging away. My bills are current, and I have luxuries that I know I take for granted but would sorely miss, were the clock turned back thirteen years.

I hope you are well and disposed to write me. I'd like to hear how you are and would like to hear what you can tell me of friends we had in common. If there is some little luxury I can provide you with, please write and tell me what and how. I would love the opportunity to show you my gratitude. I hoped, with the ascendance of the "compassionate conservative" to the White House, the corrections system would ease up on its spite-based initiatives. But I see the popularity of Jerry Falwell, and I mourn for Virginians. One day they will learn that cruelty is not a show of strength, but rather of weakness. Perhaps I am speaking out of turn because it has been so long. You are forever in my thoughts and prayers.

Your grateful friend, Rusty

CONCLUSION

As you can see from Rusty's second letter, incarceration does not end with the convict's physical release. More than a decade after his discharge, Rusty was still struggling to free himself from the beast. And if you reflect further on Rusty's second letter and some of the other things you have learned in this volume, you will come to see something else: the prison-industrial complex not only takes away the freedom of inmates but also diminishes the lives of all Americans. Here I am not referring to all the teachers who are not being hired and all the roads that are not being repaired because $63 billion is wasted each year on jails and penitentiaries. Nor do I mean the individual psychological benefits that are lost by the refusal to forgive. All these losses are important—but even worse is the spiritual damage wrought by this country's fatal attraction to prisons.

As the nine scriptural convicts and criminals in this book have reminded us, we followers of Jesus are members of an assembly of felons, the Church of the Second Chance. Our self-definition as the people of God is based on the admission that each of us is a sinner, that we all need spiritual parole—the Pope and Billy Graham no less than Charles Manson and Jeffrey Dahmer. If you declare yourself to be essentially different from killers like Manson and Dahmer, you declare yourself to be essentially different from murderers like Moses and David and the apostle Paul. And ultimately you declare yourself to be different from Christ, who died a convict's death for you and Manson and Dahmer.

So all those penitentiary walls and razor wire fences have the ironic effect of locking you out of the fullness of God's community and God's love. Without those 2.3 million prisoners, you are incomplete both on the human and the divine level. You have caged part of yourself and part of God.

In a very real sense, then, it is in your own interest to accept the challenge of this book and work toward "a faith-based approach to prison reform." Inviting inmates back into your life will liberate you as much as them. Like the forgiving father in the parable, you will find your own house blessed and filled with joy when your prodigal children return from prison (Luke 15:11–32).

And yes, of course, there will be those who, like the Prodigal's older brother, grumble at the unfairness of all that undeserved mercy. We Christians call this grace, and Scripture tells us that none of us can be saved without it. If we allow ourselves to become channels for that grace, moreover, we know that miracles small and large will happen.

Do you doubt it? Listen to what happened after Rusty J. wrote that second letter to Bud T., above.

In later correspondence Rusty asked Bud to let him know which of their fellow prisoners from the 1980s and early 1990s were still housed at our correctional center. Bud told him about fourteen of their old friends and caught him up on the gossip. Two weeks later, each of these men received a money order for $20 from Rusty; Bud himself got $100, to be used for the Alcoholics Anonymous group.

Please think about this: the total of $380 that Rusty sent almost certainly constituted more than a week's wages for him. Like the poor widow and her mite, Rusty "from [his] poverty has contributed all [he] had, [his] whole livelihood" (Mark 12:44). Rusty—the sex offender and drug addict, the convict, the scum of the earth.

There are 2.3 million Rustys and Georges and Carltons and Ras Talawas and Kents and Buds waiting for you. Open your arms and make miracles happen.

Appendix

The Bible and Capital Punishment

C APITAL PUNISHMENT IS a controversial subject among Christians. While some are absolutely convinced that God demands it, others are equally adamant that he opposes the death penalty. Is there any way for Christians to agree on a common position?

I believe there is: essentially, both "sides" are right.

If Jesus had opposed capital punishment, he had the perfect opportunity to say so when the elders brought the Woman Caught in Adultery to him for trial (John 8:1–11). But he never challenged the fact that she deserved to die under the Mosaic Code; while we may consider adultery a private transgression, Christ and his contemporaries saw it as a major felony. The Pentateuch treats both adultery and murder as breaches of the covenant with Yahweh and thus prescribes execution for both.

"For whoever keeps the whole law, but falls short in one particular, has become guilty in respect to all of it," the brother of our Lord explains (James 2:10). "For he who said, 'You shall not commit adultery,' also said, 'You shall not kill.' Even if you do not commit adultery but kill, you have become a transgressor of the law" (James 2:11).

However, Jesus did not impose the death penalty at the impromptu trial of the Woman Caught in Adultery, any more than Yahweh ordered the execution of Cain for the murder of Abel. Of course, this tells us something very significant about the nature of divine justice. Equally importantly, however, Christ's court ruling in the Gospel of John gives us guidance for the use of the death penalty in our human justice system.

The fact is that the Son of God enunciated a clear and specific legal principle at the woman's trial: "let him who is without sin throw the first stone" (John 8:7). What this means in practice is that—for

Christians, at least—capital punishment may be the appropriate punishment for any number of offenses; but unless we find an executioner who is "without sin," we have no one who can carry out the legally correct sentence.

Significantly, Jesus did not impose "life without possibility of parole" as an alternative punishment. Instead he simply told her to "go and sin no more" (John 8:11).

In Chapter 1, we saw that Christ's final atoning sacrifice on the cross satisfied the requirements and obligations of the law, and thus made "an eye for an eye" superfluous. For all the "eyes" in the world, he paid with his own "eye." But note that, again, the law is not being set aside here, any more than capital punishment is being set aside in the trial of the Woman Caught in Adultery. Instead, the law is *fulfilled*: all the requirements are satisfied by the death of the one sinless man.

So the Yahwistic laws that called for execution—the Noahic Covenant of Genesis 9 and the Mosaic Covenant of Exodus and Deuteronomy—remain true standards of divine justice, as Christian advocates of the death penalty correctly point out. But they no longer apply to us! We have been "released from [that] law" by the blood of our Savior and now are subject to "the law of freedom," the law of love (Romans 7:6; James 2:12, 1:25; cf. Romans 8:2, John 13:34, 15:12 et seq.). "[L]ove is the fulfillment of the law" (Romans 13:10)—love, not capital punishment.

In the New Testament, we find a number of references to the death penalty that can be (and have been) interpreted as endorsements. But do these passages really approve of execution—or do they merely acknowledge that human societies practice capital punishment? When parents see their sons misbehaving, they may sigh, "Boys will be boys," without thereby wishing to express support.

Let us take a closer look at the four New Testament passages most frequently cited by death-penalty advocates, and let us consider whether they do in fact endorse executions:

- Jesus told Pontius Pilate, "You would have no power over me if it had not been granted to you from above" (John 19:11)

Of course, our Father grants each of us the "power" to choose good or evil, so Christ was simply stating a fact, not expressing approval of Pilate's choice. Early Christians saw Pilate's use of his "power" as evil: see Acts 2:22–23, 3:13–18, 4:24–29, 7:51–53; 1 Corinthians 2:8.

- Luke's version of the Parable of the Talents ends with the execution of the king's enemies (Luke 19:27).

    If this is an endorsement of capital punishment, then we must also torture debtors and swindle our employers; Jesus told parables about those, too (Matthew 18:34; Luke 16:1–9).

- Paul told Festus, "I do not seek to escape the death penalty" (Acts 25:11).

    The execution of criminals was a fact of Paul's time and culture, and we saw in Chapter 3's discussion of slavery that Paul did not challenge such common social practices. By this reasoning, incidentally, we would also be obligated to reintroduce the Pauline oppression of women (cf. 1 Timothy 2:9–15; 1 Corinthians 14:34–35).

- Paul wrote that civil authority "does not bear the sword without purpose; it is the servant of God to inflict wrath on the evildoer" (Romans 13:4).

    Since "sword-bearer" was the Roman term for tax collector, modern commentators read this passage as advice to the early Christians not to join the tax revolt, referred to in the next three verses. Even if a "sword-bearer" is taken to be a garden-variety law enforcement official, however, we must remember that Caesar's officials were at that time persecuting the church. So the statement that the Roman occupiers of Palestine did "not bear the sword in vain" should be understood as an observation of bitter experience and a warning—much like today's dictum, "There are two things you can't avoid, death and taxes," or Jesus' admonition that "all who take up the sword will perish by the sword" (Matthew 26:52). Ideally, of course, every government bureaucrat should be "the servant of God," but some—like Pilate and Festus—abuse their authority.

In the end, I am not sure how helpful the trading of scriptural quotations can be when trying to determine whether Christians ought to support the death penalty. Should we not be asking, instead, "What would Jesus do?"

Can you picture the Son of God using a Taser to subdue an inmate so he can be strapped to a gurney? Can you imagine the Messiah searching for a vein and inserting a needle into his arm? Can you see in your mind how our Savior prepares the three drugs used for lethal injection: sodium thiopental to anaesthetize the prisoner, pancuronium bromide to induce paralysis, and potassium chloride to stop the heart? Do you believe that the Son of God would push the plunger that forces these three drugs into the condemned convict's vein?

If you can, then you are right to support capital punishment.

Notes

Introduction

1. Alan Elsner, "Inmates' 'Do Not Pass Go' Card," *Los Angeles Times*, January 29, 2004.

2. Marc Mauer, *Race to Incarcerate* (New York: The New Press, 1999), 82–84; Richard Willing, "Inmate Population Rises as Crime Drops," *USA Today*, July 29, 2003; Connie Cass, "Prison Population Grows by 2.9% in 2003," Associated Press, May 29, 2004; Richard Willing, "U.S. Prison Populations on the Rise," *USA Today*, May 28, 2004; *Report of the Re-entry Policy Council* (Washington, D.C.: Council of State Governments / Urban Institute Re-entry Policy Forum, February 2005), xvii; and Paige M. Harrison and Allen J. Beck, *Prisoners in 2005* (Washington, D.C.: Bureau of Justice Statistics, 2006), 1.

3. Roy Walmsley, *World Prison Population List*, 3rd ed. (London: Home Office Research, Development and Statistics Directorate, 2002); Cass, "Prison."

4. Walmsley, *World Prison*; U.S. Census Bureau, 2002, as cited in Peter Wagner, *The Prison Index* (Springfield, MA: Prison Policy Initiative, 2003).

5. Harrison and Beck, *Prisoners in 2005*, 2.

6. Kevin Johnson, "Study Predicts Rise in Inmate Population," *USA Today*, February 14, 2007.

7. John J. Gibbons and Nicholas de B. Katzenbach, eds., *Confronting Confinement: A Report of the Commission on Safety and Abuse in America's Prisons* (New York: Vera Institute of Justice, 2006), 89, based on American Correctional Association and Bureau of Justice Statistics data.

8. Curt Anderson, "Violent Crime Rate for 2003 Holds Steady," Associated Press, September 13, 2004; "2004 Crime Rate Hovered at Low Levels," *USA Today*, September 26, 2005.

9. Bureau of Justice Statistics Press Release, "One in Every 32 Adults Was in Prison, Jail, on Probation, or on Parole at the End of 2005," November 30, 2006, 4:30 P.M., by Stu Smith.

10. Patrick A. Langan and David J. Levin, *Recidivism of Prisoners Released in 1994* (Washington, D.C.: Bureau of Justice Statistics, June 2002).

11. Kristen A. Hughes, *Justice Expenditures and Employment in the United States* (Washington, D.C.: Bureau of Justice Statistics, 2003).

12. Johnson, "Study Predicts Rise."

13. Vincent Schiraldi, "States Are Releasing Pressure on Prisons," *Washington Post*, November 30, 2003.

14. John J. DiIulio Jr., "Two Million Prisoners Are Enough," *Wall Street Journal*, March 12, 1999.

15. Cal Thomas, "Three Strikes and You're Broke," Tribune Media Services, November 17, 2003.

16. Alan Elsner, "America's Prison Habit," *Washington Post*, January 24, 2004.

17. Harrison and Beck, *Prisoners in 2005*, 2.

1. Adam and Eve and Divine Justice

1. Cf. Mark 11:25; Ephesians 4:32–5:2; Colossians 3:12–15.

2. Oren M. Spiegler, "Letters," *USA Today*, March 22, 2005. (Scott Peterson was convicted in 2005 of murdering his wife, Laci, while she was pregnant with their son.)

3. Bob Lonsberry, *The Early Years* (New York: Canisteo Free Press, 1995), quoted in Ronald Nikkel, "In the Company of Scoundrels," *Justice Reflections* 49, 16 (© 2004 by Prison Fellowship International). Jeffrey Dahmer was convicted of murdering seventeen people and eating parts of their corpses.

4. Walter Wink, *Engaging the Powers: Discernment and Resistance in a World of Domination* (Philadelphia: Fortress Press, 1992), 146.

5. For example: Exodus 34:6, 7; Psalms 103:3, 10; Ezekiel 33:11; Micah 7:18; Matthew 5:7, 9:13, 12:7; Luke 10:37. For these scriptural references, as well as those in endnotes 7, 11, 12, 13, and 20, I am indebted to Christopher Marshall's *Beyond Retribution*, cited below.

6. Cf. Deuteronomy 8:5; 1 Corinthians 11:21.

7. St. Thomas Aquinas, *Summa Theologicae: A Concise Translation*, trans. Fathers of the English Dominican Province (Allen, TX: Christian Classics, 1947), 418.

8. J. R. Donahue, "Biblical Perspectives on Justice," in *The Faith That Does Justice: Examining the Christian Sources for Social Change*, ed. J. C. Haughey (New York: Paulist Press, 1977), 72; see also Gerhard von Rad, *Old Testament Theology*, 2 vols (London: SCM, 1962), 377.

9.   Peter Steinfels, "Lessons for Living Found in Views of the Last Judgment," *New York Times*, January 20, 2007.

10.   Christopher Marshall, *Beyond Retribution: A New Testament Vision for Justice, Crime and Punishment* (Grand Rapids, MI: Wm. B. Eerdmans Publishing Co., 2001), 48.

11.   Cf. Exodus 22:21–26, 23:6–9; Deuteronomy 24:17, 18; Psalms 82:3; Isaiah 1:17; Jeremiah 21:12, 22:3.

12.   Cf. Deuteronomy 17:7, 12, 19:19, 21:21; 22:21–22, 24; 24:7; and Judges 20:13; 2 Samuel 19:3.

13.   Leviticus 20:2, 24:14, 23; Numbers 15:35–56; Deuteronomy 21:19, 21; Joshua 7:25; 1 Kings 12:18, 21:10, 13; 2 Chronicles 10:18.

14.   Marshall, *Beyond Retribution*, 43.

15.   Charles Colson, "Colson on Jesus and the Death Penalty," Jesus Journal.com, September 6, 2004, 6.

16.   Harold J. Berman, *Law and Revolution: The Foundation of the Western Legal Tradition* (Cambridge: Cambridge University Press, 1983), 180.

17.   Marshall, *Beyond Retribution*, 60.

18.   Timothy Gorringe, *God's Just Vengeance: Crime, Violence and the Rhetoric of Salvation* (Cambridge: Cambridge University Press, 1996), 102.

19.   Gorringe, *God's Just Vengeance*, 140.

20.   J.D.G. Dunn, *The Theology of Paul the Apostle* (Edinburgh: T & T Clark, 1998), 342.

21.   Cf. Romans 5:6, 8; 2 Corinthians 1:5, 5:14; Galatians 3:13; Ephesians 5:2; Titus 2:14.

22.   Marshall, *Beyond Retribution*, 62.

23.   Lee Griffith, *The Fall of the Prison: Biblical Perspectives on Prison Abolition* (Grand Rapids, MI: Wm. B. Eerdmans Publishing Co., 1993), 28.

2. Joseph and Commonly Held Beliefs about Prison

1.   Walter Brueggemann, *Genesis* (Atlanta: John Knox Press, 1982), 313.

2.   Adam Liptak, "Study Suspects Thousands of False Convictions," *New York Times*, April 19, 2004.

3.   Ibid.

4.   "Exonerations Lead Virginia Governor to Call for Sweeping DNA Review," *Washington Post*, December 15, 2005.

5.   Roy Walmsley, *World Prison Population List*, 6th ed. (London: Home Office Research, Development and Statistics Directorate, 2006),

available at www.prisonstudies.org (International Centre for Prison Studies).

6. Paige M. Harrison and Allen J. Beck, *Prisoners in 2005* (Washington, D.C.: Bureau of Justice Statistics, 2006), 2.

7. Van Kesteren, J., Mayhew, P., and Nieuwbeerta P., *Criminal Victimisation in Seventeen Industrialised Countries: Key-findings from the 2000 International Crime Victim Survey*, cited in Peter Wagner, *The Prison Index* (Springfield, MA: Prison Policy Initiative, 2003), 40.

8. James Lynch, "Crime in International Perspective," in James Q. Wilson and Joan Petersilia, eds., *Crime* (San Francisco: Institute for Contemporary Studies, 1995), 22–23.

9. Harrison and Beck, *Prisoners*, 1.

10. Stephen A. Salzburg, Chairperson and Editor, *Justice Kennedy Commission Report*, American Bar Association, August 2004, 19–21.

11. Frank Green, "More Prisons, Less Crime?" *Richmond Times-Dispatch*, April 25, 2005; see Ryan S. King, Marc Mauer, and Malcolm C. Young, *Incarceration and Crime: A Complex Relationship* (Washington, D.C.: The Sentencing Project, 2005), citing W. Spelman, "The Limited Importance of Prison Expansion," in A. Blumstein and J. Wallman, eds., *The Crime Drop in America* (Cambridge: Cambridge University Press, 2000), 97–129.

12. Salzburg, *Justice Kennedy Commission Report*, 19–21.

13. Martin Powell, "Despite Fewer Lockups, NYC Has Seen Big Drop in Crime," *Washington Post*, November 24, 2006.

14. Turley and Jacobson: Frank Green, "More Prisons, Less Crime?"; Wilson: Wilson and Petersilia, *Crime*, 105.

15. Don Stemen, *Reconsidering Incarceration: New Directions for Reducing Crime* (New York: Vera Institute of Justice, 2007), 2, 13.

16. Salzburg, *Justice Kennedy Commission Report*, 81.

17. *After Prison: Roadblocks to Reentry*, www.lac.org/lac/index.php ; www.urban.org/content/PolicyCenters/Justice/Projects/PrisonerReentry/overview.htm; Marc Mauer and Meda Chesney-Lind, *Invisible Punishment: The Collateral Consequences of Mass Imprisonment* (New York: The New Press, 2003); Salzburg, *Justice Kennedy Commission Report*, 82.

18. R. Sapsford, "Life-Sentence Prisoners: Psychological Changes During Sentence," *British Journal of Criminology* 18, (1978), 128.

19. Kevin Johnson, "After Years in Solitary, Freedom Hard to Grasp," *USA Today*, June 9, 2005.

20. James DeFronzo, "AFDC, a City's Racial and Ethnic Composition, and Burglary," *Social Service Review*, September 1996, 464–471; James

DeFronzo, "Welfare and Homicide," *Journal of Research in Crime and Delinquency*, 34, no. 3, August 1997.

21. Etienne Benson, "Rehabilitate or Punish?" *Monitor on Psychology* (American Psychological Association) 34, no. 7, July–August 2003, 47; see also Anna Bailey, "More Police Means Strain on Corrections System," *The Examiner* (Washington, D.C.), April 17, 2006; and Kevin Johnson, "Commission Warns of Harm Isolation Can Do to Prisoners," *USA Today*, June 8, 2006.

22. Christopher J. Mumola, *Substance Abuse and Treatment, State and Federal Prisons, 1997* (Washington, D.C.: Bureau of Justice Statistics, 1997), 1; these figures are for state prisoners only.

23. Education as Crime Prevention, OSI Criminal Justice Initiative, September 1997.

24. University of Cincinnati professor Francis T. Cullen, in Warren St. John, "Professors with a Past," *New York Times*, August 9, 2003, A 13.

25. "The Impact of Incarceration: Issues Affecting Reentry" (Washington, D.C.: U.S. Department of Justice, Reentry Working Group, May 2004).

26. Sarah Karnasiewicz, "Love under Lock and Key," *Salon*, November 15, 2005, www.salon.com/mwt/feature/2005/11/15/bernstein/print.html (accessed May 9, 2007), citing Nell Bernstein's *All Alone in the World: Children of the Incarcerated* (New York: The New Press, 2005).

27. Barbara D. Whitehead, "Dan Quayle Was Right," *Atlantic Monthly* 271, no. 4 (April 1993), 47.

28. Bill Wasson, "Helping Kin Cope with Incarceration," *Richmond Times-Dispatch*, March 22, 2006.

29. Charles W. Colson, *Justice That Restores* (Wheaton, IL: Tyndale House Publishers, 2001), 201.

30. Karnasiewicz, "Love under Lock and Key."

31. According to a 2000 survey of seven Midwestern states by Ohio University. Jayne O'Donnell, "State Time or Federal Prison?" *USA Today*, March 18, 2004. Other studies confirm these figures: see Jens Soering, *The Convict Christ: What the Gospel Says about Criminal Justice* (Maryknoll, NY: Orbis Books, 2006) for more details.

32. Allen J. Beck and Timothy A. Hughes, *Sexual Violence Reported by Correctional Authorities, 2004* (Washington, D.C.: Bureau of Justice Statistics, July 2005), 2.

33. Associated Press, "Study Says Prison Rape Rare," *Richmond Times-Dispatch*, January 18, 2006.

34. Quotes compiled from Carolyn Marshall, "Panel on Prison Rape Hears Victims' Chilling Accounts," *New York Times*, August 20, 2005; Jim

Herron Zamora, "Former Inmates Tell Horror Stories of Rape," *San Francisco Chronicle*, August 20, 2005.

35. Brent Staples, "Fighting the AIDS Epidemic by Issuing Condoms in the Prisons," *New York Times*, September 7, 2004.

36. *HIV in Prison 2001* (Washington, D.C.: Bureau of Justice Statistics, 2004).

37. Brent Staples, "Treat the Epidemic Behind Bars before It Hits the Streets," *New York Times*, June 22, 2004.

38. Richard Morin, "Answer to AIDS Mystery Found behind Bars," *Washington Post*, March 9, 2006.

39. Michael Hardy, "ACLU: Prison Care Lacking," *Richmond Times-Dispatch*, May 8, 2003.

40. Staples, "Treat the Epidemic Behind Bars."

41. Laurie Garrett, *The Coming Plague: Newly Emerging Diseases in a World out of Balance* (New York: Farrar, Straus and Giroux, 1994), 523–34.

42. Jerry Seper, "Prisoners, Public at Health Risk," *Washington Post*, June 8, 2006.

43. David Brown, "Few Men Found to Get HIV in Prison," *Washington Post*, April 21, 2006.

44. "Snapshot Behind Bars," *Washington Times*, June 8, 2006.

45. John J. Gibbons and Nicholas de B. Katzenbach, eds., *Confronting Confinement: A Report of the Commission on Safety and Abuse in America's Prisons* (New York: Vera Institute of Justice, 2006), 101; see also 24–25.

46. Staples, "Treat the Epidemic Behind Bars."

47. Roberto Hugh Potter and Kera Moseley, "HIV and Corrections: Every Statistic Tells a Story," *Corrections Today* (ACA), July 2006, 76–77.

48. Ibid.

49. Dan Malone, "Cruel and Inhumane," *Amnesty International*, Fall 2005, 23.

50. Pete Earley, "Living with Mental Illness," *USA Today*, May 2, 2006.

51. Ibid.; Johnson, "Commission Warns of Harm."

52. David C. Fathi, "The New Asylum: Supermax as Warehouse for the Mentally Ill," *Prison Legal News*, 1, 6.

53. Frank Schmalleger, *Criminology Today: An Integrative Introduction* (Upper Saddle River, NJ: Prentice-Hall, Inc., 1999, 1996), 252–256.

54. Ayelish McGarvey, "Reform Done Right," *American Prospect*, December 2003, 43.

55. "Finnish Prisons," *New York Times*, January 1, 2003, cited in Wagner, *Index*, 41.

56. Jim Holt, "Decarcerate?" *New York Times*, August 15, 2004.

3. MOSES AND TURNING A BLIND EYE TO PRISON

1. Will Durant, *Caesar and Christ: The Story of Civilization, Part III* (New York: Simon and Schuster, 1944), 137, 112, 121.
2. Terrence E. Fretheim, *Exodus* (Louisville: John Knox Press, 1991), 42.
3. Durant, *Caesar and Christ*, 222.
4. Lawrence Friedman, *Crime and Punishment in American History* (New York: HarperCollins, 1993), 48.
5. *Encyclopedia Britannica: Micropedia Vol. 9* (Chicago: Encyclopedia Britannica, Inc., 1988), 710.
6. John J. Gibbons and Nicholas de B. Katzenbach, eds., *Confronting Confinement: A Report of the Commission on Safety and Abuse in America's Prisons* (New York: Vera Institute of Justice, 2006), 89, based on American Correctional Association and Bureau of Justice Statistics data.
7. All figures supplied by Peter Wagner, Prison Policy Initiative, through correspondence dated November 9, 2004. See www.prisonpolicy.org.
8. *Prevalence of Imprisonment in the U.S. Population, 1974–2001* (Washington, D.C.: Bureau of Justice Statistics, August 2003).
9. Associated Press, "Sentencing-Guideline Study Finds Continuing Disparities," *New York Times*, November 27, 2004.
10. Stephen A. Salzburg, Chairperson and Editor, *Justice Kennedy Commission Report*, American Bar Association, August 2004, 47–63.
11. Ibid., 55.
12. Ibid., 52.
13. *Race of Prisoners Admitted to State and Federal Institution, 1926–1986* (Washington, D.C.: Bureau of Justice Statistics, February 1994), 14, Table 7.
14. Associated Press, "Sentencing-Guideline Study."
15. Connie Cass, "Prison Population Grew 2.9 Percent in 2003," Associated Press, May 28, 2004.
16. Henry Ruth and Keith R. Reitz, *The Challenge of Crime: Rethinking Our Response* (Harvard University Press, 2003), 95–96; and, generally, Marc Mauer, *Race to Incarcerate* (New York: The New Press, 1999).
17. *Drug Policy and the Criminal Justice System* (Washington, D.C.: The Sentencing Project, 2001), 4; citing *Summary of Findings from the National Household Survey on Drug Abuse* (Washington, D.C.: Substance Abuse and Mental Health Services Administration, November 2000), 6–3 and 6–13.

18. Wendy Koch, "Despite High-Profile Cases, Sex Offense Crimes Decline," *USA Today*, August 25, 2005; figures supplied by the University of New Hampshire and the Department of Justice, and by David Finkelhor, director of the Crimes Against Children Research Center.

19. "Network News in the Nineties," *Media Monitor*, July–August 1997, 2.

20. *Sourcebook of Criminal Justice Statistics 2000* (Washington, D.C.: Bureau of Justice Statistics, 2000), Table 2.36, calculation based on Table 4.2.

21. Lawrence K. Grossman, "Why Local TV News Is So Awful," *Columbia Journalism Review*, November–December 1997, 21.

22. Tim Rutten, "CNN Should Not Stay Silent about Grace's Ethical Lapses," *Virginian-Pilot*, May 29, 2005.

23. Ibid.

24. Peter Johnson, "When It Comes to True Crime, Nancy Grace Is on the Case," *USA Today*, February 20, 2006.

25. Gibbons and Katzenbach, *Confronting Confinement*, 85.

26. *Bourgeois v. Wiley*, 849 So. 2d. 632 (La. App. 1 Cir. 2003); the appellate court later reinstated this particular case, without ruling on the merits, because the suit was filed before Louisiana passed its state version of the PLRA. If the inmates had tried to go to court *after* the PLRA became law, they would have been without recourse.

27. Bob Herbert, "America's Abu Ghraibs," *New York Times*, May 31, 2004.

28. Gibbons and Katzenbach, *Confronting Confinement*, 85.

29. *Farella v. Hockaday*, 304 F. Supp.2d 1076 (CD Ill. 2004).

30. *Davidson v. Texas Department of Criminal Justice, Institutional Division*, 5th Cir. 2003, Case No. 03–41185.

31. Ronald Nikkel, "In the Company of Scoundrels," *Justice Reflections*, 49, 16–17 (© 2004 by Prison Fellowship International).

32. Quoted in Timothy Gorringe, "The Church and the Prison," *Justice Reflections*, 45, 8 (excerpted from Chapter 9 of Gorringe's *Crime*, SPCK, 2004).

33. Mark Earley, "Resurrection Day: An Easter Message to Prisoners," Prison Fellowship Ministries 2004, 21.

4. SAMSON AND VICTIMS' RIGHTS

1. J. Clinton McCann, *Judges* (Louisville: John Knox Press, 2002), 95.

2. Henry Ruth and Keith R. Reitz, *The Challenge of Crime: Rethinking Our Response* (Harvard University Press, 2003), 95–96.

3. Frank Green, "Prisons in Nation Expected to Grow," *Richmond Times-Dispatch*, February 15, 2007.

4. Associated Press, "Guidelines Study Finds Continuing Disparities," *New York Times*, November 27, 2004.

5. www.jfa.net/memory.html (accessed May 9, 2007).

6. www.cjlf.org/releases/02–01.htm (accessed May 9, 2007) and *Voice of Justice* 10, no. 2 (March 2002).

7. Andrew Sun Park and Susan L. Nelson, eds., *The Other Side of Sin: Woundedness from the Perspective of the Sinned Against* (Albany, NY: SUNY Press, 2001), 138–139.

8. Contact the Office for Victims of Crime at (202) 307-5983 or www.ojp.usdog.gov/ovc, as well as the National Criminal Justice Reference Service at (800) 627-6872 or www.ncjrs.org.

9. Barb Toews, "Listening to Prisoners Raises Issues about Prison-based Restorative Justice," *VOMA Connections* 11 (Summer 2002), 1.

10. Marie Sue Penn, "Leaven of Forgiveness," *Sojourners*, May–June 1995.

11. Rachel King and Barbara Hood, eds., *Not in Our Name: Murder Victims' Families Speak Out against the Death Penalty* (Rutgers, NJ: Rutgers University Press, 2003), Introduction.

12. Penn, "Leaven of Forgiveness."

13. www.murdervictims.com/Impact/CubenasImpact.htm (accessed April 21, 2007), ©2005 Justice For All.

14. www.murdervictims.com/Impact/FreitagImpact.htm (accessed April 21, 2007), © 2005 Justice For All.

15. http://www.journeyofhope.org/pages/bill_pelke.htm (accessed May 9, 2007).

16. David Briggs/Associated Press, "The Freedom of Forgiveness," *The Standard Times*, © 1997/98.

17. www.jfa.net (accessed May 9, 2007).

18. See www.deathpenaltyinfo.org and L. Kehler et al., *Capital Punishment Study Guide* (Winnipeg, Canada: MCC Victim Offender Ministries, 1980).

19. "Death Penalty Support Ebbs as Tough New Option Arises," *USA Today*, December 12, 2005.

20. www.prodeathpenalty.com/DP.html, paragraph 16 (accessed May 9, 2007).

21. Peter Carlson, "It's All in the Execution," *Washington Post*, November 29, 2004.

22. Jim Krane, "The Graying of American's Prisons: An Emerging Corrections Crisis," A.P.B. News, April 12, 1999.

23. "Can Parole Cut Crime?" Parade, December 10, 2003, 17.

24. Stephen A. Salzburg, Chairperson and Editor, Justice Kennedy Commission Report, American Bar Association, August 2004, 79.

25. Jens Soering, An Expensive Way to Make Bad People Worse: An Essay on Prison Reform from an Insider's Perspective (New York: Lantern Books, 2004), 37, based on Virginia Department of Correctional Education data.

26. www.murdervictims.com/Impact/FreitagImpact.htm (accessed April 21, 2007), © 2005 Justice For All.

27. Marc Mauer, Ryan S. King and Malcolm C. Young, The Meaning of "Life" (Washington, D.C.: The Sentencing Project, May 2004), 24, citing A. Langan and D.J. Levin, Recidivism of Prisoners Released in 1994 (Washington, D.C.: Bureau of Justice Statistics, 2002), Table 10.

28. Wendy Koch, "Despite High-profile Cases, Sex Offense Crimes Decline," USA Today, August 25, 2005.

29. Mark Memmott, "Girl's Death Raises Questions about Tracking of Sex Offenders," USA Today, March 25, 2005; graph by Adrienne Lewis, USA Today.

30. Cal Thomas, "Three Strikes and You're Broke," Tribune Media Services, November 17, 2003.

31. Mauer, The Meaning of "Life," 24, citing Langan and Levin, Recidivism of Prisoners, Table 10.

32. Ibid.; 127,677 x 20.6% x 18% = 4,734.

33. "Nursing Homes Surrounded by Razor Wire: Geriatric Prisons," Justice Matters 7 (Summer 2005), 23, emphasis added.

34. Paige Akin, "Juvenile Petersburg Killer Spared Death after Ruling," Richmond Times-Dispatch, March 2, 2005.

35. Laurence Hammack, "Many Inmates Remain under Parole System," Roanoke Times, September 26, 2004.

36. Frank Green, "McCollum Appointed to Parole Board," Richmond Times-Dispatch, January 20, 2007.

37. Calculation based on figure of 6,000 and average annual cost of incarceration of $22,650.

38. Virginia Mackey, Restorative Justice: Toward Non-Violence (Louisville, KY: Presbyterian Church U.S.A., 1992).

39. Howard Zehr, Changing Lenses: A New Focus for Crime and Justice (Scottdale, PA: Herald Press, 1990).

40.   Vince Beiser, "Extreme Mercy," *Psychology Today*, May–June 2006, 84.

5. David and Rehabilitation

1.   Walter Brueggeman, *First and Second Samuel* (Louisville: John Knox Press, 1990), 280.

2.   Amit R. Paley, "A Positive Prison Experience," *Washington Post*, March 8, 2006.

3.   Poll of 1,039 respondents conducted February 15–18, 2006, by Zogby International for The National Council on Crime and Delinquency; margin of error +/- 3.1%; www.zogby.com/news/ReadNews.dbm?ID=1101 (accessed May 10, 2007).

4.   *Los Angeles Times* news service, "Prisons Begin Focusing More on Rehabilitation," *Virginian-Pilot*, March 28, 2005.

5.   C.T. Woody, "Community Can Learn to Fight Crime Proactively," *Richmond Times-Dispatch*, March 13, 2006.

6.   "What's the Matter with Louisiana?" *Louisiana CURE Newsletter*, May 2005, 8.

7.   Joan Petersilia, "A Crime Control Rationale for Investing in Community Corrections," *Prison Journal* 75, no. 4, 1995, 479–496.

8.   Gary Fields, "To Cut Prison Bill, States Tweak Laws, Try Early Release," *Wall Street Journal*, December 21, 2005; figure for 2001.

9.   Steve Aos, "Using Taxpayer Dollars Wisely," in E. Gross, B. Friese and K. Bogenschneider, eds., *Correction Policy: Can States Cut Costs and Still Cut Crime?*, Wisconsin Family Impact Seminar Briefing Report Nr. 19, 2003, University of Wisconsin Center for Excellence in Family Studies, 26. This is an abridged version of Steve Aos, Polly Phipps, Robert Barnowski and Roxanne Lieb, "The Comparative Costs and Benefits of Programs to Reduce Crime," Washington State Institute for Public Policy, May 2001. The full report and executive summary may be obtained at http://www.wsipp.wa.gov/pub.asp?docid=01-05-1201.

10.   Ibid., 25.

11.   Ibid., 23–26.

12.   Caylor Roling, "Let's Invest in Programs That Make Prisons Unnecessary," *Justice Matters*, Fall 2006–Winter 2007, 16–17; the study *Evidence-based Public Policy Options* may be obtained at www.wsipp.wa.gov.

13.   Aos et al., "The Comparative Costs and Benefits," 6.

14. Thomas O'Connor, "What Works, Religion as a Correctional Intervention: Part I," *Journal of Community Corrections* XIV, no. 1 (Fall 2004), 20, citing J. McGuire, "Evidence-based Programming Today," paper presented at the International Community Corrections Association Annual Conference in Boston, MA, 2002.

15. James Lynch and William J. Sabol, *Prisoner Reentry in Perspective*, Urban Institute, *Crime Policy Report* 3 (September 2001), 19.

16. Kathleen Kenna, "Justice for All," *Greater Good*, Spring–Summer 2005, 22–25.

17. Shawn Bushway, "Reentry and Prison Work Programs," paper presented at the Urban Institute's Reentry Roundtable, May 2003; Kim A. Hull et al., "Analysis of Recidivism Rates for Participants of the Academic/Vocational Training Education Programs Offered by the Virginia Department of Correctional Education," *Journal of Correctional Education* 51, no. 2 (2000), 256–261; Kenneth Adams et al., "A Large-Scale Multidimensional Test of the Effect of Prison Education on Prisoners' Behavior," *Prison Journal* 74, no. 4 (2001), 433–449; Gerald G. Gaes et al., "Adult Correctional Treatment," in M. Tonry and J. Petersilia, eds., *Prisons* (Chicago: University of Chicago Press, 1999).

18. Steven Steurer, Linda Smith and Alice Tracey, *Three-State Recidivism Study* (Lanham, MD: Correctional Education Association, 2001); Wayne Thompson, "Readers Forum: We All Need a 'Second Chance,'" *Tulsa World*, June 26, 2005.

19. Adams, et al., "A Large-Scale Multidimensional Test"; Steurer et al., *Three-State Recidivism Study*; David Wilson, Catherine Gallagher and David MacKenzie, "A Meta-Analysis of Corrections-Based Education, Vocation and Work Programs for Adult Offenders," *Journal of Research in Crime and Delinquency* 37 (2001), 347–68.

20. Patrick A. Langan and David J. Levin, *Recidivism of Prisoners Released in 1994* (Washington, D.C.: Bureau of Justice Statistics, June 2002).

21. Caroline Wolf Harlow, *Education and Correctional Populations* (Washington, D.C.: Bureau of Justice Statistics, 2003), 1, 3.

22. Ibid., 4.

23. *Report of the Re-entry Policy Council* (Washington, D.C.: Council of State Governments / Urban Institute Re-entry Policy Forum, February 2005), Policy Statement 15.

24. Nancy G. La Vigne et al., *A Portrait of Prisoner Reentry* (Washington, D.C.: Urban Institute, 2003).

25. Haslow, *Education*, 4.

26. "Governor's Task Force Recommends Changes in Florida's Prison System Mission," *Prison Legal News*, July 2007, 32; the report is available at www.prisonlegalnews.org.

27. Samantha M. Shapiro, "Jails for Jesus," *Mother Jones*, November–December 2003; Brigitte Sarabi, "Sentencing Policy in the Twenty-First Century," *Justice Matters*, Winter 2005, 11–12.

28. John J. Gibbons and Nicholas de B. Katzenbach, eds., *Confronting Confinement: A Report of the Commission on Safety and Abuse in America's Prisons* (New York: Vera Institute of Justice, 2006), 27.

29. Wendy Erisman and Jeanne Bayer Contardo, "Learning to Reduce Recidivism: A Fifty-state Analysis of Postsecondary Correctional Educational Policy," Institute for Higher Education Policy, 2005.

30. James Gilligan, *Preventing Violence: Prospects for Tomorrow* (New York: Thames and Hudson, 2001), 98–99.

31. Jon M. Taylor, "Post Secondary Correctional Education: An Evaluation of Effectiveness and Efficiency," *Journal of Correctional Education* 43 (September 1992).

32. "The Impact of Correctional Education on Recidivism, 1988–1994," Office of Correctional Education, U.S. Department of Justice.

33. www.changingminds.ws/brochure (accessed January 3, 2003); cited in Peter Wagner, *The Prison Index* (Springfield, MA: Prison Policy Initiative, 2003), 30.

34. "Few Prisoners Get College-Level Courses," *USA Today*, November 3, 2005.

35. "News in Brief: Utah," *Prison Legal News*, July 2007, 42.

36. James Hemm, "Challenges and Opportunities in the Field of Community Corrections," *Journal of Community Corrections*, Spring 2006, 7.

37. Christopher J. Mumola, *Substance Abuse and Treatment of State and Federal Prisoners, 1997* (Washington, D.C.: Bureau of Justice Statistics, 1999), 8.

38. Ibid., 5.

39. *Policy Brief: Offender Reentry*, National Association of State Alcohol and Drug Abuse Directors (Washington, D.C.), 1; see also Kevin Knight, D. Dwayne Simpson and Matthew Miller, "Three-Year Reincarceration Outcomes for In-Prison Therapeutic Community Treatment in Texas," *Prison Journal* 79 (1999), 337–351.

40. Thompson, "Readers Forum."

41. Ibid.

42. Aos, "Using Taxpayer Dollars Wisely," 7.

43. Tara Andrews, "Nonviolent Drug Offenders Belong in Treatment, Not in Maryland Prisons," *Washington Post*, January 6, 2006.

44. Mumola, *Substance Abuse and Treatment*, 10.
45. "Study Shows Prison-Based Treatment Benefits Everyone," *Justice Matters*, Spring 2005, 8.
46. Rogers, "Which Will Legislators Choose," 19.
47. Matthew T. Clarke, "Arbitrary Draconian Restrictions on Texas Parolees," *Prison Legal News*, July 2005, 7–8.
48. Mumola, *Substance Abuse and Treatment*, 10.
49. Catherine Kemp and Arian Campo-Flores, "A 'Meth Prison' Movement," *Newsweek*, April 24, 2006.
50. "People with Mental Illness in the Criminal Justice System: Fiscal Implications," Criminal Justice / Mental Health Consensus Project, 2005, consensusproject.org.
51. "Myths and Facts about Sex Offenders," Center for Sex Offender Management, 2000, www.csom.org/pubs/mythsfacts.html (accessed May 10, 2007).
52. Matthew T. Clarke, "Registered Sex Offenders Murdered by Vigilante in Washington," *Prison Legal News*, February 2006, 40.
53. Emily Bazar, "Website Led Shooter to Sex Offenders' Home," *USA Today*, April 18, 2006.
54. *Louisiana CURE Newsletter*, 8.
55. www.lac.org/lac/index.php; www.urban.org/content/PolicyCenters/Justice/Projects/ PrisonerReentry/overview.htm; Marc Mauer and Meda Chesney-Lind, *Invisible Punishment: The Collateral Consequences of Mass Imprisonment* (New York: The New Press, 2003); Stephen A. Salzburg, Chairperson and Editor, *Justice Kennedy Commission Report*, American Bar Association, August 2004, 82.
56. U.S. Senator Arlen Specter (R-PA), Statements on Introduced Bills and Joint Resolutions. *Congressional Record* 130 (October 7, 2005), S12015.
57. Michelle Washington, "Program Aims to Ease Ex-Cons Back into Society," *Virginian-Pilot*, September 4, 2005.
58. "Studies Show Addicts Often Return to Jail," *Richmond Times-Dispatch*, February 20, 2005.
59. Esther Griswold, Jessica Pearson and Lanae Davis, *Testing a Modification Process for Incarcerated Parents* (Denver CO: Center for Policy Research), 11–12.
60. Darrell Laurant, "Is the Prison System Right?" *Lynchburg News and Advance*, April 17, 2006.
61. Matthew T. Clarke, "Ex-prisoners Barred from Nursing in Texas," *Prison Legal News*, January 2006, 25.

62. Alan Elsner, "Inmates' 'Do Not Pass Go' Card," *Los Angeles Times*, January 29, 2004.

63. Lynch and Sabol, *Prisoner Reentry in Perspective*, 16–18.

64. T.R. Clear, D.R. Rose, E. Waring and K. Scully, "Coercive Mobility and Crime: A Preliminary Examination of Concentrated Incarceration and Social Disorganization," *Justice Quarterly* 28, no. 3 (2003), 369–404.

65. "News in Brief: Oregon," *Prison Legal News*, February 2006, 43.

66. Calculation based on figure of $22,650; see Fields, "To Cut Prison Bill."

67. "Virginia Serious and Violent Offenders Re-Entry Initiative," Virginia Department of Corrections and Fairfax County Office of the Sheriff, 2005; see www.oarfairfax.org.

68. Washington, "Program Aims to Ease."

69. Fields, "To Cut Prison Bill."

70. Ernesto Lonoño, "With Job Training, Inmates Find Doors Opening," *Washington Post*, April 30, 2006.

71. "Building Relationships, Changing Lives," Rochester Network for Reentry, October 2005, www.rnfr.org; "Lighting the Pathway through Transition," Exodus Transitional Communities, Inc., 2005, www.etcny.org.

72. "Lighting the Pathway," Exodus Transitional Communities.

73. "Reintegrating Ex-offenders, Family and Community," Project Return, Inc., October 2005, www.projectreturninc.org.

74. Pat Nolan, Testimony to the Subcommittee on Crime, Terrorism and Homeland Security, "The Second Chance Act: Making Safer Communities and Fewer Victims by Helping Prisoners Reenter Society Successfully," November 3, 2005, 2.

75. Les Kimlee, "A Lesson in Mentoring," "Building Relationships, Changing Lives," Rochester Network for Reentry, October 2005, www.rnfr.org.

76. Ellis Cose, "The Dawn of a New Movement," *Newsweek*, April 24, 2006.

77. Nancy Ritter, "No Shortcuts to Successful Reentry: The Failings of Project Greenlight," *Corrections Today* (American Correctional Association), December 2006, 95–97.

78. "Prisoner Reentry Research at the Urban Institute: A Prospectus," Urban Institute, 2005, www.urban.org.

79. *Report of the Re-entry Policy Council* (Washington, D.C.: Council of State Governments / Urban Institute Re-entry Policy Forum, February 2005), www.reentrypolicy.org.

80. Woody, "Community Can Learn."
81. Nolan, Testimony, 2.
82. Salzburg, *Report*, 84.
83. Ibid.
84. Ibid.
85. Ibid.
86. Susan B. Tucker and Eric Cadora, "Justice Reinvestment," *Ideas for an Open Society* 3, no. 3 (November 2003).
87. Cose, "The Dawn of a New Movement"; Jennifer Gonnerman, "Million-Dollar Blocks," *Village Voice*, November 16, 2004.
88. Matt Apuzzo / Associated Press, "It May Not Be the Economy, Stupid," *Richmond Times-Dispatch*, August 27, 2004.
89. Tucker and Cadora, "Justice Reinvestment."
90. Ellen Perlman, "Where Will Sex Offenders Live?" *Governing Magazine*, June 2006. See also *The Impact of Residency Restriction on Sex Offender and Correctional Management Practices: A Literature Review*, Marcus Nieto and David Jung, Hastings Law School, California Research Bureau No. 06-0008 (August 2006).

6. DANIEL AND CORRECTIONAL MAMMON

1. W. Sibley Towner, *Daniel* (Louisville: John Knox Press, 1984), 52.
2. Robert S. Mueller III, *Preliminary Semiannual Uniform Crime Report, January through June 2006*, (Washington, D.C.: Federal Bureau of Investigations, December 18, 2006).
3. In 2005, there were 1,390,695 violent crimes and 10,166,159 nonviolent property offenses. See Robert S. Mueller III, *Crime in the United States, 2005*, (Washington, D.C.: September 18, 2006).
4. A 3.7% increase in 1,390,695 violent crimes means 51,456 more violent offenses. A 2.6% decrease in 10,166,159 property crimes means 264,420 fewer non-violent offenses. The net decrease in the number of violent and non-violent crimes would be 213,964—if the preliminary rate of 3.7% and 2.6% hold for all of 2006.
5. Dan Eggen, "Violent Crime, a Sticky Issue for White House, Shows Steeper Rise," *Washington Post*, September 25, 2007.
6. Mueller, *Preliminary Semiannual Uniform Crime Report*.
7. Howard N. Snyder, "Not This Time: A Response to the Warnings of the Juvenile Superpredator," *Corrections Today* (American Correctional Association), April 2007, 116–117.

8. Kathleen Kingsbury, "The Next Crime Wave," *Time*, December 11, 2006.

9. Dan Eggen, "Violent Crime in the U.S. Continues to Surge," *Washington Post*, December 19, 2006.

10. "Violent Crime Rose in First Half of Year," *USA Today*, December 19, 2006.

11. Silja J.A. Talvi, "Inside the American Correctional Association," *Prison Legal News*, September 2005, 5.

12. "2004 Crime Rate Hovered at Low Levels," *USA Today*, September 26, 2005.

13. Paige M. Harrison and Allen J. Beck, *Prisoners in 2005* (Washington, D.C.: Bureau of Justice Statistics, 2006), 2.

14. Commonwealth of Virginia Board of Corrections meeting minutes, November 16, 2005, 2.

15. Anna Bailey, "More Police Means Strain on Corrections System," *The Examiner* (Washington, D.C.), April 17, 2006.

16. Kevin Johnson, "Study Predicts Rise in Inmate Population," *USA Today*, February 14, 2007.

17. "U.S. Prison Population Passes That of Houston," *FAMMGram* (Families Against Mandatory Minimums), Winter 2005, 6, based on Bureau of Justice Statistics data.

18. Raphael Sperry, Ariel Bierbaum, Juan Calaf, Karen Kearney, and Kathleen Monroe, "Prison Design Boycott: A Challenge to the Professional Business of Incarceration," *Prison Legal News*, November 2005, 4, citing American Correctional Association data.

19. Private Adult Correctional Facility Census, 1996 and 2001 editions, quoted in Peter Wagner, *The Prison Index* (Springfield, MA: Prison Policy Initiative, 2003), 6.

20. Talvi, "Inside the American Correctional Association," 4; Patrick O'Driscoll, "Menu Swap a Turkey, Cattlemen Say," *USA Today*, January 19, 2001; "CEO Leads Investors' Bid for Aramark," *USA Today*, May 2, 2006; see also John E. Dannenberg, "Aramark: Prison Food Service with a Bad Aftertaste," *Prison Legal News*, December 2006, 10–17.

21. Paul von Zielbauer, "Prison Health Services: As Health Care in Jails Goes Private, 10 Days Can Be a Death Sentence," *Prison Legal News*, August 2005, 3; reprinted from the *New York Times* series cited in this volume's Chapter 7.

22. Meredith Kolodner, "Private Prisons Expect a Boom," *New York Times*, July 19, 2006.

23. John E. Dannenberg, "Los Angeles County Jail Tests Prisoner Radio I.D. Tags," *Prison Legal News*, January 2006, 27.

24. "Private Prison Firms Stumble: Hire Former California Officials to Lobby for For-Profit Facilities," *Prison Legal News*, January 2006, 20–21; and "Audit: California Private Prison Contracting Tainted by Conflicts of Interest," *Prison Legal News*, July 2006, 23, citing California State Auditor's Report No. 2005-105 (Sept. 2005), www.bsa.ca.gov.

25. Talvi, "Inside the American Correctional Association," 4.

26. Matthew T. Clarke, "State Auditor Blasts Colorado DOC's Private Prison Oversight Failures," *Prison Legal News*, March 2006, 18–19.

27. Matthew T. Clarke, "Colorado Expands Private Prisons While Fining CCA for Understaffing," *Prison Legal News*, November 2006, 24.

28. Ibid.

29. Clarke, "State Auditor."

30. "Buying Power," *Coalition for Prisoners' Rights Newsletter* (PO Box 1911, Santa Fe, NM 87504) 31, no. 9 (September 2006)—based on information from the Institute of Money in State Politics in Helena, MT.

31. Matthew T. Clarke, "Former Connecticut Governor Rowland Pleads Guilty to Corruption Charges in Juvenile Prison Kickback Scheme," *Prison Legal News*, July 2005, 8.

32. Joe Garner, "Beef Is Back Behind Bars, at Least for a While," *Rocky Mountain News*, December 21, 2005.

33. Kelly Harp, Senate Republican Communications, "Kester to Corrections Officials: 'Where's the Beef?,'" December 13, 2005, @ 12:39 P.M.

34. David M. Reutter, "Private Prisons Bilk $13 Million from Florida; State Awards More Contracts," *Prison Legal News*, February 2006, 8–9; the Inspector General's report, #2005–61, is available at www.myflorida.com/administration/inspectorgeneral.

35. Michael Rigby, "Maryland's PHS Prison Health Care under Fire, New System Implemented," *Prison Legal News*, February 2006, 14–15; $2,722 is the 2002 national average for states' per capita correctional health care expenditure.

36. Karyl Kicenski, "The Corporate Prison: The Production of Crime and the Sale of Discipline," (2002), 4, at www.csun.edu/~hfspc002/karyl.prison.pdf.

37. Jon Swartz, "Inmates vs. Outsourcing," *USA Today*, July 8, 2004.

38. Michael Rigby, "Prisoners Labor at Wisconsin Wal-Mart Site," *Prison Legal News*, February 2006, 37.

39. Clayton Mosher, Gregory Hooks, and Peter Wood, "Don't Build It Here—The Hype Versus the Reality of Prisons and Local Employment," *Prison Legal News*, January 2005, 11–15; see G. Hooks, C. Mosher, T. Rotolo and L. Labao, "The Prison Industry: Carceral Expansion and Employment in U.S. Counties, 1969–1994," *Social Science Quarterly* 85 (2004), 37–57.

40. Swartz, "Inmates vs. Outsourcing,"; Mosher et al., "Don't Build It Here."

41. Ian Urbina, "Prison Labor Fuels American War Machine," *Prison Legal News*, January 2004, 1–3; Urbina is a reporter for the *New York Times*, which published parts of this article.

42. "Company Uses Prison Slave Labor for $100 Million Military Contract," *Prison Legal News*, February 2006, 39.

43. Mosher et al., "Don't Build It Here."

44. Michael Rigby, "Modern Slavery in North Carolina: Another Peculiar Institution," *Prison Legal News*, October 2005, 4.

45. "California Auditor: Prison Industries Loses Money and Fails to Demonstrate Rehabilitative Success," *Prison Legal News*, June 2006, 22.

46. Swartz, "Inmates vs. Outsourcing"; Mosher et al., "Don't Build It Here"; "Company Uses Prison Slave Labor."

47. "Alabama Supreme Court Sidesteps Merits of Suit Challenging Contracted Prison Labor," *Prison Legal News*, June 2006, 40; Laura Magnani and Harmon L. Wray, *Beyond Prisons: An Interfaith Paradigm for Our Failed Prison System* (Minneapolis: Fortress Press, 2006), 40.

48. David M. Reutter, "Florida's Privatization of Prisoner Canteen Services under Scrutiny," *Prison Legal News*, February 2006, 22; the Auditor General's report, #2005–044, is available at www.prisonlegalnews. org.

49. Michelle Groenke, "Prison Chief Admits Kickback Scheme," UPI, July 6, 2006.

50. Talvi, "Inside the American Correctional Association," 4.

51. Bill Sizemore, "Whatever Happened to... the Prepaid Prison Telephone System?" *Virginian-Pilot*, March 6, 2006.

52. John E. Dannenberg, "Phone Companies Gouge California Jail Prisoners' Families," *Prison Legal News*, April 2005, 11.

53. John E. Dannenberg, "NY DOC's 60% Telephone Call 'Surcharge' Violates First and Fourteenth Amendments," *Prison Legal News*, March 2006, 11; effective April 1, 2007, New York eliminated the state commission provision of its contract—a decision that does not impact MCI's share of the profits from overpriced phone calls, of course.

54. Bill Sizemore, "Prisoners' Calls Prove Revenue Boon for Virginia," *Virginian-Pilot*, February 1, 2004.

55. MCI *WorldCom Network Services, Inc. v. Jones*, Record No.s 021262, 021247, 020859 (Vir. 2003).

56. Sizemore, "Prisoners' Calls."

57. Bill Sizemore, "Bill That Would Lower Phone Rates for Prisoners Advances in House," *Virginian-Pilot*, January 22, 2005.

58. Sizemore, "Whatever Happened to…." (Please note that the figures of $9.20 and $8.40 are what have been published in Virginia newspapers. The *actual* bill paid by my out-of-state friends is $12.39 per call.)

59. Christina Nuckols, "Prison Supporters Rally," *Virginian-Pilot*, August 30, 2002.

60. Fox Butterfield, "With Longer Sentences, Cost of Fighting Crime Is Higher," *New York Times*, May 3, 2004.

61. Fox Butterfield, "Study Tracks Boom in Prisons and Notes Impact on Counties," *New York Times*, April 30, 2004.

62. Angela E. Pometto, "Prisons in Appalachia," *Arlington Catholic Herald*, November 18, 2004.

63. Mosher et al., "Don't Build It Here."

64. Nuckols, "Prison Supporters Rally."

65. Linda McNatt, "Talk of Prison Closings Worries Townspeople," *Virginian-Pilot*, August 9, 2002; Nuckols, "Prison Supporters Rally."

66. Warren Fiske and Christina Nuckols, "2 Southside Prisons to Stay Open, Officials Say," *Virginian-Pilot*, September 20, 2002.

67. Ken Stolle, "Virginia's Sentencing Guidelines Are a Model for the Nation," *Virginian-Pilot*, December 14, 2003.

68. Nicholas Confessore, "Spitzer Seeks Commission to Study Prison Closings," *New York Times*, February 5, 2007.

69. Ibid.

70. Ibid.

71. John J. Gibbons and Nicholas de B. Katzenbach, eds., *Confronting Confinement: A Report of the Commission on Safety and Abuse in America's Prisons* (New York: Vera Institute of Justice, 2006), 65.

72. Mosher et al., "Don't Build It Here."

73. Joelle Fraser, "An American Seduction: Portrait of a Prison Town," in Tara Herivel and Paul Wright, eds., *Prison Nation: The Warehousing of America's Poor* (New York: Routledge, 2003); see also the *excellent* graphic nonfiction book by Kevin Pyle and Craig Gilmore, *Prison Town: Paying the Price* (Northampton, MA: Real Cost of Prison Project, 2005).

74. Marvin Mentor, "Pay to Play: Guard Union Spreads the Wealth," *Prison Legal News*, March 2005, 5.

75. "The Guards Own the Gates," *Los Angeles Times*, November 24, 2003.

76. "Reject It—Now," *Sacramento Bee*, August 7, 2006.

77. John Pomfret, "California's Crisis in Prison System a Threat to Public," *Washington Post*, June 11, 2006.

78. "The Guards Own the Gates."

79. Ibid.

80. "Audit of California's 'Failed' Intermediate Parole Sanctions Program Blames Lack of Benchmarks and Data Analysis," *Prison Legal News*, June 2006, 21.

81. Associated Press, "AP: Parole Violators Crowd Calif. Prisons," *New York Times*, March 7, 2004.

82. Pamela Maclean, "Strong Arm of the Law," *San Francisco Bay Guardian*, December 4, 2002; cited in Wagner, *Prison Index*, 36.

83. Mentor, "Pay to Play."

84. Associated Press, "California Guards' Union Facing Changes," *New York Times*, May 23, 2004; Pomfret, "California's Crisis."

85. "Federal Judge Enforces 'Valdivia Remedial Plan' for California Parole Violators," *Prison Legal News*, January 2006, 9–10.

86. Marvin Mentor, "California Corrections System Declared 'Dysfunctional'—Redemption Doubtful," *Prison Legal News*, March 2005, 5, 1; see Corrections Independent Review Panel (CIRP), *Reforming Corrections*, June 30, 2004, 359 pgs.

87. See *Madrid v. Woodford*, C 90-3094-T.E.H., Special Master's Final Report, June 24, 2004; and Judge Henderson's twenty-seven–page ruling of November, 2004, and Special Master Hagar's report of July, 2006; and Andy Furillo, "Governor: Deal with Prisons Now," *Sacramento Bee*, July 27, 2006; and Jennifer Warren, "State Prisons' Special Master Won't Be a Slave to System," *Los Angeles Times*, July 16, 2006.

88. Furillo, "Governor: Deal with Prisons Now."

89. "The Pandering Pair," *Sacramento Bee*, July 11, 2006.

90. Christoph Hinckeldey, ed., *Criminal Justice Through the Ages* (Rothenburg ob der Tauber, Germany: Mittelalterliches Kriminalmuseum, 1981), 172.

91. Charles Campbell, *Doing Easy Time: Including a Stretch as Warden of a Coed Prison* (Tucson, AZ: Fenestra Books, 2005).

92. Robert Martinson, "What Works: Questions and Answers about Prison Reform," *Public Policy* 35 (Spring 1974), 25–54.

7. Jesus and Prison Conditions

1. Karl Rahner, "The Prison Pastorate," *Justice Reflections*, 39, 8. (Copyright © by Continuum, trans. Cecily Hastings.)
2. Ibid., 2.
3. Ibid., 7.
4. Ibid., 10, 11, 13.
5. Judith Greene, "Examining Our Harsh Prison Culture" *Ideas for an Open Society* 4, no. 1 (October 2004), 4.
6. www.prisoncommission.org; Kevin Johnson, "Commission Warns of Harm Isolation Can Do to Prisoners," *USA Today*, June 8, 2006.
7. Fox Butterfield, "With Longer Sentences, Cost of Fighting Crime Is Higher," *New York Times*, May 3, 2004.
8. Information provided by R. Hawthorne, FOM#B, Brunswick Correctional Center food services.
9. Eric Rich, "For Victims, a Glimpse of Life behind Prison Gates," *Washington Post*, April 21, 2004.
10. "States Trim Prisoners' Diets," *USA Today*, May 21, 2003.
11. "Food Budgets" (chart), *Richmond Times-Dispatch*, August 3, 2004 (dividing per diem figure of $4.15 by three); calculation, "USDA Per Capita Food Expenditures 2001," Table 15 (dividing per diem figure of $8.12 by three), cited in Peter Wagner, *The Prison Index* (Springfield, MA: Prison Policy Initiative, 2003), 29.
12. Paul von Zielbauer, "Private Health Care in Jails Can Be a Death Sentence," *New York Times*, February 27, 2005. For an excellent overview, see John E. Dannenberg, "PHS Redux: Sued In a Dozen States, Contract Losses, Stock Plummets, Business Continues," *Prison Legal News*, November 2006, 1–10.
13. Will S. Hylton, "Sick on the Inside: Correctional HMO's and the Coming Prison Plague," *Harper's Magazine*, August 2003.
14. *Woodward v. Correctional Medical Services of Illinois, Inc.*, 368 F.3d. 917 (7th Cir. 2004).
15. Elizabeth Dede, "TB or Not TB: Disease, Lies, and the Georgia Department of Corrections," *Hospitality* (Open Door Community, Atlanta, GA), February 2006, 1.
16. Robert Sillen, "Cruel and Unusual Prison Health Care," *Sacramento Bee*, October 8, 2006.
17. Ibid.
18. Marvin Mentor, "Federal Court Seizes California Prisons' Medical Care; Appoints Receiver with Unprecedented Powers," *Prison Legal News*, March 2006, 6.

19. Sillen, "Cruel and Unusual."

20. John J. Gibbons and Nicholas de B. Katzenbach, eds., *Confronting Confinement: A Report of the Commission on Safety and Abuse in America's Prisons* (New York: Vera Institute of Justice, 2006), 54.

21. Michael Rigby, "Report Lambastes New York Lockdowns," *Prison Legal News*, February 2005, 9.

22. Paul von Zielbauer, "Report on State Prisoners Cites Inmates' Mental Illness," *New York Times*, October 23, 2003.

23. Gibbons and Katzenbach, *Confronting Confinement*, 59.

24. Rigby, "Report Lambastes New York Lockdowns."

25. Kevin Johnson, "After Years in Solitary, Freedom Hard to Grasp," *USA Today*, June 9, 2005.

26. Rigby, "Report Lambastes New York Lockdowns."

27. Gibbons and Katzenbach, *Confronting Confinement*, 59.

28. Ibid., 65.

29. Michael Rigby, "Georgia Prison Guards Plead to Misdemeanors in Prisoner Beatings," *Prison Legal News*, November 2006, 32.

30. "Shakedown," *Hospitality* (Open Door Community, Atlanta, GA), August 2005, 7.

31. Bob Herbert, "America's Abu Ghraibs," *New York Times*, May 31, 2004.

32. Peter Carlson, "It's All in the Execution," *Washington Post*, November 29, 2004.

33. "Turning the Spotlight on Prison Conditions," *Roanoke Times*, March 13, 2005.

34. According to the Department of Justice, the number of inmate-on-inmate assaults rose from 23,715 to 30,344 (+27.9%) between 1995 and 2000, while the total penitentiary population grew from 925,949 to 1,101,202 (+18.9%). Jayne O'Donnell, "State Time or Federal Prison?" *USA Today*, March 18, 2004.

35. Gibbons and Katzenbach, *Confronting Confinement*, 24–25.

36. A. Langan and D.J. Levin, *Recidivism of Prisoners Released in 1994* (Washington, D.C.: Bureau of Justice Statistics, 2002), Table 10.

37. Richard Morin, "Time In and Time Out," *Washington Post*, February 2, 2006. Yale and the University of Chicago both make this study available on their Web sites.

38. "Turning the Spotlight."

39. Gibbons and Katzenbach, *Confronting Confinement*, 84.

40. James Q. Whitman, "Prisoner Degradation Abroad—and at Home," *Washington Post*, May 10, 2004.

41. Jim Hold, "Decarcerate?" *New York Times*, August 15, 2004.

42. Ibid.
43. Gibbons and Katzenbach, *Confronting Confinement*, 68.
44. Ibid., 67.
45. "Winston Churchill's Speech 1910," *Justice Reflections*, 90, 12, 2.
46. Frank Green, "Inmates: Grooming Rules Violate Faith," *Richmond Times-Dispatch*, September 28, 2005
47. Ibid.
48. Frank Green, "Prisons Segregate Rastafarians," *Richmond Times-Dispatch*, September 17, 2005.
49. Joan Biskupic, "Court: Let Prisoners Have Access to Religion," *USA Today*, June 1, 2005.
50. Frank Green, "ACLU Can Move Ahead in Va. Lawsuit." *Richmond Times-Dispatch*, June 1, 2005.

8. Paul and Prison Ministry

1. John Stott, *The Spirit, the Church and the World: The Message of Acts* (Downers Grove, IL: InterVarsity Press, 1990), 172.
2. See Chapter 3 and A. Skotnicki, *Religion and the Development of the American Penal System* (Lanham, MD: University Press of America, 2000).
3. http://kairosprisonministry.org
4. Thomas O'Connor, "What Works, Religion as a Correctional Intervention: Part II," *Journal of Community Corrections*, 14, no. 2 (Winter 2004–2005), 4.
5. Ibid., 6.
6. Candace Rondeaux, "ACLU Seeks End to Jails' Deal with Ministries," *Washington Post*, May 22, 2006.
7. Mike Warren, "Texas Church Leading the Way in Prison Ministry," *Restorative Justice News* (www.rjmn.net/news.html, viewed April 25, 2005).
8. John E. Dannenberg, "Nebraska Native American Prisoners' Religious Program Reinstated," *Prison Legal News*, February 2006, 30.
9. Kim Workman, "Resolving Conflict and Restoring Relationships: Experiments in Community Justice within a New Zealand Faith-Based Prison" (paper presented to "New Frontiers in Restorative Justice: Advancing Theory and Practice," December 2–5, 2004, Massey University, Albany, New Zealand).
10. *Americans United for Separation of Church and State v. Prison Fellowship Ministries*, 432 F. Supp. 2d 862 (S.D. Iowa 2006).

11. Charles Colson with Anne Morse, "Bad Judgment," *Christianity Today*, August 2006, 72.

12. Diana B. Henriques and Andrew W. Lehren, "Religion for Captive Audiences, with Taxpayers Footing the Bill," *New York Times*, December 10, 2006, quoting Prison Fellowship Ministries' Web site.

13. Ibid.

14. Samantha M. Shapiro, "Jails for Jesus," *Mother Jones*, November–December 2003.

15. Alan Cooperman, "An Infusion of Religious Funds in Fla. Prisons," *Washington Post*, April 29, 2006.

16. David M. Reutter, "Florida's Faith-Based Programs Under Watchful Eyes," *Prison Legal News*, April 2005, 30.

17. Alan Cooperman, "Single-Faith Prison Program Questioned," *Washington Post*, April 29, 2006.

18. Shapiro, "Jails for Jesus."

19. Warren Fiske, "Mark Earley Returns to His First Calling, the Ministry," *Virginian-Pilot*, November 8, 2004.

20. O'Connor, "What Works," 20, 21, 23.

21. Daniel P. Mears, "Faith-based Reentry Programs: Cause for Concern or Showing Promise?" *Corrections Today* (American Correctional Association), April 2007, 30–33.

22. Charles W. Colson, *Justice that Restores* (Wheaton, IL: Tyndale House Publishers, 2001), 137.

23. William A. McGeveran, Jr., ed., *The World Almanac and Book of Facts, 2001* (Mahwah, NJ: Almanac Education Group, 2001), 689–690. Calculation excludes Seventh Day Adventist, Christian Scientist, Jehovah's Witness, Latter-Day Saints and all non-Christian faiths.

9. Onesimus and Death by Incarceration

1. Raymond E. Brown, *An Introduction to the New Testament* (New York: Doubleday, 1997), 505–506.

2. *Lockyer v. Andrade*, 123 S.Ct. 1166 (2003); see also *Ewing v. California*, 1234 S.Ct. 1179 (2003).

3. Marc Mauer, Ryan S. King, and Malcolm C. Young, *The Meaning of "Life": Long Prison Sentences in Context* (Washington, D.C.: The Sentencing Project, 2004), 19.

4. Peter Greenwood, *The Cost-Effectiveness of Early Intervention as a Strategy for Reducing Violent Crime* (Santa Monica, CA: RAND Corp., 1995), 20.

5.   Karen Olsson, "Ghostwriting the Law," MotherJones.com, September–October 2002.

6.   Larry O'Dell / Associated Press, "Ten Years Later: Abolition of Parole Has Not Created a Building Frenzy," *Virginian-Pilot*, January 3, 2005.

7.   Michael O'Shear, "Passion Still High on Va. Ban of Parole," *Washington Post*, October 14, 2004.

8.   Olsson, "Ghostwriting the Law,"

9.   O'Dell, "Ten Years Later,"

10. B. Jaye Anno, Camelia Graham, James E. Lawrence and Ronald Shansky, *Correctional Health Care: Addressing the Needs of Elderly, Chronically Ill, and Terminally Ill Inmates* (Washington, D.C.: Department of Justice / National Institute of Corrections, February 2004), 7; see www.nicic.org.

11. O'Dell, "Ten Years Later."

12. Steve Aos, Polly Phipps, Robert Barnawski and Roxanne Lieb, "The Comparative Costs and Benefits of Programs to Reduce Crime," Washington State Institute for Public Policy, May 2001, 59. The full report or an executive summary can be downloaded at www.wsipp.wa.gov/pub.asp?docid=01-05-1201.

13. Chris L. Jenkins, "Va. Expands Use of Sentencing Tool for Judges," *Washington Post*, April 23, 2005.

14. O'Dell, "Ten Years Later."

15. *A Little Good News* (Durham, NC: Human Kindness Foundation), Summer/Fall 2005, 5.

16. Frank Green, "McCollum Appointed to Parole Board," *Richmond Times-Dispatch*, January 20, 2007; Paige M. Harrison and Allen J. Beck, *Prisoners in 2004* (Washington, D.C.: Bureau of Justice Statistics, October 2005), 4.

17. The figure of 200,000 is the roughest estimate of all the numbers cited in this volume. Here is my calculation: 1,400,000 penitentiary prisoners (parole does not apply to jail inmates) x 80% (only forty out of fifty states adopted "truth in sentencing") x 20% (percentage of "old law" convicts in Virginia's penitentiaries) = 224,000. I subtracted 24,000 as a wide margin of error.

18. Laurence Hammack, "Many Inmates Remain under Parole System," *Roanoke Times*, September 26, 2004.

19. John E. Dannenberg, "New York Parole Rates Plunge under Governor Pataki's Policy," *Prison Legal News*, November 2006, 36.

20. Hammack, "Many Inmates Remain."

21. In the first six months of 2006, the Virginia Parole Board reviewed 2130 male prisoners' cases, denied parole in 2,069 cases, and granted parole to 61.

22. Ibid.

23. "Parole Practices—Trends in Parole," Colorado Criminal Justice Reform Coalition, undated; based on Colorado Department of Corrections, "Parole Board Hearings and Decisions," November 1, 2002, and meeting with Mr. Van Pelt, Chairman, Colorado Parole Board, February 2002; figure of 96% based on figures of 23.4% "granted parole but not released until mandatory" and 0.8% "paroled."

24. Name and details have been changed.

25. James Lynch and William J. Sabol, *Prisoner Reentry in Perspective* (Washington, D.C.: Urban Institute, 2001), 14, citing Bureau of Justice Statistics data.

26. Michael Rigby, "Georgia Prisons: A Blight on the Peach State," *Prison Legal News*, March 2006, 6; Gary Hunter, "Former Georgia Parole Chairman Loses Appeal of Corruption Conviction," ibid., 10; *Whitworth v. State*, 622 S.E.2d. 21 (Ga. App. 2005).

27. Mauer, et al., *The Meaning of "Life,"* 30.

28. Ibid., 8.

29. Emily Bazelon, "Sentencing by the Numbers," *New York Times*, January 2, 2005; Jenkins, "Va. Expands Use of Sentencing."

30. Jenkins, "Va. Expands Use of Sentencing."

31. C.G. Camp and G.M. Camp, *The 2000 Corrections Yearbook: Adult Corrections* (Middletown, CT: Criminal Justice Institute, 2000), 54; calculation based on 2004 *adult* correctional population of 2.1 million.

32. See for instance Mauer, et al., *The Meaning of "Life,"* 28; James Q. Whitman, *Harsh Justice: Criminal Punishment and the Widening Divide between America and Europe* (New York: Oxford University Press, 2003); James Lynch, "Crime in International Perspective," in James Q. Wilson and Joan Petersilia, eds., *Crime* (San Francisco: Institute for Contemporary Studies, 1995); Marc Mauer, *Comparative International Rates of Incarceration: An Examination of Causes and Trends* (Washington, D.C.: The Sentencing Project, 2003); Roy Walmsley, *World Prison Population List*, 3rd ed. (London: Home Office Research, Development and Statistics Directorate, 2002).

33. Adam Liptak, "To More Inmates, Life Term Means Dying Behind Bars," *New York Times*, October 2, 2005.

34. Richard Bernstein, "Germany Frees Hijacker Who Killed U.S. Sailor," *New York Times*, December 20, 2005.

35. Michelle Boorstein, "Earley Finds New Calling, Post-Politics," *Washington Post*, December 19, 2004; "Mark Earley's Prison Epiphany," *Virginian-Pilot*, November 24, 2004; O'Dell, "Ten Years Later."

36. Stephen A. Salzburg, Chairperson and Editor, *Justice Kennedy Commission Report*, American Bar Association, August 2004, 27.

37. *FAMMGram* (Families Against Mandatory Minimums), Winter 2005, 20.

38. Salzman, *Justice Kennedy Commission Report*, 26; *FAMMGram*, 20–21.

39. Vincent Schiraldi, "States Are Releasing Pressure on Prisons," *Washington Post*, November 30, 2003.

40. *FAMMGram*, 20–21.

41. Mauer et al., *The Meaning of "Life,"* 13.

42. 24,000: calculation based on Mauer et al., *The Meaning of "Life,"* 15; 9,700: Adam Liptak, "Jailed for Life after Crimes as Teenagers," *New York Times*, October 3, 2005; 10,000: Mauer et al., *The Meaning of "Life,"* 19; "indeterminate": Mauer et al., *The Meaning of "Life,"* 18.

43. Mauer et al., *The Meaning of "Life,"* 9.

44. Ibid., 11.

45. Calculation based on figure of 127,677 in Mauer et al., *The Meaning of "Life,"* 9, and estimate of 132,000 in Liptak, "To More Inmates."

46. Liptak, "To More Inmates."

47. Adam Liptak, "Serving Life, with No Chance of Redemption," *New York Times*, October 5, 2005.

48. Mauer et al., *The Meaning of "Life,"* 11.

49. *Coleman v. Board of Prisons and Terms*, No. 2: 1996 cv 00783, E.D. Cal., May 20, 2005, unpublished; for related rulings, see *Irons v. Warden*, 358 F. Supp.2d. 936 (E.D. Cal. 2005); *Biggs v. Terhune*, 334 F.3d. 910 (9th Cir. 2003); *In re Dannenberg*, 34 Cal. 4th 1061 (2005); *In re Rosenkrantz*, 29 Cal 4th 616 (2001); *Sass v. Board of Prison Terms*, 376 F. Supp.2d 975 (U.S.D.C., E.D. Cal. 2005, 9th Cir. Case No. 0516455 (pending); *Irons v. Carey*, 408 F.3d. 1165 (9th Cir. 2005); *Dannenberg v. Brown*, U.S. Supreme Court No. 04–10299, October 3, 2005 (unpublished).

50. "Federal Court Finds California Murder Paroles Blocked by Illegal 'No Parole' Policy," *Prison Legal News*, January 2006, 33.

51. "California's New Governor Has Paroled 102 Lifers, but Rejected Twice That Many," *Prison Legal News*, January 2006, 18.

52. Liptak, "Serving Life."

53. Mauer et al., *The Meaning of "Life,"* 7.

54. News release, Georgia State Board of Pardons and Paroles, "More Violent-Crime Lifers Die in Prison Than Are Paroled," June 1, 1998.

55. Liptak, "Serving Life."

56. Harrison and Beck, *Prisoners in 2005*, 4; Mauer et al., *The Meaning of "Life*," 10.

57. "2005 Audit of California Parole Board Reveals Ongoing Deficiencies," *Prison Legal News*, February 2006, 16; Mauer et al., *The Meaning of "Life*," 10.

58. Associated Press, "Schwarzenegger Paroling Lifers Whom Davis Wouldn't," *USA Today*, June 16, 2004.

59. "2005 Audit."

60. Liptak, "To More Inmates"; "California's New Governor."

61. "California's New Governor."

62. Liptak, "Serving Life."

63. "Former Florida Warden Calls for End to Death Penalty," *Tallahassee Democrat*, June 29, 2007.

64. Carie Lemack, "Let Moussaoui Live," *USA Today*, March 6, 2006.

65. Fr. Richard John Neuhaus, "The Public Square," *First Things*, June–July 2006, 68, quoting *OpinionJournal*, April 14, 2006.

66. Fr. Gregory Jordan, "Red Repentance," *Justice Reflections* 79, reprinted from *The Tablet* (U.K.).

67. Liptak, "Serving Life."

68. Mauer et al., *The Meaning of "Life*," 28.

69. Heather Blumenthal, "Lifers Helping Lifers Swim Not Sink," *Let's Talk* (Correctional Services of Canada) 24, no. 2.

70. Richard Willing, "Death Row Population Is Graying," *USA Today*, February 15, 2005; Patrick McMahon, "Aging Inmates Present Prison Crisis," *USA Today*, August 10, 2005.

71. Anno et al., *Correctional Health Care*, 9.

72. Gary Fields, "As Prisoners Age, Terminally Ill Raise Tough Questions," *Wall Street Journal*, September 29, 2005.

73. Mauer et al., *The Meaning of "Life*," 25.

74. Fields, "As Prisoners Age."

75. Keith Gutierrez, "Aging out of Crime," *Fortune News*, Summer 2005, 14.

76. *Plata v. Schwarzenegger*, U.S.D.C. (N.D. Cal.), Case No. C-01-1351 TEH, and associated rulings, special master's reports, etc.

77. Marvin Mentor, "Federal Court Seizes California Prisons' Medical Care; Appoints Receiver with Unprecedented Powers," *Prison Legal News*, March 2006, 6; see also Andy Furillo, "Receiver Rips Prison-Reform Obstructions," *Sacramento Bee*, December 6, 2006, which gives a figure of $3 billion; and Andy Furillo, "Prisons' Legal Strain," *Sacramento Bee*, February 4, 2007.

78. Andy Furillo, "Governor Backs Prison Medical Sites," *Sacramento Bee*, August 15, 2006.

79. McMahon, "Aging Inmates."

80. "California Struggling with Growing Numbers of Elderly Prisoners," Associated Press, June 9, 2002.

81. Anno et al., *Correctional Health Care*, 10, 11.

82. Ibid., 11.

83. Willing, "Death Row Population Is Graying."

84. Gutierrez, "Aging Out"; see *Making the Walls Transparent*, www.angel-fire.com/fl3/starke/.

85. Laurence Hammack, "Aging Behind Bars," *Roanoke Times*, September 26, 2004; the article gives a figure of $42 per week, but that cannot be accurate; the top pay in the Virginia D.O.C. is $54 per month.

86. Willing, "Death Row Population Is Graying."

87. McMahon, "Aging Inmates."

88. Lane Nelson, "Unexpected Benefits," *The Angolite*, August–September 2004, 41–43.

89. Anno et al., *Correctional Health Care*, 39, 40.

90. Fields, "As Prisoners Age."

91. Gary Fields, "To Cut Prison Bill, States Tweak Laws, Try Early Releases," *Wall Street Journal*, December 21, 2005.

92. Liptak, "To More Inmates."

93. Ron Humphrey, "They Were Soldiers," *Inside Journal* (Prison Fellowship Ministries), July–August 2004, citing C. J. Mumola, *Veterans in Prison or Jail* (Washington, D.C.: Bureau of Justice Statistics, 2000); see also Art Beeler, "When Johnny or Jane Comes Marching Home," *Corrections Today* (American Correctional Association), February 2007, 60.

94. Ibid.

95. Gregg Zoroya, "Iraq Veterans Reaching Out for Help," *USA Today*, March 1, 2006.

96. ABC World News, April 13, 2006, 6:43 p.m.

97. Humphrey, "They Were Soldiers."

98. Janet Reitman, "Surviving Fallujah," *Rolling Stone*, March 10, 2005.

99. William M. Welch, "Trauma of Iraq War Haunting Thousands Returning Home," *USA Today*, February 28, 2005.

About the Publisher

LANTERN BOOKS was founded in 1999 on the principle of living with a greater depth and commitment to the preservation of the natural world. In addition to publishing books on animal advocacy, vegetarianism, religion, and environmentalism, Lantern is dedicated to printing books in the U.S. on recycled paper and saving resources in day-to-day operations. Lantern is honored to be a recipient of the highest standard in environmentally responsible publishing from the Green Press Initiative.

www.lanternbooks.com

2011

Publisher certification awarded by Green Press Initiative.
www.greenpressinitiative.org